THE COMPLETE BOOK OF STEP-BY-STEP

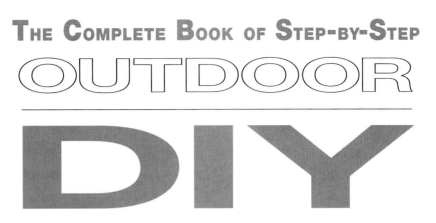

OUTDOOR DIY

**Over sixty stylish and easy-to-build
projects for your garden area**

Mike Lawrence, Penny Swift and Janek Szymanowski

NEW
HOLLAND

Contents

THE COMPLETE BOOK OF STEP-BY-STEP

OUTDOOR
DIY

Over sixty stylish and easy-to-build projects for your garden area

STONEWORK

Introduction

No building material has a longer pedigree than stone; after all, the Stone Age was the first recognized period of human culture, and early man used stone not only as a source of invaluable tools but also as a building material of unparalleled strength, durability and versatility. Stone can be used as it occurs naturally, in boulders or random blocks and slabs split and shaped by the forces of nature, or it can be worked into precisely-cut blocks that slot together as snugly as jigsaw pieces. Above all, it offers the infinite variety that only a naturally-occurring material can exhibit.

The earliest use of stone as a building material was probably the casual gathering of loose-lying surface stone to form simple enclosures for defence and to pen animals. It would soon find a use as a paving material for consolidating soft ground, and by Egyptian times records show that it was being used in the design of decorative gardens as well as for the construction of the many meticulously-engineered pyramids and temples of the period. The Greeks and Romans loved their ornamental sacred groves and public gardens, and by the Middle Ages there was a strong tradition of landscape architecture that was to spread across every culture and every continent. In every case, stone was the predominant structural feature.

Today, stone is as popular as ever for creating a wide range of garden features, from the humblest carved ornament to the most elaborate walls, arches, terraces and steps. No longer are garden landscapers restricted to using just the types of stone provided by the accident of local geology; they can within reason obtain whatever type of stone is required so long as they are prepared to pay for the inevitably high transport costs of one of the densest building materials around.

With this point in mind, perhaps the most significant development as far as garden stonework is concerned has been the growing use of man-made stone products. These are formed by the

Below: Stone lends itself to all sorts of outdoor uses, either in its natural form or as cut blocks and sculpted ornaments.

vibration or compression of selected crushed aggregate to produce walling blocks, paving stones and even ornamental mouldings such as balusters and bird-baths. Not only is the product uniform in size and structural characteristics, unlike natural stone, and therefore easier for the amateur to work with; it is also generally both less expensive and more readily available. But it lacks something: the natural beauty and variety of stone is a quality that even the most ingenious manufacturer cannot hope to copy completely faithfully.

What to build

Whether you choose to work with natural stone or its man-made equivalent, there

arch, whether it is built as a free-standing feature or is contained within a high wall. Building one is a good test of your skill as a stonemason, and the results can provide a stunning centrepiece in any garden.

Every garden also needs hard surfaces for its occupants to walk on, and stone in its infinite variety is the perfect material to choose for patios, terraces, paths and steps. Large square or rectangular slabs can create paved areas on a grand scale, while the more informal pavers and setts are ideal both for paving smaller areas and for adding detail to larger schemes. Surface colour and texture have an important part to play here too, helping the paving to blend in well with its surroundings.

Stone is also the perfect material to choose for a whole host of other garden features. A garden pond set about with rocks, perhaps with a small cascade running into it, is not only an eye-catching garden feature in its own right; it also adds a third dimension – the restful sound of running water – to the twin delights of sight and smell. The presence of water allows you to broaden the variety of plants you can grow, and also encourages wildlife to visit the garden.

Lastly, you can use stone for a wide range of other garden projects, too, from rockeries to garden furniture. All are easy – and rewarding – to build and will enhance any garden design. You need few special skills or tools – just the vision to create the effect you want – and the time and patience to put it into practice.

Left: Stone can be split into large slabs for paving, into medium-sized blocks for walling or into smaller setts for paving – here contrasted with rounded cobbles.

Below: Reconstituted regular stone slabs and blocks in the foreground contrast well with the mass of natural stone used for the rockery on the lawn.

is a huge range of garden projects to which you can turn your hand.

Walls are an obvious first choice, and there is no finer walling material than stone. Finely-dressed blocks can be used to create the neatly-detailed formal look, while randomly-shaped pieces can be turned into the most attractive of all garden features, the dry-stone wall, with its rugged natural appearance and plethora of planting pockets. Unlike brickwork, stone always looks as though it belongs in the garden, especially when it has begun to weather, and is therefore the perfect choice for boundary walls, earth-retaining walls, even low-level planters.

Another stone feature that can look particularly fine in the garden is the

WALLS

THERE IS MORE TO ENCLOSING YOUR PROPERTY THAN SIMPLY MARKING THE BOUNDARY LINES. YOU GAIN PRIVACY FROM PRYING EYES; YOU CAN KEEP CHILDREN AND FAMILY PETS FROM STRAYING; YOU CAN CONCEAL EYESORES — IN YOUR OWN GARDEN, OR NEXT DOOR; ABOVE ALL, YOU CREATE A BACKDROP AGAINST WHICH YOUR GARDEN CAN BE DISPLAYED IN ALL ITS GLORY. NOTHING DOES THIS SO WELL AS A STONE WALL. IT IS DURABLE, NEEDS LITTLE MAINTENANCE IF IT IS WELL CONSTRUCTED AND CAN GREATLY ENHANCE THE LOOK OF THE HOUSE AND ITS SURROUNDINGS IF A LITTLE CARE IS PUT INTO ITS DESIGN AND CONSTRUCTION.

WALLING MATERIALS

The first stage in planning any sort of walling project is to choose your materials. How much choice you have often depends on where you live; country areas are likely to offer local stone in abundance, while in town you may be restricted to a selection of man-made blocks unless you are prepared to foot heavy delivery bills. Wherever you live, your primary aim should be to choose materials that complement those already used for the house, for other buildings on the site and for surfaces like paths and patios. This is particularly important as far as boundary walls are concerned if you live in an area where one local building material is predominantly used.

Natural stone is without doubt the most beautiful material to use for garden walling projects, since by its very nature it looks as if it belongs in the garden. Apart from its beauty, stone is also by definition more durable than the average man-made block; after all, it has been around a long time. The most common stone walling materials are limestones, sandstones and granites; slate (shale) and flint can also be used, but are generally more difficult to work with. Colours vary from area to area, and size is really a question of pot luck. The stones themselves may be undressed (in the natural, as-quarried state), semi-dressed (cut into reasonably uniform blocks but with uneven surfaces) or fully-dressed (with square, machine-cut faces). The less dressed the stone is, the less it costs. Unless you live near quarries – which may have suitable stone in stock – you may have trouble locating supplies; because the cost of transport is so high, you will find relatively little stone stocked by suburban builders' merchants in some areas or selected garden centres – what they do stock is mainly intended for rockeries – and you may have no option but to hire a lorry and drive to a quarry yourself. However, it is a good idea to check your local classified telephone directory for any local stone merchants first.

Man-made blocks come in three main types. The most popular is best described as reconstituted stone; this is made by bonding aggregates and pigments together to create blocks with one decorative face and end, in imitation of natural quarried stone. Blocks of this sort have the advantage that they are regular and of uniform size, making planning, estimating and building easier than using natural stone. They come in a range of sizes, colours and textures and can be laid just like bricks. In some areas they are even made as multi-stone blocks complete with recessed pointing, and are quicker to build up than individual blocks – ideal for the waller in a hurry. They are stocked by builders' merchants, garden centres and specialist stockists.

Pierced screen blocks are also formed from pressed aggregate, but instead of being solid they have cut-outs in various patterns passing through the block. They are ideal for screen walls where complete privacy is not needed, but the construction can be weak unless additional reinforcement is included. They are usually about 300 mm (12 in) square and 100 mm (4 in) thick; colours may range from white through yellow to buff or just grey. Builders' merchants, garden centres, and specialist stockists such as concrete manufacturers are the likeliest sources of supplies.

Right: If you want walls with a completely natural look, a dry-stone structure is the perfect choice both for boundaries and for smaller feature walls. Its irregular stones provide plenty of planting pockets.

Plain concrete blocks are not intended to be on show and are used mainly for constructing retaining walls which will then be faced with a decorative skin. The advantage of using them in this situation is their low cost and the speed with which the wall can be built up. Sizes range from 390 mm to 600 mm (16 to 24 in) long, 150 to 300 mm (6 to 12 in) high and up to 200 mm (8 in) thick. They could be used for perimeter walls and the like if finished with a mortar rendering, especially if other materials prove too expensive. Buy them from builders' merchants or concrete manufacturers.

For more details on choosing natural and man-made stone for your garden projects, please see pages 88-89.

WALL DESIGN

Once you have settled on the materials you intend to use, your next decision is what sort of wall to build. Will it be free-standing or earth-retaining? Will it be solid or pierced with openings? Will it be straight, curved or built in bays? Will it be mortared or dry-laid? What bonding pattern will be used? And how long, high and thick will it be?

You can build free-standing walls 100 mm (4 in) thick up to a height of around 450 mm (18 in) without additional support, but over this height you should incorporate a 230 mm (9 in) square pier every 3 m (10 ft). A wall 200 mm (8 in) thick can be built up to 1350 mm (4ft 6 in) high without piers. On long straight runs of mortared wall, you should aim to incorporate an unmortared movement joint every 6 m (20 ft) to prevent ground movement from cracking the wall. Earth-retaining walls should be at least 230 mm (9 in) thick unless reinforcement is incorporated in the structure. Most walls should be mortared for strength; the only exception is if the walls are built of natural stone, where the techniques of building dry-stone walls help to ensure the structure's strength and stability. Get professional advice on the wall thickness and slope if building one higher than about 1 m (3 ft).

You can create openings in stone and block walls by using an open bonding pattern. Gaps can be left in retaining walls to encourage plants to grow for a more natural look.

The wall itself does not have to be built in straight lines, and curves or bays can help to soften its impact and help it to blend in with the contours of the

garden. It is often worth experimenting with dry-laid stones or blocks to get an idea of how different ideas will look, before you actually start laying foundations and building in earnest; it is easier to visualise what something will look like in the flesh than on paper.

Walls do not all have to be boundary walls; you can build them as screens to sub-divide the garden into different areas or to hide eyesores such as the compost heap. You can use them to create sheltered sitting areas facing a favourite view, while low walls can form terracing between different lawn or flower bed levels on sloping sites; they can even contain a raised ornamental pond or water garden.

Your walls can also be the perfect backdrop for plants, and because a well-built wall will need no maintenance (unlike the average fence), there is no reason why you should not grow plants up them, provided that you create suitable planting areas in front of the wall face. Such a wall can also provide screening from the prevailing winds, and if it faces the sun you will create a suntrap that will enable you to grow species that would not survive in the open. You can even grow plants within walls if you build them as a double skin and fill the centre with earth.

The only restraining factor when it comes to designing walls is your ingenuity. If you are stuck for ideas, do not forget the enormous wealth of ideas on

show in public gardens or stately homes all over the country; the scale may be grander than you can manage in your own back garden, but the design principles are still the same.

PROFESSIONAL HELP

Mention was made earlier of the vital importance of building walls that are strong and safe. From time to time the news media carry stories of the collapse of garden and boundary walls, often with tragic consequences for anyone in the immediate vicinity. It is therefore wise (and may in some countries be an essential requirement of local building codes) to get professional advice from a builder or structural engineer if you are building walls taller than about 1350 mm (4ft 6in), and essential if they are earth-retaining walls. This will ensure that the dimensions and constructional techniques you propose to use will result in a wall strong enough to do its job properly for the foreseeable future. The small expense will be more than justified in terms of the peace of mind such reassurance will bring.

You may decide that such large-scale projects are beyond your skill and ability to build, and that you will employ professional help for the construction as well as for the design. It is better to accept your limitations at the beginning of the project than to start work and find that you cannot complete the job.

Left: Solid walling blocks combine with pierced screen blocks to form a wind-break for a favourite stone seat.

Right: Reconstituted paving slabs and walling blocks are easier to use than natural stone for formal features.

WALLS

DRY STONE WALLS

Dry stone walls have been a feature of the landscape for centuries, and were the obvious choice for both livestock enclosure and boundary marking in areas where stone was plentiful. A well-built dry stone wall will stand for many years, and even a tumbledown one can be quickly restored to full health.

The skill in building dry stone walls lies in the waller's ability to select the right stones and to build them up into a stable, durable and good-looking wall.

WALL STRUCTURE

Since no mortar is used in building a true dry stone wall, it has to rely on a sound foundation and careful place-

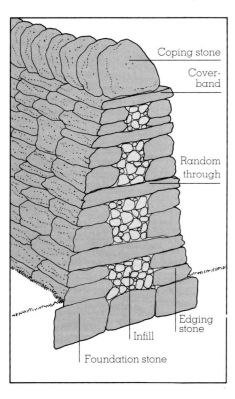

Coping stone
Cover-band
Random through
Edging stone
Infill
Foundation stone

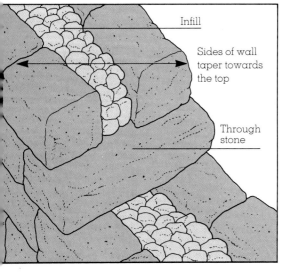

Infill
Sides of wall taper towards the top
Through stone

ment of the individual stones for its strength. At the base of the wall is a layer of large, heavy stones set in a shallow trench foundation. Above this lies the first course of the wall proper. This is built up as two separate faces, using the largest stones that are available once the foundation has been laid, to a height of about 600 mm (2 ft). The space between the two faces is filled with a 'hearting' of smaller stones, and then a course of long 'through' stones is laid so the individual stones reach from one face of the wall to the other and serve to bind them together.

Next comes a second course of facing stones, with hearting in between, a second layer of 'throughs' and, if the height of the wall requires it, a third course of facing stones and hearting.

Above and right: *If the stones used are small and regular, the structure can be built up safely without the need for through stones, using a similar bonding pattern to that used for a brick wall. Coping stones complete the wall.*

Above the final course of facing stones a layer of 'coverbands' is added. These project about 50 mm beyond the face of the wall, and help to bind the top course of the wall together; they also prevent rainwater from penetrating the core of the wall, and provide a firm base for the upright coping stones that finish the wall off.

The key feature of any dry stone wall is that each face of a free-standing wall slopes inwards from the foundation up

to the top. This slope is known as the 'batter', and may result in a wall being as much as 900 mm (3 ft) thick at the base and tapering to about 400 mm (16 in) at the top. On earth-retaining walls, the inner face slopes slightly backwards and the outer face has a rather steeper batter.

Walling materials

Since landowners are unlikely to take kindly to you loading up your car boot with stone from the local countryside, the chances are that you will have to buy stone for your walls from a local stonemason or quarry. He should be able to advise you on the best choice of stone; generally speaking harder, non-porous stone such as granite is ideal, but some limestones and sandstones are also suitable.

Estimating quantities is tricky – you cannot simply count the units as you can with a brick wall. Stone is generally ordered by the tonne, and you will find that one tonne will build about 1cu m (35cu ft) of wall including foundations. It is no bad thing to over-order slightly in any case; since carriage is very expensive, you do not want to have to send for a second delivery because you have run short of stone.

If you cannot find – or else cannot afford – natural stone, then the only alternative that looks anything like the real thing is broken paving stone, such as you would use for crazy paving. The broken edges are laid facing outwards so that they look reasonably natural. The one big advantage of using this

Below: *Hammer small pinning stones beneath individual coping stones to ensure that they are securely bedded.*

material is that the flat faces of the pieces make it easy to build the wall up evenly in courses, and you can also use slate or similar packing to avoid the appearance that the courses are too close together.

Site preparation

Make sure you have somewhere for the stone to be dumped when it is delivered, and organise helpers with wheelbarrows to transfer it to near where the wall is to be built. Then sort the stones into groups of different sizes – large foundation stones, medium-sized stones with at least one square edge for facing, long through stones and smaller infill material. It is a good idea at this stage to set aside the stones that will form the wall coping.

Apart from collecting up the tools and equipment you will need to build the wall – a spade for digging foundations, a club hammer and brick bolster for breaking the stones, a steel tape measure and a spirit level, plus gloves and stout shoes – you should also make up a batter frame to help you build the wall up to a constant and accurate slope. Make two frames from scrap battening (1) and sharpen the feet into spikes so you can set them up at opposite ends of your wall. Link them with a stringline along each face of the wall; you will move this up the frames as the wall rises.

Laying foundations

Mark out the base of the wall, and lift turf or clear surface vegetation. Then dig down to a depth of about 150 mm (6 in), or until you reach firm, undisturbed subsoil, compacting the soil by stamping or ramming it down firmly (2). In areas

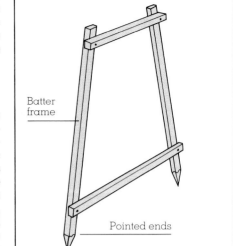

prone to prolonged frost in winter, dig even deeper – to a depth of between 450 and 600 mm (18 to 24 in).

Now you can bed in the foundation stones. These should be large and fairly flat, with the squarest edge laid at the face of the wall. Fit the stones together as best you can, and fill in gaps with smaller stones of the same thickness.

The final step before you actually start building the wall is to erect the batter frames – one at each end of the wall. Stand them alongside the foundations and use a hammer or mallet to drive their spiked ends into the ground, ready to receive their stringlines (3).

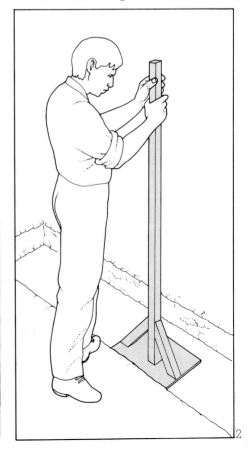

BUILDING THE WALL

Lay a course of medium-sized facing stones on the foundations along each face of the wall, again with their squarest edges facing outwards. Check with your stringline, or by 'sighting' across the batter frames, to ensure that the facing stones are set back slightly from the edges of the foundation stones. Use smaller pieces of stones to wedge the larger ones – a process called pinning – so they do not rock on the stone below. These pinning stones should always be pushed into position from the inside of the wall so they will not be seen when the wall is complete.

Pack the space between opposite faces with smaller pieces of stone, wedged as tightly as possible to ensure that the infill is well compacted and will not subside (3). Do not be tempted to use soft soil for packing; it will soon be washed out by rain, leaving the stones dangerously unstable.

Right: *A well-built dry stone wall is an object of great beauty, and need only occasional maintenance to keep it so.*

Depending on the thickness of the stone you are using, you may need to add a second or even a third course of facing stones to bring the wall height up to about 600 mm (2 ft), ready for the first course of through stones. Check that each course follows the required slope, and lay the stones so that each one overlaps a joint between the stones in the course below it (4, p17), just like stretcher bond in brickwork.

Form ends to the wall by building up a layer of long through stones at each end of the wall structure. Tie the stones into the infill at intervals with a stone laid so it projects back into the centre of the wall, and tilt the stones backwards slightly for extra stability.

Make sure that both faces and the infill are level, then lay the long through stones across the wall. They should reach from face to face for maximum strength; trim any that are over-long using your club hammer and a brick bolster. If you are short of enough stones of the right length, space those you have evenly along the length of the wall and then lay shorter 'half-throughs' between them; they should be long enough at least to reach to the centre line of the wall. Again, pin the stones inside the wall with smaller pieces of stone so they do not rock, and add infill stones in the gaps between them.

Continue building up the wall to the required height, adjusting the stringline so you keep the batter constant. A low wall may need just one more thinner layer of facing stones, followed by the layer of coverbands (the final through stones) and the coping. A taller wall (up to a maximum of about 1200 m/4 ft – higher walls may be somewhat unstable unless they are built by a specialist) will need another course of facing stones and a second layer of through stones near the top. Complete the pinning and infilling, again checking that the top of the wall is level.

Now you can add the coverbands. These are laid so that they form a sort of damp-proof course, rather like that in a parapet wall, to prevent rain from saturating the infill. They should therefore be laid so their facing edges project about 50 mm (2 in) beyond the batter slope, and their other edges should mesh as closely as possible with their neighbours like pieces in a jigsaw. Trim stones if necessary to get a good fit, and check that the coverband course is level. Pin any stones that are not perfectly bedded

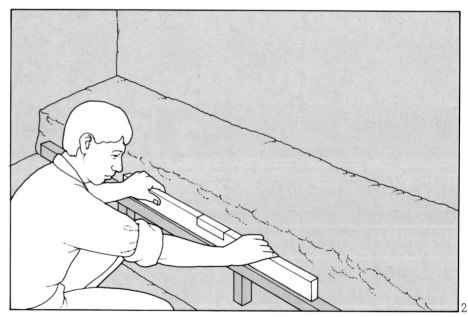

on the top course of the wall, to ensure a stable base for the coping.

If you live in an area where winters are especially severe, it is better to break·with tradition and bed the coverbands in mortar. This will help reduce water penetration and subsequent frost damage – both to individual stones, and as a result of freezing forcing the stones apart and de-stabilizing the wall.

Finally, add the coping after again adjusting the stringlines (5, p18). You can use a row of evenly-matched semi-circular stones laid on edge, lay single stones flat on top of the coverband or choose the traditional buck-and-doe coping – high and low stones which are laid alternately to give an effect that resembles a line of rabbits sitting nose to tail. It is also known as cock-and-hen coping in some areas.

Whichever type you choose, set the stones closely together. With on-edge stones, set them so they all lean slightly in one direction.

EARTH-RETAINING WALLS

If you plan to build dry stone retaining walls, follow exactly the same technique as for free-standing ones using facing stones on each face of the wall and throughs at 600 mm (2 ft) intervals. You do not need a batter frame; instead build up the ends of the wall first using long through stones, and run a stringline between the two ends to act as a guide for the batter of the front face of the wall. The only difference in construction is that the inner face slopes backwards into the bank, and it is a good idea to lay the stones with a very slight backward tilt, both to improve the wall strength and to help rainwater to drain into the bank behind.

4

5

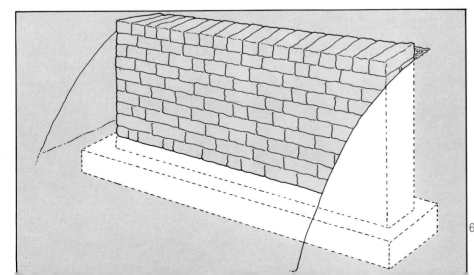

6

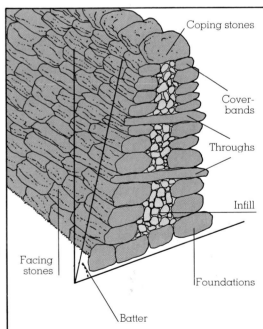

Below: *The structure of a dry-stone wall built using irregular sized stones. The most important features are the heavy foundation stones and the long through stones that bind the wall structure together. The facing stones are wedged in place with pinning stones, and the centre is filled with smaller pieces.*

Coping stones
Coverbands
Throughs
Infill
Foundations
Batter
Facing stones

Far left and left: *The first step in building a retaining wall, whether you are using random-shaped or regular stone, is to dig·out the site for the wall (1). Then check that the base on which you will be building is level (2) and add foundations for high walls. Build the wall up, using mortar to reinforce the bonding between the blocks (3), and finish off with a coping course (4). Backfill behind the wall (5) to complete the job (6).*

Raised bed wall

You can use a variation on the dry-stone walling technique to create low walls that are built to encourage an eventual clothing of plant growth. The technique is quite simple; the wall is built up using soil as the 'mortar' between the blocks, creating dozens of small planting pockets in which a variety of climbing plants can take root.

The wall can be built using either long garden walling blocks (where these are available) or pieces of broken paving slab. The former are best for a free-standing wall, with the blocks laid in two parallel rows of stretcher-bond work (end to end, with an overlap of half the block length in successive courses). Link the two halves of the wall with a header (a block laid across the two halves) after every two or three stretcher blocks.

If pieces of broken paving slab are used, the wall is best built as a cavity construction, with straight edges of slab exposed on the face of the wall and the uneven edges in its centre. The irregularities in the centre of the wall can then be filled with packed-in soil.

It must be stressed that walls built in this way should not exceed about 900 mm (3 ft) in height, and on no account should they be built as earth-retaining walls unless the blocks or slabs are set on proper concrete foundations and are bedded on mortar, with soil planting pockets only in the vertical joints.

Building the wall

Start by clearing the site, and dig a level trench to act as the footing for the wall. Compact it thoroughly with a length of fence post or similar implement, ramming pieces of broken brick or similar material into areas that are soft or have been recently disturbed. Check that the base of the trench is approximately level; any minor discrepancies can be made up by increasing or decreasing the depth of the soil bed laid beneath the first course of stones.

Build the wall up course by course, tamping each block down into a bed of loose soil about 50 mm (2 in) to compact this down to about half its thickness. This works best if the soil is slightly damp. As you complete each course, check that it is level using a long timber straightedge and a spirit level, and raise or lower any stones as necessary by adding or removing a little soil.

If you are using broken paving slabs to build the two faces of the wall, set each succeeding course back towards the wall centre by about 12 mm ($^1/_2$ in) so the face of the wall slopes very slightly inwards towards the wall centre as it rises. This will improve the stability of the wall.

Continue building the wall up course by course until it reaches the required height. Because only soil is used to bond the blocks together, it is a good idea to add mortared-on coping stones along the top of the wall to help throw rainwater clear of the wall faces and prevent it from washing out the soil. Then you can push small plant cuttings into the planting pockets.

1 Start by excavating the site for the planter, digging down until you reach firm, undisturbed subsoil.

2 Level and compact it thoroughly.

3 Build up the planter course by course, using sieved soil or peat to bed the slabs in place.

4 Check that the courses are building up truly level as the wall rises.

5 Continue adding courses, sloping the wall face backwards slightly to give the structure extra strength.

Above: This raised bed has matured over several years to become an attractive feature in an otherwise flat garden.

Moss and lichen can be encouraged by a liberal painting of natural yoghurt or pig dung diluted in water.

WALLS

REGULAR BLOCK WALLS

The main advantages of choosing blocks as the material for your garden walls are that they are comparatively inexpensive, easily obtainable, weatherproof and easy to lay because of their regular shape and size. Building a simple block wall in the garden is also the perfect way to practise your masonry skills, in readiness for some more advanced projects.

ESTIMATING QUANTITIES

Reconstituted garden walling blocks are made in a wide range of sizes. To enable you to estimate the quantities you need for a project such as building a wall, you must first decide whether you will use just one size of block, just as if you were working in brick, or whether you want to mix up a number of different sizes to create visually interesting bonding patterns. If you are using just one size it is a simple matter to estimate quantities by working out how many blocks will be needed to lay one course the length of the wall, and then to multiply this by the number of courses

required. For walls of mixed design, the best solution is to plan the bonding pattern accurately to scale on squared paper, and then to count up how many blocks of each type will be needed.

Finally, it is wise to order a few extra blocks. You may ruin some in cutting them; others may have been damaged by careless handling during delivery.

MORTAR FOR BLOCK WALLS

Mortar for building block walls is made up of cement, soft (well-graded builders') sand and either lime or a chemical plasticiser. You can mix your own mortar from separate ingredients, or buy prepacked dry ready-mixed bricklaying mortar. The latter is probably simpler for a small job, but will be expensive for a large one. If you prefer to mix your own mortar, it is easiest to buy masonry cement, which has the plasticiser added and also comes in 50 kg (110 lb) bags, plus 0.2 cu m (about 300 kg/6 cwt) of sand for each bag of cement. For smaller bag sizes, use the same 1:6 cement:sand ratio for estimating quantities. See page 92 for more details about mixing mortar.

SITE PREPARATION

Excavate your trench to a depth of about 250 mm (10 in), ram in a 100 mm (4 in) layer of hardcore and drive in timber pegs which you can level using a

straightedge and spirit level. Then, lay the concrete, tamping it down well until it is level with the tops of the pegs, (in very cold or hot, dry weather, cover it with polythene to maintain its moisture content), and leave it to harden for two or three days. Do not worry about getting a perfectly smooth surface; the first mortar course can take up any slight irregularities. If frost threatens, it is best to postpone the concreting until warmer weather is promised. See page 16 for more details about setting out wall foundations.

BUILDING THE WALL

1 Before laying any blocks, it is a good idea to dry-lay the first course on the foundation strip, with a 10 mm (¹/₂ in) gap between each block, so you can work out the precise position of end piers and corners. Then you can spread a bed of mortar on the concrete, ready to receive the first course of blocks.
2 To keep your wall straight, you should set up stringlines between pegs driven into the ground at each end of the wall. Then butter some mortar onto one end of the first block and set it in place at one end of the wall, with its face in line with the stringline. If the wall starts with a pier, lay the first block at right angles to the stringline.
3 Repeat this buttering and laying for subsequent blocks, continuing until you reach the end of the wall or the first

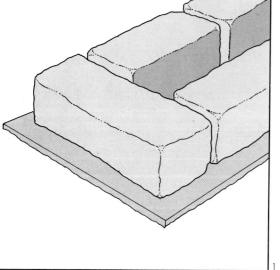

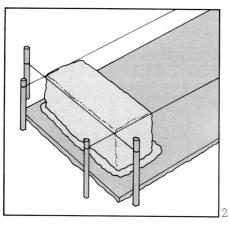

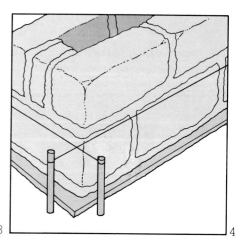

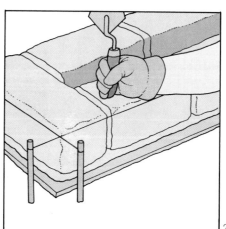

corner. At intermediate piers, lay two blocks side by side, end on to the face of the wall. Then go back and check that all the blocks are in line with the string-line, and are sitting level with each other; tamp down any that are high, and use your spirit level to check that the whole course is truly level. Trim off excess mortar from the joints, leaving it flush with the block faces for now.

4 Now you can start the second course. The blocks are staggered in a pattern called bonding to give the wall strength. On a wall one block thick, a simple overlap known as stretcher bond is used. At the end pier, lay a whole block as shown, and complete the second course of the pier with a half-block. Then continue laying the second course; note that at intermediate piers cut blocks are centred over the two end-on blocks in the first course to maintain the bonding.

5 The third course is laid out in identical fashion to the first, and the fourth is the same as the second. Simply continue building up the wall in this way, checking that each course is level and that the wall is rising truly vertically. It's a good idea to make up a gauge rod from a length of timber, marked off with alternate 65 mm (2$\frac{1}{2}$ in) and 10 mm ($\frac{1}{2}$ in) lines, so you can check that your mortar courses are even. Finish off the top of the wall with a course of coping stones, and set capping stones on top of piers.

6 On a small wall, you can leave the pointing – the neatening of the joints – until the end. On larger projects, point after every three or four courses have been completed. The simplest finish is achieved by drawing a length of rounded stick along the joints to give them a recessed rounded profile. An alternative is the struck joint, formed by drawing the pointing trowel along each joint at a slight angle. Finally, brush off excess mortar from the block surfaces with a stiff brush, and cover it with polythene sheeting if rain or frost threatens.

6

Right: The completed wall, pointed and finished off with irregular coping stones set on edge, looks massively solid.

Walls

SCREEN BLOCK WALLS

Pierced screen walling blocks are available in a range of different designs, and can be used as an attractive alternative to solid masonry blocks, especially where you want an open-screen effect. You can use them on their own in conjunction with special matching pier blocks, coping stones and pier caps where available, or

include them as decorative infill panels in walls built of other materials.

There is one big difference between screen walling blocks and other walling units. Because they are square there is no horizontal bonding between the walling units as the wall is built; instead they are simply stacked up in uniform vertical columns. This so-called stack bonding is naturally weak, and if you are building a complete wall with these blocks you have to incorporate piers (ideally built using special grooved pier blocks, although these may not be available in your area) in the wall structure at a maximum of 3 m (10 ft) intervals, as well as at the wall ends and at any corners. If the wall is more than two blocks high you should also use horizontal reinforcement in the form of expanding metal mesh strips to tie wall

and pier together after every two courses of blocks (which coincides in height with three pier blocks). The mesh strips should also be used between every course along the length of the wall.

To give the whole structure additional strength and rigidity, reinforcement can also be used within the hollow piers, in the form of 16 mm (¾ in) diameter steel rod or 50 mm (2 in) square angle iron, set in the foundation strip at each pier position. The piers are then filled with concrete as they rise.

BUILDING THE WALL

1 Start by marking out the position of the wall. Unless you are building on an existing concrete base slab, excavate the trench and pour the concrete for the foundation strip to finish at ground level.

7

8

If reinforcement is being used for the piers, set the steel rods in place in the concrete at each pier position and prop them upright while it sets (see below).

2 Then build up the first pier to the required height, checking with a spirit level as you work that the pier is rising truly vertically.

3 With the pier complete, lay a bed of mortar along the foundation strip or slab and position the first walling block in the pier's side groove after buttering mortar onto its edge. Check that it sits level and square.

4 Butter more mortar onto its other vertical edge. Use a fairly soft mortar mix which will adhere easily.

5 Add a second block next to the first and check that both are level and in line. Neaten the mortar joints with your trowel.

6 Complete the rest of the first course, using your spirit level to check that the blocks are level and also that they are in line across the face of the wall.

7 Carry on adding subsequent courses to the wall in the same way. If you are building higher than two courses, use expanded metal mesh as reinforcement between the courses. Then add two more courses and leave the mortar to harden overnight. Complete the remaining courses the next day and add coping stones and pier caps.

8 If you prefer recessed pointing, use a shaping tool to form the joint shape while the mortar is still soft.

Racking back is a technique needed when working on a large project. If you are building a second wall from one of your piers but won't finish it in one day, 'rack back' the corner to leave a stronger bond (see above).

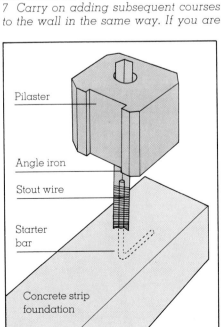

Pilaster

Angle iron

Stout wire

Starter bar

Concrete strip foundation

ARCHES HAVE BEEN USED TO BRIDGE OPENINGS IN WALLS FOR THOUSANDS OF YEARS, AND MEDIEVAL BRICKLAYERS AND STONEMASONS DEVELOPED A WIDE RANGE OF VARIATIONS ON THE BASIC SEMI-CIRCULAR ARCH THAT ARE STILL IN USE TODAY. IN THE GARDEN, AN ARCH CAN FRAME A GATEWAY, FORM AN ATTRACTIVE DIVIDER BETWEEN DIFFERENT PARTS OF THE GARDEN AND CAN EVEN PROVIDE VIEWING PORTS IN BOUNDARY WALLS. THE CONSTRUCTION TECHNIQUE IS MUCH THE SAME IN EVERY CASE.

The secret of successful arch building lies in ensuring that the arch is strong enough to support its own weight, and that the masonry below and beside it can withstand the outward thrust which the arch transmits to it. Building an arch into a run of wall ensures that the second point is safely dealt with, and accurate setting-out of the stones or

Left: *Smaller arches can be safely built using randomly-shaped stones so long as they are well bedded in mortar.*

man-made blocks that will form the arch takes care of the first.

PLANNING THE ARCH

While it is possible to form an arch in a wall one block thick (in other words, a wall built in stretcher bond), such a construction is not really strong enough for a full-height gateway. Any wall of this height should be built in 230 mm (9 in) thick masonry.

The arch itself is then formed of a semi-circle of blocks laid so that their ends (the

Above: *You can also build arches in garden walls, continuing the wall structure above and to either side of the opening.*

Left: *A large arch such as this is best built with closely-fitting dressed stones forming the arch itself.*

headers) are exposed on each face of the wall. For a typical domestic garden arch 1 to 1.2 m (3 to 4 ft) wide, the arch shape is formed by setting the blocks so that they almost touch, filling the gaps between them with wedge-shaped fillets of mortar. If the upper curve of the arch is to be left exposed, it is usual to lay two (or even three) rows of blocks to give the arch both necessary strength and pleasing proportions. However, if the arch is to be surrounded by masonry a single row of blocks can be used. In this case you will need to do some careful cutting of the blocks that will abut the upper surface of the arch to create a neat finish.

the arch blockwork while you lay it. Measure the pier separation carefully, divide the figure by 2 to get the radius of the curve and draw out two semi-circles to this radius on plywood or chipboard (particle board). The simplest method of doing this is to use a makeshift compass – a pencil, a piece of string and a nail.

Cut out the semi-circles with a jigsaw (sabre saw) or padsaw. Then cut another piece of board or softwood so its length matches the arch diameter and its width is just less than the wall thickness minus the combined thicknesses of the semi-circular former sides. Nail the two semi-circles to this.

Cut timber spacers to the same width as the base of the former, and nail these in place at intervals round the curved edge of the former to keep it rigid.

Prepare two props of scrap timber just less than the height of the piers, stand them in position and knock a brace in between them to keep them pressed against the blockwork. Lift the former into position, and check that it is level with the top of the piers and has vertical faces. Nail down through its base into the top of the props to hold it securely in place.

BUILDING THE ARCH

You can now lay the first block at each side of the arch, setting it on a wedge-shaped mortar bed so that the stretcher face which will form the underside of the arch is firmly pressed against the former.

Mark a true vertical line on the face of the former, passing through the centre of the semi-circle, and position a block (without mortar at this stage) on the centre point at the top of the former. This will form the 'keystone' of the arch.

Use another block and a pencil to mark how many whole blocks will fit in each quarter-circle between the keystone and the first block laid. Remember to allow for the thickness of the mortar joint, which should be as thin as possible at the point where the blocks will rest on the former.

Now start building up the arch, laying one block at a time at each side and adjusting the thickness of the mortar as necessary so the blocks line up with your pencil marks. Carry on until you reach the keystone position; then butter some mortar onto each face of the last block, and gently tap it into place. If you find that the keystone will not fit and you cannot reduce the spacing of the other blocks, either trim the keystone down slightly with a bolster or an angle

You are not restricted to building semi-circular arches, although these tend to look the most pleasing in a garden setting. An alternative is the so-called segmental arch, which is just a smaller part of the circumference of a larger circle. Here again, careful cutting of the surrounding blockwork will be called for.

FREESTANDING ARCHES

If you plan to finish off an opening in a garden wall with an arch, the first step is to build up the wall in blockwork to the level at which the arch will start – known as the springing point. This is usually at between 1.5 and 1.8 m (5 to 6 ft)

above ground level, to allow ample headroom beneath the centre of the arch. Make sure that the coursing at each side of the opening is level, otherwise the arch will start its life lopsided and will always look unsymmetrical. As mentioned earlier, the ideal pier separation is likely to be between 1 and 1.2 m (3 to 3½ ft); if you intend hanging a gate within the opening, measure its width carefully (including the hinges and fastenings) and leave the appropriate gap between the piers.

MAKING AN ARCH FORMER

The first step in constructing the arch itself is to make up a former to support

grinder, or use slips of roof or quarry tile instead to form the keystone.

With the ring complete, use a timber straightedge to check that the face of the ring is flat and in line with the face of the blockwork at each side of the opening. Point up the joints between the blocks on each face of the arch. Then spread a bed of mortar about 10 mm (1/2 in) thick over the upper surface of the arch, ready for the second row of blocks.

Lay these as for the first course, trying to prevent too many of the joints from coinciding with those in the inner ring by adjusting the thickness of the mortar wedges. You should aim to finish the ring with two blocks sitting either side of the arch centre line, above the keystone in the first ring.

Point the joints on the face and top surface of the second ring, and leave everything to harden for at least 48 hours. Then carefully remove the props and let the former drop down out of the way. Trim away any excess mortar from the underside of the arch and neaten the pointing there.

BUILT-IN ARCHES

If you decide to continue the wall upwards so that the arch will be completely surrounded by masonry, simply continue laying courses of blocks on top of the existing wall at each side. In each course, cut the block that will abut the arch so it will match the angle of the ring at that point, allowing for a 10 mm (½ in) thick mortar joint all round the curve. For the neatest possible effect, use a small angle grinder to cut these blocks to the precise angle required.

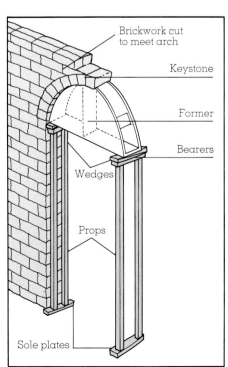

Brickwork cut to meet arch

Keystone

Former

Bearers

Wedges

Props

Sole plates

Patios

IF YOU ARE ABOUT TO START WORK ON CREATING A NEW PATIO — OR EVEN RENOVATING OR EXTENDING YOUR EXISTING ONE — SOME CAREFUL PLANNING WILL NOT ONLY HELP YOU TO MAKE THE BEST POSSIBLE USE OF THE SITE; IT WILL ALSO HELP THE JOB TO PROCEED IN AN ORDERLY FASHION AND WITH THE MINIMUM OF DISRUPTION. THIS PLANNING NOT ONLY COVERS YOUR CHOICE OF SITE AND MATERIALS; IT ALSO ENABLES YOU TO DEAL WITH OBSTACLES SUCH AS TREES AND MANHOLES.

The idea of having a hard-surfaced area in the garden on which to set your garden furniture, sunbathe, have a barbecue or create a playground for the children is a fairly recent one in countries with a cool climate. Even the word is imported – it's Spanish, and originally described a roofless courtyard.

Until the patio's import from sunnier climes, the grander sort of home had a terrace on which to walk and admire the view, while humbler abodes had a simple back yard which was little used for leisure purposes. But all that has changed now, and no self-respecting home is complete without its patio.

FIRST THOUGHTS

If you are planning a new patio, the first thing to do is to sit down and work out exactly what you expect it to do for you. Will it be used mainly as an outdoor room when the weather is fine, with chairs and a table where you can sit and read, sunbathe, eat and entertain friends? If so, will you want to include features such as a barbecue? Will the furniture be movable or built-in as part of the patio construction? Will you need space so that the children have somewhere to play when the lawn is wet? Do you want to include a washing line, so you don't have to trudge down the garden on winter days? Answers to all these questions will help you to envisage exactly what sort of patio you want, in terms of both its size and its features.

PATIO MATERIALS

At this stage it is also a good idea to start thinking about the sort of materials you want to use for your patio, since this will have a direct bearing on your design and planning. The choice is between plain concrete, paving slabs of natural or reconstituted stone, and bricks or block pavers.

Concrete is comparatively inexpensive, and can obviously be used to create a patio of any shape or size, however unusual. Its drawbacks are that the surface is visually pretty uninspiring (although a variety of textured surface finishes can be created), and it is hard work to lay, even if you do order it ready-mixed. You will need quite a lot of site preparation, plus formwork to contain the concrete as it is poured. However, it makes the most durable patio surface if it is well laid, and can always be treated as a sound base for more decorative surface materials.

Paving slabs are the most popular choice for patio surfaces. They are available in a wide range of types, shapes and sizes. Natural stone slabs are an ideal choice if you are near a quarry or other local source of supply, but if you are not they are likely to be expensive because of haulage costs. Man-made slabs, though, are relatively inexpensive and are widely available from local DIY superstores, garden centres, builders' merchants or specialist suppliers. There are squares and rectangles in a variety of sizes, colours and surface textures – including some very good imitations of natural split stone – which allow you to experiment with layouts more exciting than the traditional chequerboard or stretcher-bond arrangements. You can also buy inter-locking hexagons, and even round stones that can be intermingled with materials such as cobbles. Laying is easy – either on a sand bed or on mortar over an existing concrete base – but larger slabs can be heavy to handle. The biggest advantage of slabs over other materials is the speed with which you can lay even a substantial patio and have it ready for use. The one

Left: *Patio surfaces can complement or contrast with the materials used for the house. Here, slate set in mortar is the perfect foil for the house brickwork.*

The solution is to look elsewhere.

For example, by siting it at one side of the garden you will be able to avoid the shadow of the house, and putting it at the bottom of the garden could give you a whole new view of your property. Think too about privacy, especially if you are an ardent sunbather; picking a site that is not too overlooked will do wonders for your peace of mind!

If you're lucky enough to have a flat garden, the actual patio construction will be a strictly two-dimensional affair, but if the land slopes up, down or across your patio site you will have some heavier work to do – excavation, back-filling (or a combination of the two), plus building some earth retaining walls to keep patio and garden apart.

If the patio is to adjoin the house, you have to make sure that its finished surface will be at least 150 mm (6 in) below the level of the house damp course to avoid heavy rain splashing back above it and causing damp penetration. If the garden slopes steeply away from the house, you may be able to minimise the amount of backfilling involved by having the patio level well below the DPC, and reaching it by steps from the house. But if the garden slopes up from the house, you need to think about drainage from the patio surface; otherwise your enclosed low-level patio will turn into a pond in wet weather.

Lastly, once you have decided where your patio will be sited and how big it will be, it is time to look at whether there are any obstacles in the way of your plans – things like manholes (which can often be disguised), mature trees (which you may be able to make into a feature of the patio), even existing structures such as paths, steps and clothes lines.

Making detailed plans

For all but the simplest rectangle it pays to make a scale drawing of your proposals before you start the actual construction. This allows you to estimate materials accurately and also to work out precisely how you will overcome any site obstacles.

Work on squared paper to a scale of, say, 1:20 – this means that every 10 mm on your drawing represents 200 mm on the site. If you prefer to work in imperial measurements, use a scale of 1:24 – 1 in on the plan equals 2 ft on the ground. Measure up the site carefully so you can draw existing features onto the plan. If the site slopes and excavation and retaining walls will be needed, measure the falls carefully so you can produce

disadvantage is that it is tricky to lay them in shapes other than rectangles unless you are prepared for a lot of cutting to shape.

Block pavers are a comparatively recent arrival on the DIY scene in certain countries, although they have been used in public works for years. They are roughly brick-sized, so they are easy to handle, and come in a range of colours and textures. Most are simple rectangles, but there are also interlocking shapes which can look very attractive over small areas. They are designed to be laid over a sand bed with no mortar joints, so they can be placed and levelled very quickly (and taken up again if necessary). Because of their small size, they can also cope with curves and other unusual shapes far

more readily than slabs.

To get an idea of what is available in your area, visit local suppliers – DIY superstores, garden centres, builders' merchants or concrete manufacturers – so you can see colours and textures 'in the flesh' before making your choice.

Choosing a site

The next thing you should do is decide where the patio is going to go. Nine times out of ten, the automatic choice is to put it across the back of the house, where it acts as a sort of stepping stone between house and garden. However, unless your house faces broadly to the south in the northern hemisphere, or north in the southern hemisphere, you will not get much sun by siting it here.

PATIOS

sectional drawings as well to indicate the precise positions of steps, walls and other three-dimensional features.

If you are intending to use paving slabs, it makes sense to minimise the amount of cutting you have to do by sizing the patio so that, if possible, it consists of rows of whole slabs. This means that you need to know the size of the slabs. Most are 450 or 600 mm (18 or 24 in) across, but some ranges include half-slabs too to finish rows and, with square slabs, to enable you to stagger joints in alternate rows if you want to. With concrete and block pavers, you obviously have far greater flexibility – a concrete patio can be any size or shape you want, and block pavers are small enough for cutting not to be a major problem.

Now you can draw in the outline of the patio and add details of any other features such as walls, steps, planters and the like that you want to incorporate into it. With paving slabs, you can even draw in the individual slabs – useful for estimating quantities, as well as giving you a chance to alter the laying pattern so you can cope with obstacles such as manholes without having to do too much awkward cutting. If you are planning to lay slabs with different textures or colours to create a pattern, now is the time to colour these in – again both to help accurate estimating and to act as a guide when you start laying the slabs.

COPING WITH MANHOLES

Manholes are one of the most common obstacles when it comes to laying a patio. They are unsightly things at the best of times, and the temptation is simply to pave over them. While frowned on by professionals (and some regional authorities), this is acceptable so long as you take steps to prevent soil or sand from entering the drains and are prepared to lift the paving materials in the event of a blocked drain occurring. This means sticking to loose-laid materials – slabs or block pavers – on a sand bed (and remembering to tell your purchaser what you have done if you ever move house).

As a precaution against sand finding its way into the chamber, you should cover the manhole with a sheet of heavy-duty polythene sheeting, laid so it extends about 150 mm (6 in) beyond the chamber all round. It is also worth giving the manhole cover a generous coat of proprietary rustproofer before covering it up, especially if it is one of the lightweight galvanised types rather

RENOVATING AN OLD PATIO

If you inherit an old and run-down garden, you may be fortunate enough to discover an overgrown and derelict area of paving. A mess it may be: however, the one thing that has probably survived intact is the paving itself, and by clearing the area and then lifting and re-laying the old slabs you will be able to create a new patio with all the charm of weathered stone, and at a fraction of the cost.

1 Start by clearing the area of weeds and other foliage that has encroached on it.
2 Working from the edge of the paved area, start lifting individual stones and breaking up any old mortar pointing.
3 If the subsoil is well compacted, re-lay the slabs on pats of mortar. Otherwise use a 50 mm (2 in) thick sand bed.
4 Use square-edged pieces to form the new edge of the re-laid patio.
5 Complete the renovation by re-pointing all the gaps between the stones.

than solid cast iron.

Obviously, you cannot do this if you are laying concrete or bedding slabs or crazy paving in mortar. Here there is no alternative but to build up the walls of the chamber so that the cover will finish flush with the patio surface. You can always disguise its presence by standing a planter on top of it.

PROVIDING DRAINAGE

Any 'solid' patio should have a slight slope to stop rainwater from forming puddles on the surface, although this is not critical with slabs and pavers laid loose over a sand bed because water can drain away through the open joints. For a patio adjoining the house wall, the slope should obviously be away from the house. Where the patio will be a sunken affair in a sloping garden, you should also incorporate a surface gully at some point near the centre of the patio area and link it to a drain running to a soakaway. You are generally not allowed to drain surface water into an existing foul water drain or sewerage system.

Left and below: *Reclaimed paving stones have the attractive patina of age that modern paving materials can take years of natural weathering to acquire.*

Left: *Instead of pointing between the stones, fill the gaps with soil and plant them to encourage spreading ground cover.*

33

PATIOS

WORKING ROUND TREES

If you have a mature tree within the area your patio will occupy, aim to lay your paving material no closer to it than about three times the trunk diameter. This will ensure that the tree is not starved of water and will prevent subsequent growth from disturbing the paving materials. With slabs and pavers, set those round the opening on a mortar bed to prevent them from shifting and to form a neat edge.

USING EXISTING BASES

You can generally resurface existing concrete patios by laying slabs or block pavers on top of them so long as raising the surface level by up to 100 mm (4 in) will not cause damp problems in an adjoining house wall. If the concrete is badly cracked, aim to lay your new surface loose on a sand bed; otherwise so long as it is in reasonably sound condition you can use a mortar bed instead and then point up any of the

joints which occur between the slabs.

If you want to extend an existing area of concrete, the weak spot will be the joint between old and new areas. Break up the edge of the existing area and brush on a liberal dose of PVA or latex bonding agent to ensure a strong bond at this point.

LAYING A PATIO

Laying a patio is one of the simplest and most satisfying outdoor construction projects you can tackle, and is a golden opportunity to get the hang of some basic building techniques too. The actual job does not need a great deal of skill, just your time and effort, both of which are effectively free. Here is how to lay a patio using paving slabs, first on sand and then on mortar; block pavers are covered on page 38.

PREPARING THE BASE

Unless you are planning to use crazy paving, you will get perfectly satisfactory results by laying your slabs on a

sand base about 30 mm to 50 mm (1 in to 2 in) thick: no mortar is needed. However, this base must be flat, with a slight slope away from the house for drainage, and must be properly prepared if you are to avoid subsidence in the future. Most importantly of all, it must not be built up in such a way that the damp–proof course (DPC) in the house wall is bridged. Ideally, the finished patio surface should be about 150 mm (6 in) below DPC level, to prevent heavy rain from splashing back up the wall and causing damp penetration.

This means you will probably have to do some excavation of the patio site, even if only to remove vegetation from the area. If the subsoil is firm, do not disturb it; however, if it is at all loose, you will have to excavate to a depth of about 150 mm (6 in) and lay a 100 mm (4 in) layer of well-rammed hardcore. In this case it is then better to lay slabs on a mortar bed rather than on sand.

You can of course also lay new slabs over an existing surface – concrete, for example – so long as the finished patio surface will still be at least 150 mm (6 in) below the level of the house damp course.

Estimating quantities

With square or rectangular slabs laid in rows, working out how many you require is quite straightforward so long as you know how big the slabs are; you will need x rows, each containing y slabs – a total of x times y slabs in all. Order a few extra slabs to allow for unforeseen breakages.

Sand is sold by the cubic metre or cubic yard and parts thereof, so to work out how much you will need measure the patio area in square metres and divide the answer by 20 to get the volume required. For example, a patio 8 m (about 26 ft) wide and 5 m (16 ft) deep would need 2 cu m of sand. Order it from your local builders' merchant or transport company, who should be able to deliver hardcore too if you need it.

Laying slabs on mortar

Start by dry-laying the slabs you are using so you can work out where cut slabs will be needed. Then mark your starting point clearly, lift the slabs and the turf and excavate to a depth of about 150 mm (6 in) to expose solid, undisturbed sub-soil. Then shovel in a 100 mm (4 in) thick layer of broken brick or coarse aggregate and ram it down thoroughly to consolidate it. If you are laying your patio over existing concrete, simply

Right: The finished patio has a smooth surface that is good-looking, practical and also easy to keep clean.

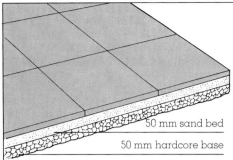

1 A typical patio cross-section – slabs laid on sand or mortar over hardcore.

50 mm sand bed
50 mm hardcore base

2 Excavate soft subsoil, then tip in a layer of hardcore about 50 mm (2 in) thick.

3 Tamp the hardcore down well into the subsoil with a heavy baulk of timber.

4 Check that the hardcore is level by drawing a batten across its surface.

Patios

sweep the surface clean and remove any loose concrete, ready to receive the new slabs.

You can lay the slabs in a continuous mortar bed, but this increases both the cost of the job and the amount of mortar you will have to mix. Instead, either put down five dabs of mortar, one under each corner of the slab and one under the middle, or lay a narrow band of mortar beneath the perimeter of the slab plus, again, one in the centre.

Bed the first slab on the mortar and tamp it down firmly with the handle of your club hammer.

Use your spirit level to check that the slab is level in one direction and that it has a slight fall in the other – away from the house if the patio adjoins it. The

degree of fall is not critical; the bubble on the spirit level should be just off-centre in the direction of the slope.

Lay subsequent slabs in the same way, butting them tightly up against their neighbours as you work and checking the levels continuously. If a slab is lying too low, lift it and add some more mortar before tamping it back. Use spacers for even joints.

Cut and fit slabs as necessary to complete the paved area, laying them in the same way as the whole ones. Make sure that edge slabs have a continuous mortar bed beneath them, and finish it

off neatly with your trowel. Then mix up some fairly dry mortar to use for pointing the joints.

Fill gaps with mortar if they are too narrow for a cut slab.

To point the joints, cut a sausage-shaped portion of mortar, lay it along the joint and use the edge of your trowel to chop it down into the gap. Alternatively, use an offcut of thin board such as hardboard held on edge to press the mortar down. Finish the joint neatly, then move onto the next one. Leave mortar droppings on the slab surfaces to dry, then brush them off; if

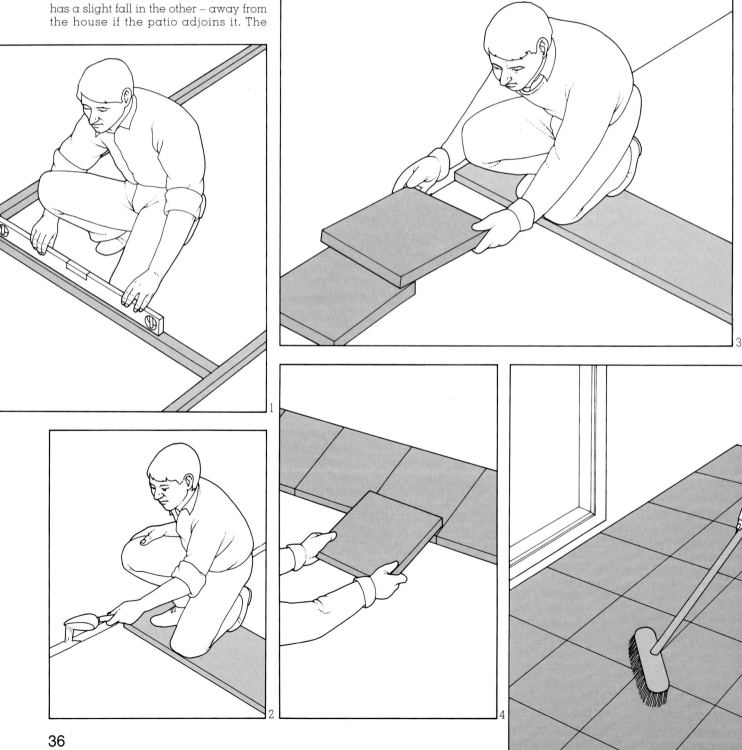

you try to remove them while they are still wet, they will stain the surface.

LAYING SLABS ON SAND

1 Begin by marking out the patio area accurately, either by dry-laying slabs or by using pegs and stringlines. Then excavate as necessary – see PREPARING THE BASE – and check that the subsoil or hardcore is roughly level. Its surface should be about 90 mm (3 in) below the surrounding ground level, so that once the sand bed and the slabs are laid the patio surface will be at the same level as the surrounding ground; actually, it is better to aim for it to be fractionally lower, so you can run your mower along the lawn edge without touching the paving.

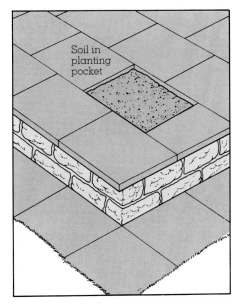

Soil in planting pocket

Save topsoil for use elsewhere in the garden; if you have to excavate a lot of subsoil, either use it to create a raised feature elsewhere in the garden, or else hire a mini-skip and have it taken away. If you are worried about weed growth, treat the patio area with a liberal dose of long-acting weedkiller at this stage.

To make it easier to get the sand bed the right depth, place 50 mm (2 in) square battens at intervals across the area to be paved. Then tip and rake out the sand between them and use a long plank spanning the battens to level it.

2 Once you have got a firm, level sand bed, lift the battens and fill in the gaps left behind with more sand.

3 Now all you have to do is to lay the slabs. Start at the edge next to the house wall, kneeling on a plank so you do not disturb the sand bed unduly, and bed the first row in place. As you work, check that each slab is level with its neighbour, scooping out or adding sand as necessary, and tamp the slab down gently but firmly with the handle of a club hammer or an offcut of heavy timber – a piece of fence post, for example.

4 Lay subsequent rows in the same way, sliding each slab into position off the edge of its neighbour in the preceding row rather than standing it on edge and then lowering it to a horizontal position.
5 Aim for closely-butted joints, and check

the alignment of the rows as you work.

If you have to cut the occasional slab, mark the cutting line with chalk and then cut a groove along the line with a brick bolster and club hammer. A few firmer blows on the line should result in a clean break along it. If you have a lot of slabs to cut, it is worth hiring a power tool called an angle grinder, which will both do the job quickly and more accurately and will also save a lot of effort and broken slabs!
5 With all the slabs laid, all you need to do now is brush some sand and sieved soil into the joints. If the perimeter of the patio will be above the level of the surrounding ground, you need some form of edge restraint to prevent the border slabs from creeping outwards. This can be provided by bedding bricks or garden walling blocks round the edge of the patio on a mortar bed, or by using lengths of preservative-treated timber – say 75 x 25 mm (3 x 1 in) in cross-section – set on edge and held in place with stout pegs driven into the ground.

Your newly-laid patio will need little in the way of maintenance. An occasional watering with weedkiller will stop weeds from growing along the soil-filled joints. If any individual slabs show signs of subsidence, simply lift them with your brick bolster and sprinkle a little more sand underneath to restore them to their original level.

Patios

Laying block paving

There are two distinct forms of block paving. The first involves bedding small but regularly-shaped stone blocks known as setts in a layer of mortar, and then pointing between them. The second uses uniformly-shaped, man-made pavers which are laid on a dry sand bed and are butt-jointed closely together (1). Dry sand is then brushed into the narrow joints to lock the blocks together.

Setts, usually of granite, have been a popular surface for centuries; indeed, the cobbled streets of medieval towns were just as likely to be paved with roughly-dressed square setts as with rounded cobbles. They are immensely durable, but laying them is a highly labour-intensive process.

Block paving has not been around for nearly so long. It first became popular some twenty years ago for use in public open spaces such as shopping precincts, and then spread to the new housing market before being discovered and taken up by the DIY market. The blocks are relatively small and manageable, unlike paving slabs, and are quick and easy to lay. They are available in a wide range of colours from buff to black, and are a standard size. Their one drawback is that since the blocks are laid on a sand bed, you need to provide some form of edging all round any paved areas – even where they abut turf – to prevent the sand from leaching away and causing the edges of the paving to spread and subside.

Interlocking pavers

Mark out, excavate and consolidate the area as for any paving project. The depth you need is 20–50 mm (¾–2 in) plus the thickness of the pavers themselves – typically around 65 mm (2½ in).

Next, position the edge restraints all round the area to be paved. You can use proprietary path kerbstones, a row of the pavers laid end to end or side by side, both bedded in concrete, or even preservative-treated timber planks secured with stout pegs. As you position the edging, check that each unit is accurately aligned and that opposite sides of square or rectangular sites are truly parallel to each other. If you are setting the edging in concrete, keep this at least 65 mm (2½ in) below the top surface of the edging to allow the sand bed to be laid right up to it.

When the concrete has hardened, lay the sand bed across the site and use a notched batten to level it to the required depth below the edge restraints. Then you can start laying the first pavers.

Right: *Small stone setts are ideal for paving this walled garden. Leaving small areas unpaved allows shrubs and small trees to be planted to soften the garden's appearance.*

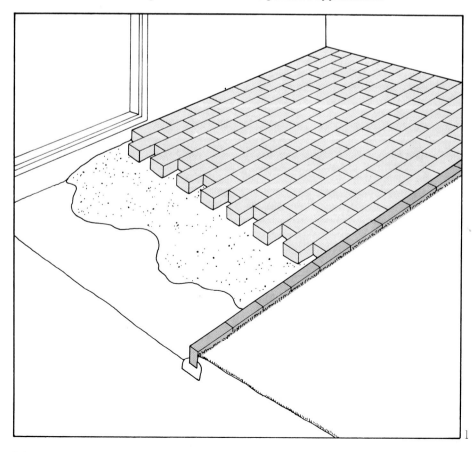

If you are working with a pattern that runs parallel to the edging, simply build it up by working across the area row by row. Set stringlines to guide you if you are working with diagonal patterns. Tamp each paver down firmly into the sand bed with a club hammer, and check that it sits level with its neighbours.

When all the whole pavers have been laid, split and fit any cut pieces that are needed to complete the pattern. It is advisable to hire a hydraulic block splitter if you have a lot of cutting to do; otherwise, you could use a brick bolster and club hammer. Finish off by brushing sand into the joints, then sweep the finished surface.

Above: *To create a stone mosaic as a feature within a larger area of paving, start by cutting a supply of roughly square stone blocks. Then bed them in soil or mortar, building up the design you want with blocks in contrasting colours. Finish off by brushing soil or dry mortar into all the joints.*

LAYING SETTS

Start by excavating the site for the setts to a depth of 25 mm (1 in) more than the average thickness of the stones you are using. Consolidate any soft areas with broken brick or coarse aggregate.

Define the edge of the area that is to be paved, and spread a layer of fairly dry mortar to a depth of about 20 mm to 50 mm (1 in to 2 in) over an area of about 1 sq m (10 sq ft). Then position the row of setts that will form the edge of the area, spacing them about 12 mm (½ in) apart. Tamp them down into the mortar bed and use a timber straightedge to ensure that the tops of the setts are level with each other (2).

Carry on laying setts in rows until you have covered the first area of mortar bed. Then spread further small areas of mortar and carry on placing and levelling setts as before until the paving is complete. Leave the mortar to set hard for 48 hours.

Pointing between the setts in the traditional manner would be impossibly time-consuming and agonisingly back-breaking. The easiest way of pointing them is to make up an almost-dry mortar mix and to brush it into the joints with a stiff broom, using the bristles to tamp the mix down between the stones. Brush off any excess mortar, then spray the whole area very lightly with water from a garden hose to dampen the mortar and help it to set hard.

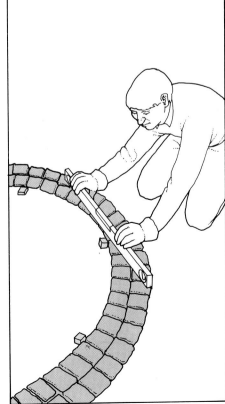

Paths

PATHS ARE VITAL COMPONENTS OF GARDEN DESIGN, PROVIDING LINKS BETWEEN VARIOUS PARTS OF THE GARDEN THAT NOT ONLY CARRY TRAFFIC OF VARIOUS SORTS — THE MEANDERING ADMIRER OF HERBACEOUS BORDERS, THE LOADED WHEELBARROW, THE CHILD ON A BICYCLE — BUT ALSO LEAD THE EYE TOWARDS INDIVIDUAL FEATURES OF THE GARDEN LAYOUT. EVEN THE MATERIALS USED TO SURFACE THEM CAN MAKE A MAJOR CONTRIBUTION TO THE OVERALL APPEARANCE OF THE GARDEN.

Right: The path through this densely-planted garden is formed by laying square paving slabs on the diagonal and infilling along the edges with gravel to encourage ground-cover plants to encroach on it.

Planning a path

Whether the path you want is to be a major garden feature or will simply enable you to walk to the garden shed without getting your feet wet, it deserves some planning. Of course, in a very small garden your options will be severely limited, and you may have no choice but to lay it as a straight line, perhaps bordering a flower bed that hugs one boundary of your property. However, if you have more space available you can experiment with different positions and also with different layouts.

Below: Planters and beds edged with natural stone blocks complement the crazy-paved paths in this walled garden.

The best way of doing this is to draw up a scale plan of your garden, with all its existing features drawn in. You can then pencil in the various options; a straight path down one side or down the centre, short straights with angled corners to change the path direction, a simple curve or a meandering S-shape are all possibilities. Whatever you draw, make the path at least 1 m (just over 3 ft) wide if possible; the absolute practical minimum width is about 750 mm (2 ft 6 in).

Once you have an outline you like the look of, move outdoors with a handful of pegs or garden canes and start transferring your plan to the garden. Then go upstairs (or climb steps to eaves level if you live in a bungalow) so you can look down on the layout and check whether it works in visual terms. Ask yourself whether it is in scale with

the garden. Does it leave awkward-to-mow patches of lawn alongside it?

Does it help to lead the eye towards a particularly attractive garden feature – a pond, a summerhouse, a showpiece shrub? Do not be afraid to alter the line and shape as you please; it is far simpler to move a few pegs now than to make alterations once you start to lay the path itself. Once you are happy with the layout, drive the pegs in securely in their final positions. Add stringlines to delineate straight edges, and use rope or lengths of garden hose to mark out curves, ready for the site preparation to begin.

Choosing materials

When you are planning a path down the garden, it is well worth thinking about the various materials available before making your final decision, since this could affect the practicality of your proposed scheme. This is particularly important if you want a path with curves, since some materials can cope better than others.

Path surfaces need to satisfy three main criteria: they should look good, wear well and be reasonably easy to keep in good condition. The materials that best satisfy these requirements are concrete, the various forms of slab and block paving, both loose-laid and mortar-bedded, gravel and tar macadam. Each has its advantages and disadvantages.

Concrete

Concrete is probably the most widely-used material for garden paths. It can be used as the final surface, or to provide a solid sub-base for other materials, and its main advantages are that it is extremely durable if it is mixed, laid and finished carefully, that it can easily be laid in curves and other complex shapes, and that it is fairly easy to keep in good condition. Its drawbacks revolve mainly around the laborious and time-consuming effort needed to prepare the site, mix and lay the concrete and finish the surface, and there is the added nuisance that the path cannot be used until the concrete has hardened fully.

Buying ready-mixed concrete reduces the labour element but will push up the price by as much as 30 per cent compared with mixing it yourself, and is really only worth considering if you are laying more than about 1cu m (1.3 cu yd) of concrete. You can find local

suppliers in your classified telephone directory under the heading Concrete – ready-mixed.

PAVING

After concrete, paving of one sort or another is the second most popular material for paths. The choice includes:
• square, rectangular or hexagonal flagstones;
• small block pavers – clay or concrete blocks and paving bricks;
• crazy paving – essentially broken pieces of paving or natural stone laid in a jigsaw pattern.

All three can be laid as 'rigid' paving in a mortar bed, ideally over a concrete base if they are to last well. The first two, flagstones and pavers, can also be laid as 'flexible' paving over a bed of sand.

The advantages of paved finishes are that you have a wide choice of surface finishes and an easy-to-maintain surface.

Left: *Plain slabs are ideal for creating regular formal paths. Here, the line is broken by spacing the slabs slightly so that grass can grow between them.*

gravel in place – paths need fixed edging of some sort to stop the stones finding their way onto lawns and flower beds. One other obvious drawback is that gravel simply does not work on sloping sites.

TAR MACADAM (ASPHALT)

Tar macadam consists of crushed stone bound together with tar or asphalt and rolled out to give a flat surface. It is usually black, but red may also be available to special order, and the colour monotony can sometimes be relieved by rolling white chippings into the finished surface to give it a speckled appearance. It can be laid like concrete as a complete path, usually about 75 mm (3 in) thick, or as a surface dressing about 15 mm (⅝ in) thick over an existing sound concrete or paved surface.

Macadam needs minimal maintenance once laid, and is easy to repair if the surface is damaged. However, it is softened by prolonged hot sunshine, and can be dented by point loads. Freshly-laid macadam needs to harden for two or three days before being used.

Left: This path features a mosaic-like pattern of small stone setts laid in diamond shapes, with the spaces filled in with gravel in a similar grey colour.

Below: Gravel is ideal for surfacing wide, sweeping paths, but care must be taken to keep stones from spreading onto adjoining lawns and flower beds.

Flexible paving has the additional advantages of being relatively quick to lay, ready for immediate use and easy to repair, while rigid paving has the major drawback of involving a lot more work – especially the pointing between the slabs once they have been laid.

GRAVEL

Gravel paths have an unmistakeably 'country house' feel about them, but there is no reason why they should not be laid on a smaller scale in the average garden. For the best looks and performance, you need well-rounded pea gravel or crushed stone between 10 and 20 mm (⅜ to ¾ in) in diameter, laid about 50 mm (2 in) thick on a sub-base of hardcore which is covered with sand to stop the gravel sinking into it.

The main advantages of gravel are that it is inexpensive, that it is very quick to lay, and incidentally that it is a not inconsiderable burglar deterrent - few would-be thieves will try tip-toeing up a gravel path at dead of night. Set against that is the need for regular raking and weedkilling to keep the surface looking smart, and the problem of keeping the

PATHS

Laying a macadam path from scratch is really a job for a specialist contractor, since the macadam must be delivered, laid (in two coats) and rolled hot. Unfortunately, there are a lot of rogue macadam operatives around, who are likely to turn up on your doorstep, lay a path that will not set for months and then disappear without trace. So if you decide you want a professionally-laid path you can trust to be of good quality, only employ firms that are members of the relevant building trade associations.

If you like the look of tar macadam and want just a surface dressing over an existing path, you can use cold-roll macadam or pre-mixed asphalt. This is sold in sacks and is simply raked out and levelled with a garden roller.

PLANNING THE WORK

Once you have decided which material to use, and whether you are laying from scratch or just resurfacing an existing path or drive, you have to make your mind up as to whether you are going to do the work yourself or employ someone to do it for you. Then you must gather information on material prices for a do-it-yourself job, or get estimates from contractors, so you can budget the job properly.

For concrete, measure the length and width of the area to be covered and multiply by the thickness to be laid. So a 20 m (65 ft) long path 1 m (3 ft 3 in) wide and 100 mm (4 in) thick will need 20 x 1 x 0.1 = 2 cu m (2.6 cu yd) of concrete.

For paving slabs and blocks, divide the total path area by the individual slab or block area to get the total number of slabs/blocks needed. Add an extra 5 per cent to allow for cutting and breakages. If they will be laid on a 50 mm (2 in) thick sand bed, use the same sums as for concrete to estimate how much sand will be needed.

If you are laying gravel, take the advice of your local aggregate supplier. Lastly, a standard-sized bag of cold-roll macadam covers about 1 sq m (11 sq ft).

LAYING CONCRETE

For a garden path you need a sub-base of well-compacted hardcore covered with a top layer of sand; this is then covered with concrete laid within timber formwork. Make both the sub-base and concrete surface layer 50 mm (2 in) thick for a path taking just light foot traffic, and 75 mm (3 in) thick if it will carry heavier loads such as a wheelbarrow.

If you are mixing the concrete yourself, the mix to use is 1 part cement to 1 parts sharp sand and 2½ parts 20 mm (¾ in) aggregate; if you are using combined sand and aggregate ('all-in aggregate'), mix 1 part cement to 3½ parts aggregate. Measure out the quantities accurately by bucket rather

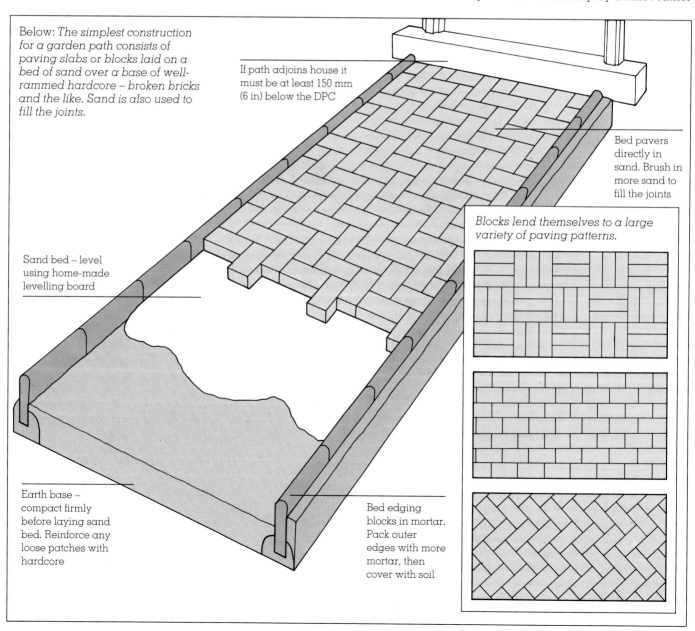

Below: *The simplest construction for a garden path consists of paving slabs or blocks laid on a bed of sand over a base of well-rammed hardcore – broken bricks and the like. Sand is also used to fill the joints.*

If path adjoins house it must be at least 150 mm (6 in) below the DPC

Bed pavers directly in sand. Brush in more sand to fill the joints

Sand bed – level using home-made levelling board

Blocks lend themselves to a large variety of paving patterns.

Earth base – compact firmly before laying sand bed. Reinforce any loose patches with hardcore

Bed edging blocks in mortar. Pack outer edges with more mortar, then cover with soil

than by shovelfuls, and hire a concrete mixer to ensure thorough, even mixing of each batch.

If you are ordering ready-mixed concrete, the specification to ask for is: minimum cement content 330 kg per cu m (20lbs per cu ft); 4 per cent entrained air; target slump 75 mm (3 in).

Excavate the path site to the required depth, set up your formwork using strong timber pegs and lay the hardcore. Then shovel the concrete into the formwork, rake it out roughly level and tamp it down with a heavy beam resting on the formwork at each side. Finish the surface with a float, a shovel back or a broom to taste. To prevent the continuous ribbon of concrete from cracking, you should then create expansion joints in the path. To do this, simply tamp a length of angle iron into the surface at roughly 2 m (6 ft) intervals and withdraw it to leave a groove about 25 mm (1 in) deep. Leave the concrete to cure under polythene sheeting or damp sacks for three days. It can then be walked on, but avoid heavy traffic for a few more days, especially in cold weather. Avoid laying concrete altogether if the ground is frozen or if frost is forecast.

L<small>AYING</small> FLAGSTONES AND PAVERS

You can lay both flagstones and pavers directly over an existing concrete base if this does not cause problems with levels (especially next to house walls), so long as the old concrete is in good condition. If it is not, it is best to break it up and use it as hardcore for a new sub-base. If you are laying a sub-base from scratch, it should be 75 mm (3 in) thick for a path taking light foot traffic, and 100 mm (4 in) or more for paths carrying heavier loads.

If you plan to bed the flagstones, crazy paving or brick pavers in mortar, use a 1:5 cement:sand mix. Place the mortar in a 'box-and-cross' pattern beneath large slabs – a line round the perimeter of the slab and crossed lines in the centre – and tamp the slab down into position. With crazy paving and small brick or block pavers, use a continuous mortar bed. When all the slabs or blocks are laid, point the joints, using a dry crumbly mortar mix so you do not stain the face of the stones. You will have to use a small pointing trowel on crazy paving, but for flagstones and pavers with narrow regular-sized joints it is easier to use a strip of plywood or hardboard to ram the mortar into the joints, finishing it about 3 mm (⅛ in) below the surface of the paving.

If you are laying flagstones or flexible paving on a sand bed, you need a thicker sub-base – about 100 mm (4 in) of well-compacted hardcore on sandy soil, more on clay soil. Follow the advice of

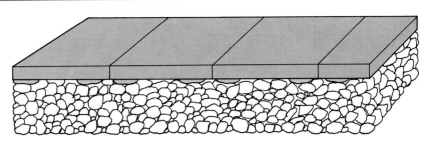

Pre-cast slabs resting on five mortar spots over compacted hardcore

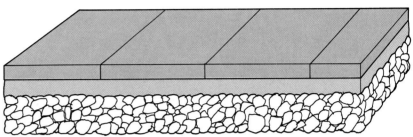

Pre-cast slabs laid on a layer of mortar over compacted hardcore

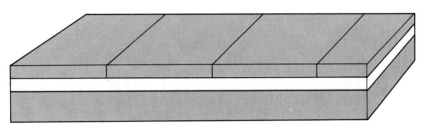

Pre-cast slabs laid on a bed of sand over compacted soil

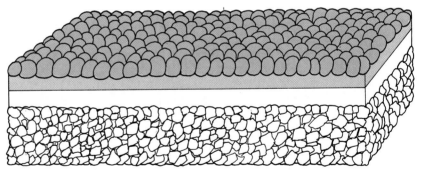

Cobble paving, embedded in mortar laid on sand over hardcore

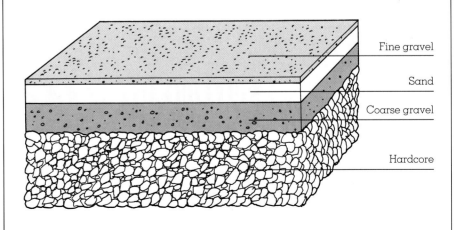

Fine gravel

Sand

Coarse gravel

Hardcore

the block manufacturers on this point. You also need some form of edge restraints – pegged timber, kerbstones or blocks set on edge in concrete – to stop the slabs or blocks from creeping outwards at the edges and to prevent the sand bed from eroding. You then top the sub-base with a 50 mm (2 in) thick layer of sharp sand, and place the slabs or blocks in position. Once they have all been bedded into place and tamped down, brush more sand over the surface to fill the joints, but remember that since the paving is laid on a flexible bed of sand they may tend to open up and crack the pointing as time goes by.

LAYING GRAVEL

This is the simplest way of laying a new path. All you need is enough 10-20 mm (⅜ – ¾ in) diameter pea gravel to form a layer about 50 mm (2 in) thick over the path area; your supplier will advise you on how much to order. You will find local suppliers listed in your classified telephone directory under Quarries or Sand and gravel suppliers, or you can ask at your local builders' merchants.

To lay a gravel path, simply excavate the area to a depth of about 150 mm (6 in) – or 200 mm (8 in) on soft clay soils – and ram in a 100 to 150 mm (4 to 6 in) thick layer of hardcore. Add some coarse gravel and then a layer of sand to prevent the gravel from sinking into the sub-base. Then install some form of

perimeter edging – pegged strips of preservative-treated timber, for example, or path edging stones or brick pavers set in concrete. Once they are in place, you can have the gravel delivered. You will probably need to barrow it to the path site, so set planks on the lawn if you have to run across it. Simply shovel it in between the edge restraints, spread it out, rake it level, and the path is ready for use.

It is a good idea to keep a couple of sacks of gravel over from the job, so you can fill ruts and top up bald patches as the path wears and settles down. It will need raking regularly, plus treatment with weedkiller two or three times a year.

LAYING COLD-ROLL MACADAM (COLD-MIX ASPHALT)

As mentioned earlier, laying hot macadam is really a job best left to professional contractors. However, you can lay cold-roll macadam over old concrete, paving or existing macadam to give it a new surface if it is sound but looks in need of a facelift. It is difficult to lay this product over hardcore with an ordinary garden roller – you need to put down two layers and use a hired plate vibrator to get good results – and so it is best not used to create new paths from scratch.

The material comes in sacks, generally containing 25 kg (55 lb) which will cover an area of about 1sq m (11sq ft) in

Below: *Place heavy-duty plastic sheeting between gravel paths to kill weeds.*

a layer 20 mm (¾ in) thick as raked out and 15 mm (⅝ in) thick after rolling and compacting. You will also need a quantity of liquid bitumen emulsion for use as a tack coat over the existing surface. A 5 kg (11 lb) drum will cover an area of about 7 sq m (75 sq ft).

Start by preparing the old path surface, filling potholes with macadam after brushing in some bitumen emulsion to improve the adhesion of the repair. Then pour the bitumen emulsion onto the surface, brush it out with an old broom and leave it to become tacky – this takes a couple of hours. Throw the broom head away afterwards.

Next, tip out the bags and rake the macadam out to a thickness of about 20 mm (¾ in). It is best to work in imaginary bays about 1 m (3 ft) wide. Use the back of the rake to break down any lumps, and check the surface as you work for slopes, bumps and hollows using a spirit level and a timber straightedge. When you have got it reasonably level, roll the surface with a garden roller, filling in any hollows that appear using some extra macadam. Keep the roller wet by sprinkling water onto it from a watering can so it does not pick up lumps of macadam. Finish off by scattering contrasting stone chippings over the surface and rolling them in.

You can walk on the path surface immediately, but avoid heavy traffic for two or three days to allow the binder to harden fully.

STEPS

IF YOU HAVE A GARDEN THAT SLOPES STEEPLY OR IS ALREADY ON SEVERAL DIFFERENT LEVELS, STEPS ARE THE OBVIOUS WAY OF COPING WITH THE SLOPE OR OF GETTING FROM ONE LEVEL TO THE NEXT. APART FROM THEIR PRACTICAL VALUE, THEY CAN ALSO BE A PLEASING GARDEN FEATURE IN THEIR OWN RIGHT. YOU CAN USE THEM EITHER TO LINK SEPARATE FLAT AREAS OF THE GARDEN, SUCH AS LAWNS AND TERRACES, OR TO MAKE PATHS UP STEEP SLOPES EASIER TO NEGOTIATE.

You can build steps as free-standing structures, usually where a wall separates the higher and lower areas, or cut them into the slope of the land itself. You can, of course, also have 'cut-in' steps where a wall occurs, by cutting back into the upper level so that the bottom step is flush with the face of the wall instead of being some distance away from it. Cut-in steps are generally easier to build, because the ground provides most of the support for the treads and very little complicated masonry is involved, but you do not have to be highly skilled to create perfectly satisfactory free-standing steps if that is the type you prefer.

The easiest ways of building garden steps are either to use garden walling blocks and paving slabs, or to cast them in concrete. The former method is far simpler than the latter, which tends to look aesthetically ugly anyway. The two

Above: *If you leave narrow planting pockets at the rear of each tread on a flight of natural stone steps, low-level plants will soften their appearance.*

most important factors to remember are that the materials you choose should suit the style of your garden – in other words, they should blend in with walls, paved areas and other masonry features – and that they should be safe to use.

PRELIMINARY PLANNING

Start by deciding what materials you are going to use, since this could affect the dimensions of the steps. For example, risers in blockwork should ideally be two blocks (about 150 mm/6 in) high. The size of the paving slabs you choose will dictate the tread width (and perhaps its depth, although cut slabs at

Left: *If possible, build your steps with materials that match those used for other features of the garden, such as retaining walls and raised planters.*

the rear of the tread are perfectly acceptable). Remember that for safety, treads should measure at least 300 mm (12 in) from front to rear, so that your toe or heel does not catch the edge of the step above as you ascend or descend the flight. Furthermore, the flight should have a minimum width of 600 mm (2 ft), and 1200 mm (4 ft) or more if people will want to pass each other on the flight.

The next stage is to work out how many steps the flight needs, by measuring the vertical height between the two levels and dividing this by the height of an individual riser. Remember that the bottom step height will include the tread thickness, but the others will not. If the answer you get from this piece of arithmetic is not close to a whole number, vary the riser height; for comfortable (and safe) walking combine shallower risers with deeper treads, higher risers with shallower treads. Do not build risers higher than about 170 mm (7 in); they are tiring to climb on all but very short flights, and can be a trip hazard.

Now you can make some simple sketches showing the plan and the front and side elevations of the flight, so you can work out the bonding pattern for the masonry and therefore estimate how many blocks and pavers you will need for the job.

As you make your plans, remember that free-standing steps should be toothed into the wall from which they are built out, to prevent them from pulling away from it if the flight should subside slightly. Cut-in types are not so prone to movement, but on steep slopes it is a good idea to set the lowest riser on a concrete strip foundation for extra stability. Where a flight will exceed about seven steps, you should include a landing – a wider flat area – at the half-way point.

Do not forget to provide drainage so water does not collect on the treads; this will make them slippery and potentially dangerous, and will also encourage the growth of algae and moss on their surfaces. Standing water will also freeze in winter – an obvious but oft-forgotten hazard, as any hospital casualty department will confirm. You should allow a fall of about 12 mm (½ in) towards the front of each tread.

Think too about drainage from paved areas at the bottom of the flight; in wet weather the steps can act as a small waterfall and may carry water from an upper area down to the lower one in unexpectedly large quantities. A gully leading to a nearby soakaway may be the answer.

STEPS

It is essential to fit a handrail or build parapet walls beside long flights, especially if they will be used by children or the elderly. Ensure that tread nosings project beyond the face of each riser, to throw a shadow and accentuate the edge of the tread. Provide lighting if the steps will be used at night.

SITE PREPARATION

Once you have completed the planning and taken delivery of the materials you ordered, you can start to mark out and excavate the site of your steps. How you proceed depends on the type of steps you are building.

For free-standing steps you need a concrete strip foundation beneath the perimeter of the lowest flight. This should be 100 mm (4 in) thick and 230 mm (9 in) wide for stretcher-bond blockwork. For flights more than five treads high, the individual risers need to be supported too, so rather than laying individual strip foundations for them it is better to lay a concrete foundation slab big enough to support the whole flight. For both strip and slab foundations, allow the concrete to set hard before building on it – 24–48 hours is usually enough, but in cold climates allow three days in summer and up to six in winter. Cover it with polythene or damp sacking to stop it from drying too quickly in hot weather.

For cut-in steps, the slope itself is cut away into steps to support the individual treads. Use string lines to mark the width of the flight and the position of the nosing of each tread. Then dig out the rough shape of each step in turn, working from the bottom of the flight upwards. Check as you work that each step is approximately the same depth and height, and take care not to break down the leading edges of the steps as you work. To lessen the risk of step edges crumbling as you excavate them, stand on a short board or plywood offcut slightly smaller than the tread itself to spread your weight.

Use a tamping post to pack down any small patches of loose subsoil you come across. If you find larger 'soft spots', dig them out until you reach firm subsoil, and pack in hardcore to restore the level.

For long or steep flights, cast a concrete strip foundation across the line of the lowest riser for extra support. It should be 100 mm (4 in) thick and twice as wide as the riser thickness.

THE FIRST STEP

Once you have completed the site preparation and laid the foundations, you are ready to start building your steps. Check first that you have all the necessary tools and materials to hand.

For laying garden walling blocks, use a 1:5 mortar mix with added plasticiser, or else buy bagged dry ready-mixed bricklaying mortar – a 50 kg (112 lb) bag makes enough mortar to lay about 60 bricks. If you are mixing your own mortar, one 50 kg bag of cement plus soft bricklaying sand will yield enough mortar for at least 450 bricks.

For free-standing steps, start by setting out pairs of string lines over the centre of your strip foundations to mark the outline of the first course of blocks (1). Then lay mortar along the front of the foundations and bed the first course of the riser in it. Check that the front edge of the riser is the correct distance from the wall; then complete the first course, working back towards the wall at each side and cutting the last block to size if necessary.

Use your builder's square to check the corners for accuracy, and adjust them if they are out of square.

You can now add the second course (2), in whatever bonding pattern you have decided to adopt. Where the course meets the wall, chop out a wall block and tooth in the last whole block of the step course (3, p52).

Allow the mortar to harden, then shovel in hardcore behind the riser and tamp it down. Take care not to disturb the new work as you do this.

On long flights of steps, you should build up walls off the foundation slab beneath the positions of subsequent risers to provide support for the treads (4, p52). Then add hardcore as before.

Right: *This unusual flight of steps zig-zags its way up the bank, with the individual treads supported on separate cast concrete blocks. The risers are kept low for safety reasons.*

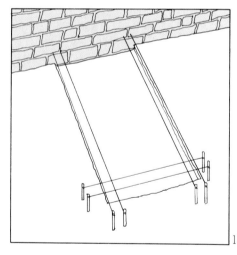

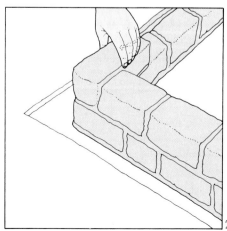

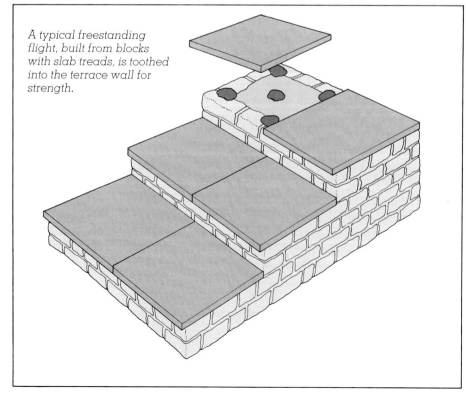

A typical freestanding flight, built from blocks with slab treads, is toothed into the terrace wall for strength.

Steps

If the steps are to be flanked by parapet walls, you are likely to be working in 230 mm (9 in) thick blockwork. Here the treads will rest on the inner half of the wall, with the outer 'skin' continuing unbroken past each tread position. With risers two blocks high, it is best to use English bond – alternate courses of stretchers and headers – with the stretcher course being used alongside each tread position so that the treads rest on the inner half of the headers on every other course.

With cut-in steps, all you have to do is to spread a bed of mortar over the compacted subsoil (or on the strip foundation if one is being used) and build up the riser in stretcher bond, cutting blocks as necessary to match the tread width. Then back-fill behind the riser with subsoil if there is a gap, tamping it down to just below the level of the top of the riser.

With free-standing steps the treads are added when the flight is completed (see COMPLETING THE FLIGHTS opposite), but with cut-in steps the second riser is usually built off the back edge of the first tread. Bed the slabs that form the tread in position, with a continuous mortar bed on top of the riser and generous dabs of mortar on the hardcore. Tamp the slabs down, check that they are level from side to side and ensure that there is a slight fall from back to front. Remember that for safety the front edge of the tread – the nosing – should project beyond the face of the riser below by a distance of about 25 mm (1 in).

The second step

Building the second step of your flight is just a repeat of the previous stage, except that for free-standing steps the U-shaped retaining wall is shallower from front to back.

For free-standing steps, you once again build the riser first - off the hardcore packing on short flights, on top of the honeycomb supporting wall you built within the previous flight on long ones. Check that the riser's front edge is

the correct distance from the wall behind, then complete the blockwork according to your plans. Again, tooth in the second course of the riser to the wall, and back-fill with hardcore (5). Continue raising honeycomb supporting walls to support the remaining risers further up the flight as necessary.

For cut-in steps, you simply bed the blocks to form the second riser on the rear edge of the first tread, then back-fill behind it and bed the second tread in place. Again, check that the tread is level from side to side and that it slopes

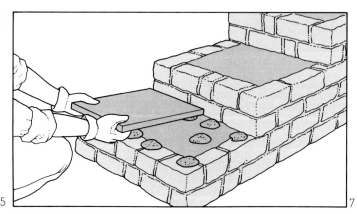

slightly from front to back. Spread your weight as you work on the second tread by laying a board on top of the first one.

COMPLETING THE FLIGHTS

Continue this sequence of operations to build the rest of the flight, adding risers (and treads on cut-in steps) until you reach the top (6).

With free-standing steps, the last riser you build will usually finish one step below the upper level; the wall itself will form the last riser, and the top tread will be level with (or will be part of) the upper level.

When you have finished all the brick-laying and the backfilling is consolidated, you can lay the treads. Start with the bottom step, laying a generous dabs of mortar on top of the supporting block-work and adding dabs of mortar on top

of the hardcore (7). Then set each tread in position, tamping it down as described for cut-in steps and checking the level and the drainage slope (8). Point the gap between the rear edge of the tread and the next riser neatly, or add cut pavers at the rear of deep treads. Then add subsequent treads in the same way, and finish off by neatening off all the pointing. As before, use a board to spread your weight when standing on treads you have just laid to avoid disturbing them.

If the flight is flanked by parapet walls, continue to build these up to the required height. Cut blocks at an angle as necessary if the line of the wall is to match the slope of the flight, and finish off the wall with pre-cast coping stones or a soldier course of blocks set on edge and neatly pointed. If you are adding a soldier course of blocks, use small

galvanised ties to secure the end block in place; it is prone to being dislodged accidentally otherwise.

With cut-in steps, all that remains is to neaten the pointing on the risers and between the treads, and to fill in the edges of the flight with turf or soil as appropriate.

Try to avoid using your new steps for at least 48 hours after you have finished building them, to allow the mortar to set hard. Set up simple rope barricades to remind the forgetful.

CONCRETE STEPS

As already mentioned, steps built with block risers and slab treads are probably the most popular form of garden step construction, but cast concrete steps are an alternative. However, setting up the timber formwork is quite complicated and the finish is utilitarian, to say the least, unless it is faced with some other material. However, concrete steps are very durable and may be worth considering as part of a patio or path project involving the use of lots of concrete for the other surfaces.

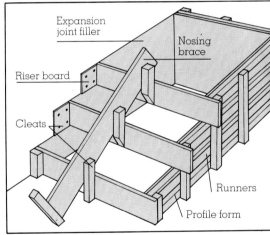

Left: *Concrete steps are an economical alternative to masonry, especially for longer flights. A coat of masonry paint can give them a brighter look.*

STEPS

If you are casting concrete steps in a bank, excavate the slope as for cut-in paved steps. Then cast a 150 mm (6 in) thick concrete foundation strip beneath the position of the first step. Position the formwork so that the front of each tread will overlap the back of the one below it by about 150 mm (6 in), so that each tread is bonded to its neighbours. Remember to give the formwork at the sides of each tread a slight slope towards the front. Start placing the concrete at the foot of the flight, laying each succeeding step in turn. Tamp the concrete down level with the tops of the formwork, and leave this in place for at least 48 hours before removing it. Give the steps a further two or three days to harden fully before using them.

To cast free-standing concrete steps the formwork must be much stronger and the whole flight must be built on a 150 mm (6 in) thick concrete foundation. The practical maximum height for a flight of this sort is about five treads.

Use 12 mm (½ in) plywood cut to the shape of the flight for the sides, bracing them upright with braces and stakes, and nail on the formers for the tread fronts. Start filling the formwork with concrete, then top this with a layer of steel reinforcing mesh. When the rest of the concrete has been poured in, it will set round the mesh and help to bond the flight together. Again, leave the concrete to harden – this time for four or five days because of the mass of concrete involved – before carefully removing the formwork.

In areas where winter frost is very cold and prolonged, foundations may need to be considerably deeper than the measurements given above to ensure that they are below the frost line. Consult local building codes for guidance, or take professional advice.

Right: *Steps are the natural way to link different levels of sloping gardens.*

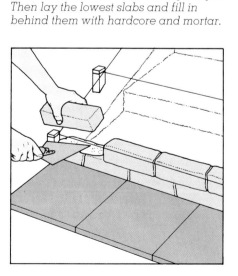

1 Mark out the flight with pegs and stringlines, and excavate the step shapes. Then lay the lowest slabs and fill in behind them with hardcore and mortar.

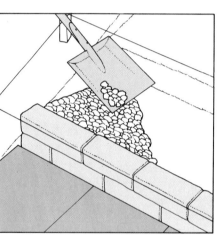

3 Fill in behind the first riser with hardcore, and check that the step cut in the bank is roughly level with the top of the masonry. Dig deeper if necessary.

2 Build up the brickwork or blockwork to form the first riser, checking that the masonry is level and neatening the pointing as you complete each course.

4 Tamp a little hardcore into the step to consolidate the soil, and to provide a slight fall from the back to the front of the step cut-out for drainage.

5 Back-fill the next step with more hardcore and tamp down as before. Then lay the slabs to form the second tread, again with a slight overhang at the front.

Below: *Even a shallow flight of built-in steps makes an attractive garden feature.*

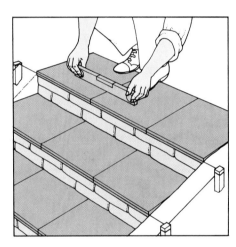

8 Carry on building risers and laying treads until you reach the top of the flight, setting the last tread level with the ground at the top of the bank.

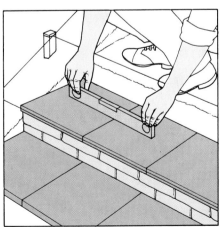

6 Lay the next course of bricks or blocks to form the second riser on the back edge of the first tread. Keep mortar off the rest of the slab to avoid staining.

7 Place pats of mortar on the hardcore, plus more on the first riser, and lay the slabs that will form the next tread. Check that they are level across the tread.

9 Neaten the pointing on the risers and brush a dry sand/mortar mix into the joints between the slabs. Leave for about seven days to set before using them.

PLANTERS

APART FROM HAVING MASONRY FEATURES ON A GRAND SCALE, SUCH AS WALLS, PATIOS, PATHS AND STEPS, EVERY GARDEN NEEDS SMALLER DETAILS TOO TO PROVIDE SOME VARIATION IN SCALE. PLANTERS ARE A PERFECT EXAMPLE, AND BY WORKING WITH SUITABLE RAW MATERIALS YOU WILL SOON BE ABLE TO CREATE A WHOLE RANGE OF DIFFERENT-SIZED AND SHAPED PLANT CONTAINERS THAT WILL ENHANCE THE CORNER OF THE PATIO OR SIT TANTALISINGLY AT THE EDGE OF A FLOWER BED OR SHRUBBERY. SO LONG AS THEIR SOIL IS WATERED REGULARLY, WHATEVER YOU CHOOSE TO GROW IN YOUR PLANTERS WILL THRIVE AND HELP TO PRODUCE AN ATTRACTIVE GARDEN ORNAMENT.

If you are going to carve stone, as opposed to just cutting it, you will need some special mason's tools and a club hammer to drive them. The basic cutting and shaping tool is a chisel, an all-steel construction with a hexagonal cross-section and a square-ended cutting blade; it is available in sizes ranging from 12 to 50 mm (½ to 2 in) wide. The point chisel or punch, as its name implies, has a pointed cutting tip, and is used to concentrate the force of the hammer on a small area of the stone during the initial roughing-out of the workpiece. The pitching tool has a wide single-ground blade, and is used for removing larger amounts of stone when trimming a workpiece down to the required size.

For carving the sort of cut-out necessary to create a stone planter, the most versatile tool of all is a mason's scutch holder, a special chisel-like tool with a replaceable cutting edge known as a scutch. This is double-sided, and may have plain or toothed edges. It is used after the initial roughing-out, and the toothed version leaves a series of furrows in the stone which can either be left as

Right: *Simple carved planters blend well with the garden, and are an ideal introduction to stone-carving techniques.*

Below: *You need only the simplest carving tools to create both formal and irregularly-shaped planters.*

the final finish or can be smoothed off using either the plain mason's chisel or the wider mason's bolster.

CHOOSING STONE

The best types of stone to use for carving objects such as garden planters are the various sandstones and limestones. Both can be liable to frost damage in the long term if they are used in a permanently damp situation, while limestone will be gradually eroded by rainwater action. However, the latter will do minimal damage over the likely life of the planter, and will have the beneficial effect of rendering it self-cleansing.

In order to minimise the amount of cutting and wastage involved in carving the planter, try to choose stones that are already rough-cut to about the size and

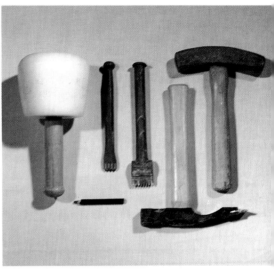

Above: *Basic carving tools include hammers, mallets, mason's chisels, and a scutch holder and scutch.*

overall depth you want. As far as colour is concerned, both types of stone can be found in shades ranging from creamy white to deep ochre; limestones may contain visible shell and other fossil formations, betraying their submarine origins, while the sandstones may have bands of colour resulting from the depositing of different-coloured sediments during their formation. These can look particularly attractive as an edge detail to small pieces of ornamental stonework such as a garden planter.

When selecting stones, remember that even small pieces can be surprisingly heavy – the typical density of limestones and sandstones is between 2,000 and 2,500 kilograms per cubic metre (125 to 155 pounds per cubic foot). Turn stones on the ground to inspect them, with the help of a sturdy lever and fulcrum if necessary to get extra power, and do not lift heavy stones without

PLANTERS

help. When it comes to transporting them, take great care not to overload and damage the suspension of the typical family car, which was not designed to carry such loads.

See pages 88-89 for more details about selecting stone.

CARVING A PLANTER

When you have found a suitable piece of stone in an appropriate size, shape and colour for your garden, examine it carefully to see which way the 'bed' of the stone runs (see below). Although limestone and sandstone are both relatively soft, you will find carving much easier if you are working with the bed horizontal, cutting into it and then hollowing out along it rather than the other way round.

Before starting to mark out and carve the stone, set it at a comfortable height on a sturdy support; a tailor-made timber carving table 600 to 750 mm (24 to 30 in) square is ideal.

1 Start by marking the outline of the recess you want to cut in pencil on the top surface of the stone. Leave a margin between the cutting line and the edge of the stone of at least 50 mm (2 in), to avoid any risk of the edge breaking away as you work.
2 Use a club hammer and mason's chisel – or better still a toothed scutch in a mason's scutch holder – to outline the recess. Work all round the cutting line, chopping vertically downwards first, then lower the tool's cutting angle to about 45° to start breaking away the

stone within it. Always work towards the centre of the recess, walking round the workpiece as you do so.
3 As the recess deepens, brush out the stone chippings and dust so you can keep a close eye on your progress.
4 Continue carving in the same way, gradually deepening the recess by cutting down the sides further to create a smooth bowl in the stone. Check the depth of the recess as you work, to avoid any risk of cutting too deep and cracking the stone or breaking through the base.
5 Either leave the stone with the ridged finish left by the toothed scutch, or smooth off the ridges using a plain scutch, a mason's chisel or a bolster. Brush out the debris for the last time and the planter is ready for use.

PLANTERS

MAKING A WORK TABLE

Use workshop scrap wood and a blockboard offcut to assemble a sturdy carving work table with a comfortable working height. Cut the pieces to length and nail them securely together.

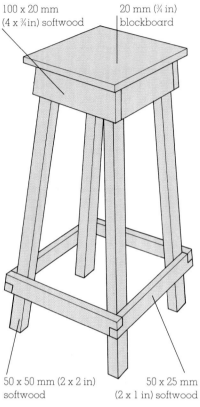

100 x 20 mm (4 x ¾ in) softwood

20 mm (¾ in) blockboard

50 x 50 mm (2 x 2 in) softwood

50 x 25 mm (2 x 1 in) softwood

Left: *Working at ground level is always possible, but it can cause back-ache, so a custom-made table (Above) is best.*

ROCKERIES

CREATING A ROCKERY OR ROCK GARDEN NOT ONLY ADDS A WELCOME THIRD DIMENSION TO THE EXPANSE OF LAWNS AND FLOWERBEDS FOUND IN A TYPICAL GARDEN. IT ALSO BRINGS A VARIETY OF TEXTURE TO THE GARDEN AND ALLOWS YOU TO GROW A VARIETY OF SPECIES SUCH AS ALPINE PLANTS WHICH WILL MAKE THE ROCKERY A COLOURFUL AND INTERESTING GARDEN FEATURE ALL THE YEAR ROUND.

In their natural habitat, rock plants grow and thrive in the wind-blown soil and broken-down stone chippings that always accumulate in pockets in the rocks and around the base of the outcrop. The contrast between the mass of stone and the delicacy of the tiny plants makes a striking contrast, and is one that gardeners everywhere have long striven to emulate on a smaller scale in their own gardens.

The secret of success in creating a rock garden is not to try to emulate the sometimes strikingly massive rockeries on view in large parks and botanical gardens. There is still space for a rock garden in even a small plot, but it must be in scale with its surroundings.

CHOOSING A SITE

A successful rock garden should look just like a natural outcrop of rock, so it will work best if surrounded by an expanse of lawn or other open space. It should be kept well away from formal features such as regular flower beds, paths and geometrically-shaped ponds, since its own informality will sit uneasily alongside them. However, including a rock pool in a rock garden, perhaps with a cascade or waterfall, can look most attractive.

If you are too short of space to site your rock garden in the open, you can build it up against a garden wall or in a corner between two walls, although this

Right: On sloping sites, use the largest blocks you can find to create a rockery in scale with the bank. Make sure the stones are securely bedded.

Below: On level sites, keep the rockery structure relatively low; tall mounds look out of place, and nature would have quickly eroded a high outcrop of rock.

never quite looks as natural as it should. Never build one against a house wall, where it can cause damp penetration.

If the garden slopes, this gives you the opportunity to use the slope to good effect, letting the rocks break through the natural ground level, and if the slope is steep you can build the rocks up as a natural outcrop that in practice also acts as an earth-retaining wall if the stones are big enough.

Choose a site which gets plenty of sunshine, since most alpine plants prefer full sun to shade (where, in their natural habitat, they would freeze to

for the rock gardener, but are likely to prove comparatively expensive.

When choosing stones, look mainly for flattish slabs rather than rounded boulders, and pick pieces in a range of sizes which will help to give the rockery a natural appearance. Do not attempt to take them home by car, even in several separate trips; you risk damaging its suspension. If the supplier's delivery charges seem excessive, it may be worth hiring a truck and collecting the stones yourself. Take one or more strong helpers with you to assist in lifting the heavier stones.

You will also need soil for your rockery, and unless you are planning any major landscaping work in your garden and will have soil to spare, you will have to order this from your garden centre or other supplier. The ideal material is good-quality topsoil mixed with coarse sand to improve drainage.

PLANNING THE ROCKERY

The shape of rockery you build will depend to a certain extent on the size of the available site. As a general rule, avoid pure geometric shapes such as circles, rectangles or ovals; nature is never that symmetrical. Instead aim for something more random such as a tapering wedge shape, wider at the front and narrowing down as the stones rise towards the rear, which at least gives the impression that they were exposed naturally by the effects of wind and rain.

The ideal rock garden is built up in tiers, each smaller than the one beneath it. Apart from mimicking nature, this ensures that the structure is stable and will not suffer from any unexpected avalanches. On a flat site, try to ensure that the tiers look different when viewed from different angles; they should not look like the symmetrical layers of a wedding cake. On a sloping site, set each succeeding tier back into the face of the slope to create a basically triangular layout.

Do not make the mistake of building the rockery too high. To keep things in proportion, the overall height should never be more than half the diameter of the base.

PREPARING FOUNDATIONS

A rockery is more than just a random pile of stones and soil, built up on your chosen site. It needs a suitable foundation and, more importantly, good drainage, especially on a flat site or where the soil is clay rather than sand or chalk. Clay soils tend not to drain freely, and this can mean that your rockery becomes a sticky waterlogged mess after heavy rain.

Start by marking out the approximate shape you want the rockery to have. Do

death). Some will tolerate light shade, however, and you can place these on the least sunny side of the rock garden. Keep it well away from overhanging trees. Not only will they shade the rockery; if they are deciduous their annual leaf fall will be difficult to clear from the rockery and an accumulation of dead leaves will smother the plants. Watch out too for large shrubs nearby with greedy root systems, since they will rob the rock garden of moisture in hot weather.

Last of all, site your rock garden where it can be seen and enjoyed – in the front garden, or at the back in full view of the living-room window.

CHOOSING STONE

Since transport charges make up most of the cost of natural stone, it makes sense to shop for it locally. If you have any quarries nearby, they will be your best (and cheapest) sources, and will offer stone that is in keeping with the local geology. Otherwise garden centres or builders' merchants are likely to be your only source; some now stock quantities of stone in several varieties specifically

not bother with pegs and stringlines; trickling sand out round the perimeter of the area will be perfectly adequate.

Next remove any turf or vegetation from the site, and excavate it to a depth of about 150 mm (6 in). Set topsoil aside in a heap unless it is heavy clay, in which case remove it to another part of the garden. Then trample the subsoil firmly to consolidate it and create a solid base for the rockery.

The solution to poor-draining clay soils is to create a drainage sump or soakaway beneath the rockery. The natural backward tilt of the stones will tend to channel water down into the centre of the rockery, so dig out a hole there about 900 mm (3 ft) square and

450 mm (18 in) deep. Fill this with hardcore and then cover it with a layer of coarse gravel or some upturned turf to prevent topsoil from washing down into the soakaway and clogging it up.

Next, prepare the bedding material – a mixture of five parts topsoil to one part sand. The quickest way of doing this is by the shovelful, mixing five of one and one of the other in a wheelbarrow and then dumping it straight into the hole. Carry on mixing and tipping until the bedding reaches ground level (1).

BUILDING UP THE ROCKERY

Start by selecting the largest stone from your stack (2) to form the keystone of the rockery. It will be too heavy to lift unless you have help, so use a baulk of stout timber and a fulcrum to lever it end over end from the stack to the site. You may be tempted to use a pickaxe to do this; however, it was not designed to withstand leverage between head and handle, and using it in this way will weaken the fixing and may well break the handle completely.

Once the stone is in its approximate final position, look at it from every angle to check its orientation, and to make

sure that any visible strata are roughly horizontal. One face may be more presentable than another, and now is the time to swing it round to get the best face forward. As you adjust the stone's position, swivel it from side to side to settle it into the bedding material. Then insert your lever under the front edge and raise it slightly so you can shovel some more soil underneath its front edge and thereby give it a slight backward tilt. This mimics the way natural rock outcrops lie, creates natural planting pockets above each stone and also helps to guide rainwater back into the rockery instead of making it cascade down over the stones and wash the soil away. Compact the soil round the base of the stone thoroughly using a baulk of timber, then stand on it to check that it is securely bedded with no tendency to rock from side to side.

Select two slightly smaller stones next and lay them in the same way either side of the keystone. Set them back slightly to give the front tier of the rockery its desired shape, and butt them tightly up against the keystone. Wedge small pieces of stone into any gaps to help retain soil behind the stones. Again tilt each stone backwards slightly,

each stone will safely bear your weight as proof that it is well bedded.

At this stage, stand back and review your progress. Now is the time to make any alterations to the appearance of the stones, before you start building the second tier behind them, so look carefully at the way each stone lies. Does it look as if its front face is emerging naturally from the soil beneath as if by erosion? Are its strata running at a natural-looking angle? Are the stones closely butted together so the joints look like natural fissures? Make any necessary adjustments, then shovel in more of the bedding mix behind the stones ready for the second tier to be built (3).

Stamp this bedding mixture down well to form a solid base for the next tier before starting to place the stones. Again use large stones near the centre of the tier and smaller ones at the edges (4). Experiment by setting some of the stones slightly in front of their neighbours to give the tier a jagged and more natural appearance and to vary the sizes of the planting pockets. Again set the stones with a slight backward tilt, wedge small pieces of stone between the larger ones to help retain the topsoil, and check their stability by standing on them. Rebed any that move, and make

packing soil under its front edge, and consolidate it in position.

Lay the rest of the stones in the first tier of the rockery in the same way, tapering them down in size as you work outwards towards the ends of the tier. Check that

sure that you are happy with the way the individual stones are arranged.

Add more soil behind the tier to build up the height gradually, and create as many further tiers as the design of your rockery requires,

ROCKERIES

completing the structure by placing one or two stones at the pinnacle.

The next stage is to add the growing medium – three parts of good topsoil, two parts of compost or peat and one part of coarse sand. Add some bonemeal, mix it thoroughly and spread the mixture over all the exposed soil surfaces of the rockery to a depth of about 75 mm (3 in). Firm it into place ready for planting to begin (5, p63).

Below: *If you are fortunate enough to have running water in your garden, create a series of natural rock falls and let it cascade over them.*

Once you have planted the rockery, water it well using a fine spray setting on your garden hose or sprinkler. Check whether water is running visibly through any gaps between the stones, and block them with small stone wedges. Then spread a 25 mm (1 in) thick layer of coarse stone chippings over all exposed soil surfaces. This keeps weeds down and prevents the soil from drying out in summer.

ROCKERY MAINTENANCE

A well-built rockery (6, p63) will not move significantly, although some of the stones may settle slightly as the back-fill

is compacted by rain. If individual stones do show signs of movement, lift them slightly with a lever and pack smaller pieces of stone beneath them. Add fresh chippings as necessary to cover any soil that becomes exposed through natural erosion or after a cloudburst.

VARIATIONS ON A THEME

You can extend the rockery principle in many ways. For example, if you have an open boundary at the front of your property, laid at present to lawn, a linear rockery along the boundary will not only look most attractive; it will define the border clearly, and help to

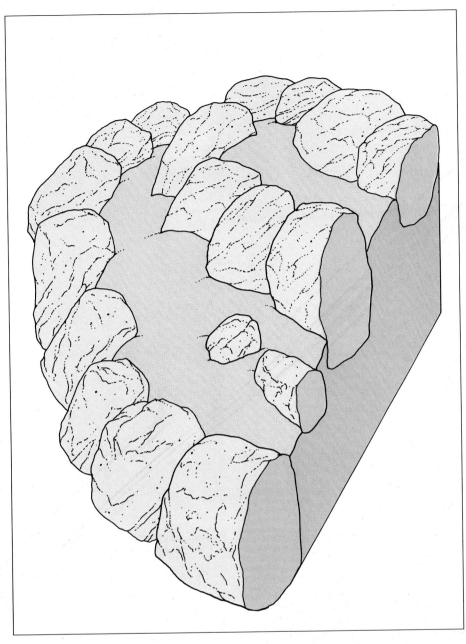

dissuade passing children or dogs from trespassing on it. Such a boundary rockery need be no more than about 1m (about 3 ft) deep and perhaps 500 mm (20 in) high, and the plants it can support will make a most unusual display all year round.

If you have a steeply sloping back garden, a vertical rockery incorporating a cascade could be a stunning centrepiece. The basic construction involves creating a closed loop for the water to run round with the aid of a pump, discharging at the top of the cascade and flowing down over the stones to a collecting pool at the foot of the slope. To keep the water from seeping away into the subsoil, this loop must obviously be waterproofed, and the best way of doing this is to use flexible pond lining material (see pages 76-78 for more details) to create a watercourse from the top of the slope down to the pool at the bottom. The pump can be submerged in this pool, and the hose is run beneath the liner up to its discharge point.

A cascade of this sort works best using fairly large stones, which must be set in steps cut in the slope to keep them in position. Work from the bottom upwards, excavating the collecting pool first; this should be as wide as the cascade but can be fairly shallow from front to back so it can be almost concealed by overhanging stones; it should also be deep enough to conceal the pump and to provide a reasonable reservoir of water for the cascade. Then cut out the steps and lay the liner in position over them, funnelling its bottom end over the lip of the collecting pool.

Spread some rounded gravel on each step to provide a bedding for the stones (and to prevent them from puncturing the liner if they have any sharp projections). Then set the stones in place, building them up so they touch each other in the random arrangement of a natural rock outcrop and so conceal the liner beneath. Set each stone so its top surface slopes downwards towards the front.

At the top, lay a flattish stone with a slight forward tilt to act as the top discharge lip of the cascade. Bring the circulating hose from behind it to near its front edge, then conceal it with a final capping stone bedded in gravel on top of the stone forming the discharge lip. Complete the cascade by wedging smaller stones into any gaps.

Now you can fill the reservoir and start the pump. Water will flow over the discharge lip and will tinkle down over and between the other stones, eventually being funnelled by the liner into the collecting pool for recirculation.

Left: *A combined rockery and pool lets you grow aquatic plants alongside your favourite rockery alpines.*

65

Seats & Tables

WHILE STONE MIGHT NOT APPEAR TO BE AN OBVIOUS CHOICE AS A MATERIAL FOR CREATING GARDEN FURNITURE, THERE IS TREMENDOUS SCOPE FOR USING ITS STRENGTH, DURABILITY AND RUGGED NATURAL APPEARANCE TO CREATE SEATS AND TABLES THAT CAN REMAIN AS A PERMANENT PART OF THE LANDSCAPE EVEN WHEN THEY ARE NOT BEING USED FOR THEIR PRIMARY PURPOSE.

Building stone seats

For anyone who has ever walked in the countryside and has looked for a natural seat to rest on from time to time, it takes relatively little imagination to transplant that welcome shelf of stone on the open hillside into the garden. The stone bench – perhaps a ledge at the side of a sheltering cave – was probably early man's first seat, and the fact that many stones split naturally into manageable slabs along their bedding planes makes the construction of simple garden seating a relatively straightforward task.

The simplest structure, a bench, needs nothing more than a horizontal slab for the seat, resting on two or three securely-set supporting stones. Unless you are prepared for some laborious dressing work on the seat supports to ensure that the seat is level and will not rock, it makes sense to use cement mortar not only to bond the components together but also to take up any irregularity in their fit, effectively providing a

Right: A massive tabletop set on a stone drum is surrounded by a stone bench.

Below: A slate slab set on heavy stone blocks makes an unusual outdoor table.

Above: *Natural stone slabs set on sturdy legs create a sitting-out area with an eerily prehistoric look about it; only the stone trolls are missing.*

Left: *A little ingenuity is all it takes to turn even the most unlikely stone shapes into unusual garden seats.*

essential for bedding the stones and bonding the joints, and some additional reinforcement in the form of galvanised metal pins may be needed to give the seat extra strength.

Perhaps the most satisfying type of masonry seating to construct is a shelf seat and back slab built into a surrounding masonry wall. This acts as both back support and armrest, as well as supporting the seat itself, and the resulting structure combines the function of seat and wall in one potentially very attractive garden feature.

To build such a seat, you should plan the perimeter walls first. The structure is basically a masonry box; the front wall will support the front edge of the seat, the side walls will rise a little higher and act as armrests, while the back wall will rise to shoulder height and will support the angled back slabs. As the walls are built up, stones are set to project as corbels from the side and rear walls into the box level with the top of the front wall to provide supports for the seat

joint that can be compressed when the mortar is wet to ensure a level seat.

A variation on the simple bench seat is the cantilevered slab, built into a stone wall so that the seat projects from it at a comfortable height. The wall itself obviously needs to be fairly massive in width, since you need to set about one quarter of the slab (measured from front to back) within the wall structure to provide adequate

support to the slab. The additional weight of the rest of the wall, sitting on the rear edge of the seat slab, then helps to counteract the leverage imposed by someone sitting on the seat.

Slightly more elaborate is the slab seat – a bench with stone blocks set on it to form back and arm supports. Careful choice of the stone blocks used is essential if the seat is to be comfortable as well as structurally secure; mortar is

slabs. The side and rear walls are then built up to their required heights, and are topped off with capping stones to prevent rainwater from penetrating the wall structure.

Once the basic box has been completed, the next step is to use mortar to bed the seat slabs in place, resting their front edges on the top of the low front wall and setting their side and rear edges on the corbels built into the wall structure. Once the seat is in place, similar slabs can be added to form the back support. Set the slabs so that their lower edges rest on the seat slab, and lay them back at a slight angle so their top edges rest against the back wall. Use mortar to bond them in position and to point the gaps between both the seat and back slabs.

You can build a monumental seat of this sort as a straight bench, in a gentle curve or as a more steeply-curved horse-shoe shape, depending on its site.

The comfort factor

It must be said that unless a stone seat has been warmed up by standing in full sunlight for an hour or so, it is likely to be a cold and potentially rather damp place to sit. You can overcome this either by making individual slatted timber panels to suit each seat, or by making seat cushions. The former can obviously be left outside so long as they are made from preservative-treated timber, while the latter should be covered with waterproof fabric even if they are brought out only when they are required, to counteract any dampness in the stone. Latex foam is the ideal cushion filling for this situation, since it is itself moisture-resistant.

Building stone tables

Creating stone garden tables is really a variation on the simple bench principle. The basic ingredient is a single stone to act as the table top. This can either be a roughly-hewn and irregularly-shaped slab of sandstone or limestone, or a more highly-finished piece of slate or marble; it all depends on the visual effect you want to achieve and on what type of stone is most readily available locally.

To support the table top you have several options, each the masonry equivalent of tried-and-tested indoor furniture designs. One of the most spectacular is the centre pedestal, which works particularly well with the more massive and irregular table-top slabs. This is nothing more than a square block or a roughly cylindrical drum set on the ground to support the table top, which should be securely bedded on mortar to ensure that it cannot be toppled.

The second option is best for rectangular slabs, and involves setting the table top on two end supports – blocks or slabs set securely in the ground with their tops level ready to receive the table top.

The third option, more difficult to construct than the other two, requires the positioning of a sturdy stone column at each corner of the table. This method is ideal for supporting both square and rectangular table tops.

Using loose stone

There is obviously no substitute for large flat slabs when it comes to forming the working surfaces of garden seats and tables, but there is no reason why their supports should not be built up using small individual stones rather than more massive monoliths. This applies particularly to supports for tables, where you can build up end or corner supports as columns or panels of masonry bonded together with mortar. However, it is wise to incorporate some form of internal reinforcement within the supports to withstand lateral move-ment, since the table top itself is still likely to be fairly massive and a collapse of the supports could have serious consequences.

The best way of constructing such a support is to start by laying a shallow concrete foundation pad beneath the chosen support position. Then decide on the height of the support and prepare one or two steel reinforcing rods long enough to match this and to allow for the L-shaped end of the rod to be bedded in the concrete pad. Set the rods in the concrete immediately after placing it, and prop them upright while the concrete sets. You can then build up the masonry support round the reinforc-ing rod(s) to the required height, concealing them within the column or wall as you work. When you reach the top of the rod, add a generous pad of mortar on top of the pier and bed the table top in place.

Below: *Dressed slabs forming a flight of steps, a table and a bench have supports fashioned from contrasting stonework. The latter need internal reinforcement.*

Ponds

A POND IS ONE OF THE MOST ATTRACTIVE FEATURES YOU CAN CREATE IN YOUR GARDEN, BECAUSE IT BRINGS AN EXTRA DIMENSION: WATER. APART FROM PROVIDING A HOME FOR A COLLECTION OF ORNAMENTAL FISH, A POND ALLOWS YOU TO GROW A RANGE OF AQUATIC AND MARSH-LOVING PLANTS AND PROVIDES A NATURAL ATTRACTION FOR WILD LIFE OF ALL SORTS — BIRDS, AMPHIBIANS, INSECTS, EVEN THE OCCASIONAL CAT! BY SITING IT CAREFULLY, YOU CAN ALSO MAKE IT THE CENTREPIECE OF THE GARDEN, AND A SENSIBLE CHOICE OF SHAPE AND SIZE MEANS THAT IT WILL COMPLEMENT ANY GARDEN LAYOUT, FORMAL OR INFORMAL.

The one thing to remember about creating a pond is that it is more than just a construction job. While you can make a watertight hole in the ground and fill it with water almost overnight, the plants will take time to establish themselves and so it may take a season or two for the pond to become self-supporting. Once it has done so, however, it will be perfectly capable of looking after itself.

A CHOICE OF TYPES

The essential ingredient of any pond is a waterproof lining, and you can provide this in one of three common ways.

The simplest, if available, is a rigid pond liner. These are moulded from either reinforced glass fibre or PVC, and come in a wide range of shapes and sizes, up to a maximum of about 4 m (13

ft) long. Most are a neutral grey colour, but cream and blue are also available; some have edges moulded to resemble rocks or paving, while others need a natural stone surround to conceal their edges and help them to blend in with their surroundings. To install one, all you have to do is dig a hole of the right shape in the ground and lower the liner into place, checking that it is level and well supported with soil round the sides. A rigid liner is likely to be the most expensive type of pond; glass fibre types

Right: *A raised pond, here built with natural stone and incorporated within a rockery, is the simplest type to build.*

Below: *Minimalist water gardening, with a small fountain cascading over a bed of cobbles within a semi-circular screen.*

Above: *Incorporating a pond into your patio allows you to grow an attractive array of aquatic plants.*

cost a little more than PVC ones, but are stronger (although you should not stand in either type during installation or planting). Both can be repaired if they develop cracks, and should last for at least ten years.

A flexible liner placed in an in-ground excavation or within a retaining wall above ground is a better bet if you want a pond larger than the off-the-shelf sizes available in rigid liners, or if you want to create an unusual shape without too much hard work. The cheapest is 500-micron polythene, available in various shades and used as a double layer to line the excavation. This is easily punctured by stones, cats' claws and the like, virtually impossible to patch successfully and becomes brittle at the water line quite quickly because of the action of ultra-violet light in the sun's rays; expect a maximum life of three to five years. The maximum width of this type depends on its thickness.

PVC sheet is more expensive than polythene, but lasts on average about twice as long. Two types are available; ordinary liners have two layers of PVC bonded together, while reinforced types have fabric mesh sandwiched between the two layers for extra strength. The PVC layers may be neutral or coloured. Various widths are available; larger sizes will have welded seams.

PVC sheet suffers from the same drawbacks as polythene; it is readily punctured (though reinforced types are fairly strong and holes in either type are easily mended with a vinyl repair kit), and it is also gradually degraded by sunlight. However, it makes a more natural-looking liner than polythene because the material stretches as the pond is filled, pulling out most of the creases and folds.

Butyl rubber is the most expensive type of liner available, but is by far the most durable; manufacturers claim a life of up to 50 years. It comes in black, charcoal grey and stone colours, and is highly resistant to puncturing (unless over-stretched) and degradation by sunlight.

The third type of liner you could choose is concrete. It is the best bet for large or ornately-shaped ponds, because large flexible liners can be very expensive. Obviously, using concrete means much more work than if a liner is fitted, and a lot of care has to be taken to make the pond waterproof. Even then, leaks may occur due to soil shrinkage in summer, frost and ice damage in winter, even growing roots from nearby plants. It is therefore a good idea to line the hole with heavy-duty polythene first so that hairline cracks do not result in leaks, and to reinforce the concrete with metal mesh on large ponds.

Concrete ponds cannot be stocked immediately, since the lime in the mix is harmful to plants and fish. You have to neutralise this by filling and emptying the pond three times, leaving it to stand full for about a week each time. An alternative is to brush on a special neutralising agent, or to use a heavy-duty bituminous waterproofer (which also helps guard against leaks).

POND SIZE

The size of pond you construct depends largely on personal preference – and on the size restrictions noted above for individual pond types. It depends as much as anything on the size of your garden and on how large a feature you want the pond to be. In general terms, the bigger the pool can be, the better; tiny ponds not only look ridiculous, but they also tend not to develop into self-supporting life systems as well as larger ponds where nature quickly establishes a balance between plant life and the pond's inhabitants.

The only formal size guideline to bear in mind concerns the number of fish you plan to have. As a rough guide allow one square metre (11 sq ft) of surface area for every ten 50–75 mm (2–3 in) fish. If you are buying larger (and more expensive) fish, check the stocking level with your supplier.

POND SHAPE

Once you have settled on which type of pond you want to install, it is time to think about the shape. In a formal garden layout a square, rectangular or round pond usually looks best, while irregular shapes will suit an informal layout. Rigid liners come in regular and irregular shapes; if you are using a flexible liner you can drape it into almost any shape you want, but there will be unavoidable folds and overlaps at sharp internal corners.

With concrete, formal shapes are best cast in two stages; the base of the pond is laid first, and then plywood shuttering is set up to form a mould for the pond walls. These should be placed as soon as the base concrete is firm. The edges of the base should be keyed while the concrete is still wet to improve the bond between base and walls, and it is also a good idea to bed in some reinforcing mesh along the join as the base is laid. Informal pond shapes with sloping sides can be cast continuously or in stages, but again the joint between sections should be reinforced to prevent cracking.

ABOVE OR BELOW GROUND?

Most people automatically assume that a pond will be below ground, and one that sets out to imitate nature will obviously be installed in this way. But if you are creating a formal pond there is no reason why it should not be above ground, enclosed by raised retaining walls which can also incorporate other features such as planters, seats and steps, and could have a fountain or several levels linked by waterfalls. It is also worth considering this option in a garden designed for a disabled person, or where there is a danger of small children falling into a below-ground pond.

A variation on this idea involves setting the pond, perhaps again with a waterfall, into a raised bank or rockery. Such treatment certainly helps to make the pond even more of an eye-catching feature.

Right: On sloping sites you have the opportunity to use running water, by pumping water to the top of the cascade from a holding pool at the bottom.

CHOOSING THE SITE

Where your pond is sited is just as important as what it is made of or what shape it is. The main thing to avoid is shade, since this will prevent aquatic plants from developing properly. You should also steer clear of trees that drop their leaves, since they will clog up the pond every autumn and foul the water unless they are removed before they begin to decompose. The best position is one that will receive plenty of sunlight, yet is reasonably sheltered from any strong prevailing winds.

If you want to have lights round (or in) the pond, or plan to install a pump to run a fountain or waterfall, it is wise to consider a site fairly near to the house so the electricity supply is easy to install. You will then be able to enjoy the sight and sound of your pond from the house or patio, in the evening as well as during the day.

CARE AND MAINTENANCE

A well-balanced pond will look after itself for the most part, with a natural balance quickly establishing itself, keeping the water clear and the fish

PONDS

and plants healthy. As mentioned earlier, you will need to remove dead leaves and the like blown into the pond before they sink and decompose; it may be worth netting the pond in autumn to keep most debris out. If the water becomes murky, you can treat it with algicidal chemicals, available from pond equipment suppliers or pet shops; however, this is often just a passing phase, and it may clear of its own accord.

Cats (and birds in country areas) can be a menace, since both will poach fish. You can net the pond, but this rather detracts from its appearance. A better way of deterring cats is to surround the pond with a low ornamental wire fence of the type popular for edging flower beds; it needs to be no more than about 150mm (6in) high to keep them away. Herons wade into ponds to make their catch, so deny them access by netting the shallows or stringing black thread across it; the latter method has the advantage of being virtually invisible.

Ice is the fishes' biggest enemy in cold climates. If the pond is iced up for more than a day, gases from decomposing vegetation cannot escape and the fish may die. The best method of keeping at least part of the pool ice-free in cold weather is with a small pool heater. In no circumstances should the ice be broken by force, since this could stun or kill the fish; if you cannot keep a small ventilation opening clear with pans of boiling water or similar means, then it is better to leave any thick ice to thaw naturally.

Ice can also be a problem with steep-sided concrete pools, because the expansion across the surface can cause cracking. Avoid absolutely vertical sides if possible, since this allows the ice sheet to expand up the slope as it forms.

PROFESSIONAL ADVICE

The best places to visit for specialist advice about installing and managing a garden pond are water gardens suppliers. They can provide you with everything you need, from the pond itself to plants, fish, food, in-pond equipment such as planting containers, pumps and fountains, pond chemicals, repair kits and so on. Some also publish helpful leaflets and books on the subject, and are happy to deal with queries about any aspect of pond care.

BUILDING A CONCRETE POND

Ther are two particular circumstances in which concrete is the best choice for a garden pond. Firstly, you may want a formal-style pond in a shape or size that is not available as an off-the-shelf rigid liner. Secondly, your plan for a large free-form pond could mean having to buy a large very expensive liner; using concrete would be much cheaper.

The main drawbacks of using concrete are that your pond will take much longer to create (and you will not be able to stock it immediately unless you are prepared to seal the concrete surface in some way), and it may give more problems in the future than a rigid or flexible liner type.

Obviously, you can create any shape you want with concrete, but there are one or two practical limitations to take into consideration. If you plan a formal pond, you will need timber shuttering to support the sides of the pool, and this could be expensive and difficult to set up for a large pond. If you are having an informal shape, you will have to be prepared to work fast in placing and finishing the concrete if potentially weak joins are to be avoided. Whichever type you choose, make sure that the central part of the pond is at least 400 mm (about 16 in) deep so it cannot freeze solid in winter; a deep end around 600 mm (2 ft) deep is ideal for fish to stay cool in hot weather. Use the shallows for plant containers.

THE CORRECT MIX

Concrete for a pond needs to be a fairly strong mix – 1 part cement to 1 part sharp sand and 2 parts coarse aggregate (or 1:3 if you are using all-in aggregate). For a job of this size it is well worth hiring a small concrete mixer; you will save time as well as effort. If you are planning to use ready-mixed concrete, your supplier will advise you on the best mix to use for the job. Make sure that you are equipped to shift the concrete quickly from where it has been tipped to the pond site so you can place it all before it starts to set.

Estimating quantities is easiest for a rectangular or other regular shape. The base and walls should be a minimum of 100 mm (4 in) thick, so you can work out the volume of the concrete one section at a time. With irregular-shaped bowls, estimate the area of the pond at ground level and double it to get the surface area of the bowl itself; then multiply this area by the thickness to arrive at an overall volume.

If you are mixing the concrete yourself, aim for a mix that is slightly on the

maker's instructions regarding coverage and number of coats.

Finish off the pond by bedding stone slabs or pavers all round the perimeter, and pointing the joints for a neat finish.

MAINTENANCE

The main problem with concrete ponds is that cracks can develop due to ground movement (more likely with rectangular types than free-form bowls, which tend to 'float' over subsidence like a boat). This means leaks, and all you can do if they occur is to empty the pond and patch them with a proprietary sealant or with mortar; in the latter case, rake out the cracks to at least 10 mm (⅜ in) wide so you can form a substantial repair, and coat the crack edges with PVA building adhesive or latex bonding agent first to improve the bond. Then re-apply a coat of pond sealer over the entire pond surface.

If the leaks persist or you cannot track them down, the best course of action is to empty the pond completely and fit a flexible liner inside the concrete shell.

dry side, especially if you are not using formwork. Too sloppy a mix will be difficult to place on sloping surfaces.

THE CONSTRUCTION

Once you have planned the shape and size of your pond and chosen its site, mark the outline with string and pegs and start digging. Remember to allow for the thickness of the concrete. With rectangular pools, cut the sides at an angle of about 20° to the vertical, and level the base.

If the subsoil is soft, put down a 100 mm (4 in) thick layer of well rammed hardcore in the base of the excavation, and blind it with sand. Otherwise, simply compact the base of the excavation thoroughly.

Lay a sheet of metal reinforcing mesh in the hole, covering just the base of a rectangular one, the whole of a freeform one. Cut and bend the mesh if necessary to get a good fit, and wire overlapping sections together.

Pour the concrete. In a rectangular pond, cast the base slab first, and check that it is level and well compacted. With a free-form pond, start in the centre (1) and build up the concrete layer round the pond sides. Work from a scaffold board spanning the pond.

With rectangular ponds, add reinforcement round the sides and erect the formwork for the sides using shuttering plywood and softwood braces. Check carefully that the shuttering is level; once the pool is filled, any errors will be glaringly obvious.

Pour the concrete into the formwork and tamp it down well. Finish it off level with the top of the formwork, and add the ledge all round which will support the perimeter paving. Float the concrete smooth in a free-form pond, then cover the concrete with polythene sheeting so it cannot dry out too quickly.

Next, add features such as small top feeder pools (2) and waterfalls (3), and finish the concrete surface with coloured rendering if you wish (4).

Where formwork has been used, remove it after about 14 days and apply a 25 mm (1 in) thick 1:3 mortar render over the pool sides and base. Add a waterproofer to the mix as an extra safeguard.

Before adding plants or fish, condition or seal the concrete to remove the harmful lime from the surface. Conditioning means filling the pool, leaving it to stand for two or three days and then emptying it again; repeat this twice more. Alternatively, brush on a proprietary pond sealer, following the

Below: *Even the smallest pool can be given life by the addition of a pumped cascade and some low-level landscaping.*

CONSTRUCTING A LINER POND

Flexible liners offer the easiest, quickest and most adaptable way of creating a garden pond; all you need is a hole in the ground – or a retaining wall structure if you want an above-ground pond – and a liner big enough to fill it.

PLANNING

Before you can work out how big a liner you need, you have to decide on the site, style and shape of your pond. Most people simply dig a hole in the lawn, but you may prefer to create a raised pond – either an informal one, perhaps within a rockery, or a formal one surrounded by masonry walls and a parapet. You will need a combination of hole in the ground and retaining wall on sloping sites.

For in-ground ponds, the simplest way of planning the position and shape is to use rope or the garden hose (1). Lay it out and move it around until you get the shape you want; then check how it will look from further away by viewing it from an upstairs window.

For raised ponds you will have to carry out some or all of the preliminary construction work first. The big advantage of this type of pond is that you are working mainly above ground level, so there is less stooping involved, and with walled types you can conceal the edges of the liner neatly beneath the final course of capping.

At the planning stage, you should also think about the depth of the pond. This should be a minimum of 380 mm (15 in) for the smallest ponds, increasing to 450 mm (18 in) for ponds with a surface area of between 2.5 and 9 sq m (25 and 100 sq ft) and to 600 mm (24 in) for areas up to 20 sq m (220 sq ft). Remember that these are recommendations for the deep centre of the pond; if you want marginal plants, you can have shallower shelves round the pond perimeter.

MEASURING UP

Most manufacturers of pool liners use a standard formula for finding the size of liner you need. The length is the overall pond length plus twice the maximum depth, the width the overall pond width plus twice the maximum depth. Because of the stretchiness of the sheeting, no extra allowance is needed for the overlap round the perimeter. So a pond 3 x 2 m (10 ft x 6 ft 6 in) in size and 450 mm (18 in) deep will need a 4 x 3 m (13 x 10 ft) liner.

OTHER MATERIALS

Unless your subsoil is relatively free from stones, you should line the pond excavation with a cushioning layer of sand about 25 mm (1 in) thick. A cubic metre (1.3 cu yd) of sand will cover about 37 sq m (400 sq ft) to this thickness.

In addition, you may like to ensure the longest possible life for your new pond by laying special fabric matting over the sand bed before fitting the liner itself. This is generally 2 m (6 ft 6in) wide, and is simply draped into the excavation and overlapped at the joins.

For an in-ground pond, you can simply turf up to the edge... so long as you do not mind fishing grass cuttings out of the water every time you mow the lawn. It is better to provide a paved area surrounding the pond, so you will need some suitable slabs, plus sand and cement for bedding and pointing them.

For raised pools with perimeter walls, or ponds with retaining walls above and below on sloping sites, you will need concrete for strip foundations as well as suitable stone or garden walling blocks (plus mortar) for the walls themselves.

BUILDING A LINER POND

With your pond outline marked and your liner delivered, you are ready to start work on the actual installation.

Clear turf and other vegetation from the pond site, and start excavating it (2). Save topsoil in one heap (on a tarpaulin or boards so you do not spoil the lawn) for use elsewhere in the garden, and dispose of the subsoil separately – either by using it to create a raised garden feature, or by having it taken away.

Work out towards the pond edges, forming a flat base to the excavation and sloping the sides at an angle of about 20° as you near the edge (3). Cut planting shelves as required, making them about 230 mm (9 in) wide and

5

7

230 mm or so below the final water level. Finally, cut back the turf at the pond edge as necessary to accommodate the edge paving.

Complete the final shaping of the excavation, and carefully remove any sharp stones protruding from the sides or base. Then cover the base and sides with a 25 mm (1 in) thick layer of damp sand (4) to act as a cushion and protect the liner from punctures. Pat it into place, and also use it to fill any holes left by prising out sharp stones.

Check that the pool edge is precisely level by driving short wooden pegs into the plateau where the paving will go, and holding a spirit level across them (use a long straightedge if

Right: *The finished pond, complete with oxygenating plants and submerged planters, ready for the fish to arrive.*

6

PONDS

Right: Even the smallest garden has room for a pond. Here, a simple raised version adjoins a matching patio.

you have only a short level). Remove or add soil as necessary. If you do not do this, the filled pond will show up any high spots.

Drape the liner loosely into the hole (after laying fabric matting, if you have decided to use it). Aim for an even overlap all round. Then anchor the overlap at intervals with stones to ensure that the liner stretches evenly as you fill it with water.

Start running the water in (5), easing off the stones to ensure that the liner fits snugly as the water level rises. Some creasing is inevitable, but you can smooth out major creases by hand as they occur.

Once the pool is full, you can go round the perimeter and cut off the liner

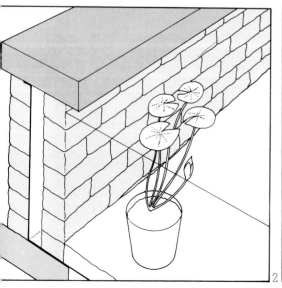

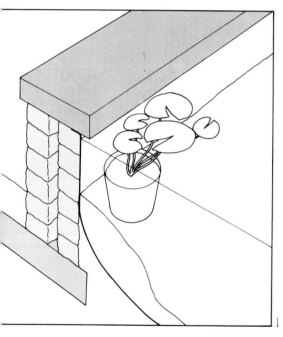

overlap (6), leaving about 150 mm (6 in) all round to lie on the perimeter plateau. Save some small offcuts in case you need to patch a puncture in the liner at any time in the future.

Lay the perimeter paving on a generous bed of mortar so that it overlaps the pond edge by about 50 mm (2 in), and point the joints (7). Where lawn adjoins the paving, set the slabs with their surface just below ground level so you will not damage the mower blades. Top up the pool so that the final water level is about 25 mm (1 in) below the under-

side of the overhanging slabs, so that the area of liner exposed to view (and to potentially damaging sunlight) is kept to an absolute minimum.

Leave the pond to stand for a few days before introducing the plants, and give these (especially the vital oxygenating ones) time to become established before finally adding the fish.

BUILDING A RAISED POND

Whether you are building a complete perimeter wall or just a short retaining

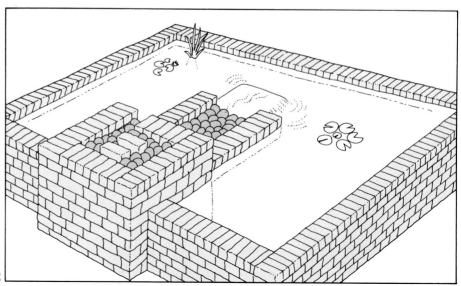

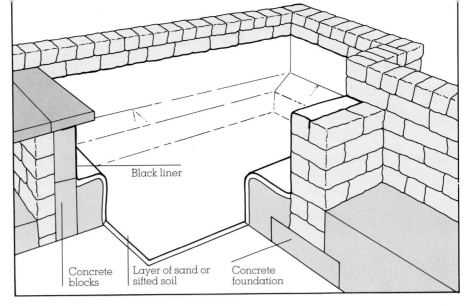

one, you need proper foundations to ensure that it stays where you put it. The technique is the same as for building any garden wall.

You can build these walls in one of two ways – as a single thickness of masonry with the liner draped inside it (1), or as a double-skinned construction with the inner skin added once the liner has been installed (2). The advantage of the latter method is that the liner is invisible at the sides of the pond – all you see is the attractive masonry – and so is less prone to accidental damage or degradation by the weather.

Plan the position, size and shape of the pond carefully, and excavate the trenches for the foundation concrete. Place this and leave it to harden for at least 48 hours.

If the pond is to be half-raised, excavate the deeper central portion at this stage, leaving the plant shelf at roughly the same level as the foundation concrete. Remove stones, and lay a sand cushion as with in-ground ponds.

Build up the perimeter or retaining walls as per your design, checking carefully as you build that each course is precisely level – vital with a complete perimeter wall. When you reach the final height, check the levels again. Allow the mortar to harden for 48 hours before fitting the liner. With a raised pond, lay a sand cushion over the base of the 'hole'.

Lay the liner in place, with an even overlap all round, and with a square or rectangular pond form neat 'hospital corner' folds at each internal angle. Anchor the liner with stones placed on top of the wall.

If you are using the concealed liner technique mentioned earlier, build up the inner leaf of masonry now, working from outside the pool if possible so you do not risk puncturing the liner by standing on it. Check the coursing as the wall rises; its last course should obviously be

Diagram labels: Black liner · Concrete blocks · Layer of sand or sifted soil · Concrete foundation

level with the outer wall. Neaten the pointing and remove any mortar droppings.

Fill the liner with water, easing off the anchor stones and neatening the internal corner folds as the water level rises. When it is full, trim off the overlap all round, leaving a flap about half the masonry width in size to be covered by the capping stones.

Finish off by laying the capping stones in place to secure the edges of the liner, and top up the pond so the water level is just below the underside of the overhang.

With the double-skin type, empty and refill the pond a couple of times to get rid of the alkalinity caused by the mortar pointing. Then introduce first the plants, then the fish, just as for in-ground ponds.

OTHER WATER FEATURES

The traditional way of creating moving water in the garden is to install a fountain or waterfall in an existing garden pond. However, if you do not have a pond or your garden is not big enough for one, you can still enjoy the pleasures of a water feature in a very small space.

The secret is to create a miniature version of a full-scale pond-and-fountain installation. All you need is a reservoir (usually at or just below ground level) to supply the water, a small pump to circulate it and some hosepipe or small-diameter tubing to connect everything up and complete the circuit. The water can emerge by overflowing from a container of some sort (perhaps an ornamental urn, a pre-cast concrete birdbath or a wall-mounted gargoyle), from a fountain head or from a free-standing decorative garden ornament such as a spouting dolphin. It then runs down and is collected in the reservoir, from where it is simply recycled by the pump back to its discharge point. The whole system is self-contained, so you will not get a waterlogged garden and you will simply need to top it up occasionally to replace losses from evaporation and spray.

Many water garden suppliers now offer a range of these water features, ready for you to install. All they need is a power supply to run the pump. The simplest have a reservoir that stands above ground, like a planter, and are filled with large pebbles in the middle of which a small fountain discharges. Larger versions feature centrepieces such as imitation millstones (with the water discharging upwards through the centre hole in the stone), or ornate fountain centrepieces which often do double duty as a birdbath. Both types are designed to stand within a ground-level or above-ground reservoir.

If you prefer to create your own water feature, you can do so by combining your own choice of cascade, fountain or other discharge point with an in-ground or above-ground reservoir. This can be a flexible liner or a rigid moulded pool, and can be left as 'open water' or filled with pebbles, just like the ready-made water features mentioned above. If the feature is to be above ground, it is a simple matter to form a support for the liner in much the same way as building a raised planter.

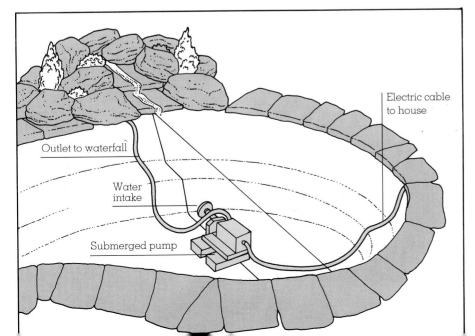

Diagram labels: Outlet to waterfall · Water intake · Submerged pump · Electric cable to house

Small weekend projects

This final section looks at some of the smaller-scale projects you can tackle. You may want to carry them out to add the final touches to a large outdoor stonework project, or just to embelish your garden with a few simple decorative features. All are quick to construct and require little in the way of expensive materials, but will enhance any garden in which they are sited.

Mounting a sundial

One of the most attractive small stone features you can add to your garden is a sundial. Apart from being a pleasing object in its own right, it will provide an amusing diversion on sunny days and will be an object of fascination for children used to telling the time from more technologically sophisticated time-keeping equipment.

The essential ingredients of a sundial are the clock face and the style of gnomon (the pointer that casts the shadow that tells the time). There is nothing to stop you from making these yourself, using trial and error to get the hour spacings correct on the dial; set the pointer at an angle to the dial equal to the degree of latitude where you live. However, it will be simpler and quicker to buy a ready-made dial – they are sometimes available in a variety of metallic and cast resin finishes – and to set it on a column and base of your own design.

The sundial shown here consists of four pieces of stone. The pedestal is formed from two square slabs, one smaller than the other, with smooth top and bottom surfaces and roughly dressed edges. The column is a slightly tapered rough-dressed pillar set on the pedestal, and the dial support is an octagon – a square with the corners cut off at 45° – again with smooth top and bottom surfaces and rough-dressed edges all round. The dial itself can be surface-mounted on the support or set in a shallow circular recess ground into the stone.

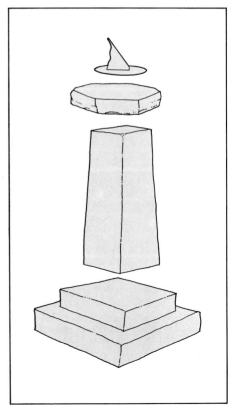

PAVING AROUND TREES

There will often be situations where you want to lay paving of one sort or another in an area already occupied by a specimen tree or two. If you are to avoid depriving the tree's roots of air and water, it is obviously out of the question to take the paving right up to the trunk itself. One solution is to lay the paving units up to a point no closer than about 300 mm (12 in) from the trunk depending on the size of the tree, with a slight slope to encourage rainwater to run into the roots, and then lay cobbles around the trunk to help discourage weeds from growing. Bed the slabs on sand, not mortar.

Stepping stones and water go well together too. If you are lucky enough to have a stream running through your garden, or you have a largish pond, then stepping stones can allow you to cross the water and continue your path. With a pond, they also make access for pond maintenance – trimming the lilies or thinning out oxygenating weed, for example – easier and safer.

CHOOSING MATERIALS

You can use any flat paving material for your stepping stones. Reconstituted stone or concrete slabs – the sort widely used for patios and garden paths – are ideal. They come in squares, rectangles, hexagons and circles, so you can use them for formal or informal arrangements, and colours range from yellows and buffs to red, green and grey.

Left: *A line of small stepping stones set in the lawn is unobtrusive, and keeps feet dry in wet weather.*

Below: *Make sure that individual stones are set low in the ground so that they do not catch on lawnmower blades.*

LAYING STEPPING STONES

You can use stepping stones in a number of different ways as an alternative to the traditional garden path. For example, a series of stones could run across the lawn – to the shed or greenhouse, for example, or to a focal point such as a seat or birdbath – and will allow traffic even in wet weather when the lawn is soft and sodden. The shapes of the individual stones, and the way in which they are arranged, allows you to create a straight and formal effect or a meandering, almost natural one.

There is another obvious advantage of having stepping stones instead of a continuous path: cost. If you need to provide a lengthy footway in your garden, continuous paving of any sort could prove quite expensive, while a few stepping stones will, literally, go a long way.

You can also use stepping stones in conjunction with other materials. For example, a path created from individual stones surrounded by cobbles, shingle or crushed bark looks most attractive, and is inexpensive to lay and easy to maintain.

Another use for stepping stones is to provide easier access within wide borders and flowerbeds. It is impossible to reach plants and shrubs at the back of the bed without compacting the soil, whereas a few strategically-placed stones could solve the problem and save you from getting muddy feet when gardening.

Natural stone looks even better – literally, more natural in appearance, as though the line of stones just 'happened' instead of being put there by man. The most common types are granites, limestones and sandstones, which range in colour from grey to a warm buff yellow and even red, and which can be readily split along the 'grain' into randomly-textured slabs. Larger boulders are ideal for use in ponds or flowerbeds. Slate can also look extremely attractive, but can be slippery when wet unless 'riven' stones with a rough surface are selected.

LAYING STONES ACROSS A LAWN

This is the simplest way of laying stones, since they are held in position by the surrounding turf.

Start by planning out the line of the path across the lawn, using pieces of cardboard cut from grocery boxes as imitation stones. With these, you can experiment with both the line the path will take and the best spacing of individual stones before spending any money. You can also count up precisely how many stones you will need.

Mark the chosen stone positions with small wooden pegs, pushed into the lawn surface. Three pegs per stone are sufficient to do this accurately.

When the stones arrive, have a dry run by simply laying them out on the lawn surface. You can check the appearance of the path best from an upstairs window, with a helper in the garden to make any last-minute adjustments that may be needed to the layout.

Use a small border spade or a turf edging tool to cut neatly round the perimeter of each stone to a depth slightly more than the stone's thickness. Then set the stone to one side, and lift the turf. Save it; it may come in useful for repairs to worn patches and crumbling edges elsewhere on the lawn.

Remove any large stones and roots from the hole, and sieve some soil or builders' sand into the bottom to a depth of about 25 mm (1 in). This will make it easier to bed the stone in place firmly and prevent it from rocking when stepped on.

Lay the stone in place, and tamp it down – either use a baulk of timber such as a fence post off-cut, or simply jump up and down on it. Check that it sits level, with its top just below the soil surface, so you will be able to mow the grass without the mower blades clipping the edges of the stone. If necessary, lift the stone and add or remove soil until you are happy with the level.

Right: Use small stepping stones set in a pond or stream to allow safe access to other parts of the garden.

Finish by trickling soil into any gaps round the edges of the stone, or use off-cuts of turf if you badly over-cut the hole to begin with. Then lay the rest of the stones in the same way.

LAYING STONES ACROSS A POND OR STREAM

The task of positioning the stones is a little more difficult here, since safety is of paramount importance.

First of all, measure the depth of the water in which your stones will be set, and find out what surface they will rest on. In natural ponds and streams the bottom will be soil or gravel; in a man-made pond you may find concrete, plastic or rubber sheeting or rigid plastic. It is best not to lay stones on flexible pond liners, since you may puncture and crack them, but concrete is fine.

Work out what sort of stones to buy. For a formal pond setting, paving slabs are probably the likeliest choice; they will be set on a built-up brick or stone plinth so their surface is just above water level. For a more natural effect in reasonably shallow ponds and streams, choose individual boulders with relatively flat top and bottom surfaces, thick enough to project about 50 mm (2 in) above the water level.

With natural ponds and streams, you can simply set the stones in place on the bottom. Use a trowel to excavate a shallow hollow, and set each stone in place. If it is too low, scoop soil back into the hollow. Then pack more soil round

the sides of the stone to help keep it in place. If you want to ensure that the stone will not move, drive metal pegs in all round it, with their heads below water level. Use non-ferrous metal if possible (aluminium tent pegs are ideal); rust will discolour pond water.

With man-made concrete ponds, you need to lower the water level so that you can build up the plinth or position the boulder on 'dry' land (you are unlikely to be setting the stepping stones in the deepest part of the pond, so you will not have to disturb the fish). Simply siphon the water out with a length of garden hose; remember to remove it when the level has dropped sufficiently, or it will continue siphoning and you will end up with an empty pond.

Now build up a plinth for each paving slab, using engineering-quality bricks or garden walling blocks and mortar made with a waterproofing additive. For a slab 450 mm (18 in) square, you need a plinth about 350 mm (14 in) square – four bricks per course, laid in herringbone fashion. Build the plinth up to roughly the normal water level, then bed the stepping stone on top. Neaten up the pointing and leave it to harden for at least 48 hours before refilling the pond.

If you are using boulders, simply set stones of the right thickness on a mortar bed laid on the pond bottom – again after lowering the water level as necessary. You can use slate or tile to pack the level up if necessary. Finish off with a collar of mortar round the base of the stone.

Building a patio planter

Another attractive weekend stonework project is the construction of a low-level patio planter. You can set it on any firm paved surface; the structure is light enough not to need full-scale foundations, making it ideal for any situation.

You can use natural stone if it is available, or man-made garden walling blocks otherwise; there is a variety of man-made blocks that could have been tailor-made for a project such as this. Each 'block' has its faces and ends moulded to resemble a section of dry-stone walling, and all you have to do is build up the structure to the required extent and height by bedding the blocks on bricklaying mortar and pointing the joints to match the recesses between the moulded stones. To finish off the wall,

5

6

use capping blocks moulded to look like the traditional on-edge stones used on dry-stone walls.

1 Work out the size of planter you want to build, and order the required number of walling and capping blocks. You will also need cement and soft sand (or pre-mixed dry-pack bricklaying mortar), plus a brick bolster and club hammer to cut the blocks, a shovel for mixing the mortar, and a bricklaying trowel and spirit level for laying the blocks.

2 Start by laying the blocks that form the first course of the planter, setting them on a mortar bed and checking that they are level. There is no need to point the vertical courses, though you can if you wish.

3 Add the second course, changing the bonding pattern of the blocks as shown to give the wall additional strength.

4 When you have completed the planter walls, add the capping stones, setting them on a narrow ribbon of mortar along the centre line of the walling blocks for extra strength. Tap each block down so it is level.

5 You will probably have to cut one or two of the capping stones to length to complete the planter. Set the block on a bed of sand and use your brick bolster and club hammer to split the block at the desired position. It should break cleanly along the plane between the individual moulded stones.

6 Complete the planter by setting the cut length of capping stone in place. Then leave the mortar to harden for 48 hours before filling the planter with soil and compost, ready for planting.

Right: The finished planter, filled with compost and planted out with variegated ivy and colourful bedding plants.

Reference

This reference section contains additional information about the tools and materials you will need for the outdoor stonework projects described earlier in the book. It also summarises the main techniques involved, including clearing and preparing sites, working with concrete and cutting blocks and slabs.

Basic building tools

You will need a selection of basic tools for jobs such as clearing, excavating and levelling sites, setting out projects, mixing, placing mortar and concrete, and so on.

The basic excavation tools are a pickaxe and a shovel. The pickaxe has a pointed tip at one end of its curved blade which is used for hacking into and breaking up solid masonry or old concrete, and a spade-ended tip at the other end for grubbing out loose materials so they can be dug out with the shovel. The pickaxe is available with a range of different head weights, commonly 2.2, 3 and 4.5 kg (5, 6½ and 10 lb), and has a strong hardwood handle about 900 mm (36 in) long.

If you are demolishing walls or breaking up concrete, you may find a sledgehammer a useful alternative to the pickaxe. This has a squared-off head weighing anything from 3.2 to 6.3 kg (7 to 14 lb), and a handle up to 900 mm (36 in) long, similar to the pickaxe.

If you have a lot of demolition work to do or have to break up thick concrete, hiring an electric breaker may speed up the process and save a lot of effort. Breakers are available with a range of inter-changeable cutting points (chipping points) and chisels.

The shovel, available with either a rounded or squared-off blade, is better than a spade for shifting loose material since the slightly raised sides help retain material on the blade. However, a spade will also be useful for a wide range of general digging, levelling and other site preparation work.

A tool that is valuable for moving heavy weights, whether you are lifting or placing heavy stone blocks, is the straight crowbar. This is a long steel rod with a point at one end and a chisel blade at the other; to use it you place one end under the object to be moved, position a sturdy fulcrum such as a block of masonry under the bar as close to the loaded end as possible, and apply downward pressure on the other end.

It is likely that you will have to move sizeable amounts of soil, rubble, concrete and stone during the construction of whatever you are creating. It is well worth buying or hiring a sturdy steel contractor's wheelbarrow with a pneumatic tyre; you will soon wreck an ordinary garden wheelbarrow, especially when moving heavy pieces of stone. Make sure you also have a supply of stout planks (scaffold boards are ideal) for use as runways and ramps if you are working on soft or broken ground, to prevent the barrow's wheel from becoming bogged down.

If your project calls for large quantities of mortar or concrete, hire a small electric concrete mixer for the duration of the job. This will save a lot of back-breaking hand mixing, and will also ensure that the mortar or concrete is evenly and thoroughly mixed to the required consistency.

TOOLS FOR SETTING OUT

The basic requirements here are pegs and stringlines, a steel tape measure and a builder's square. Make up a supply of tapered sawn timber pegs about 300 mm (12 in) long, and saw a notch all round each one just below its top to help retain the strings as you set out your site.

You can make up an accurate builder's square using three lengths of sawn or planed wood. Cut one about 1 m (3 ft 3 in) long and another about 1.3 m (4 ft 3 in) long, and connect them at right angles using a halving joint. Then cut the third piece about 1.6 m (5 ft 3 in) long, and nail it across the other two pieces to form a triangle. Cut off the excess wood from the ends of the angled length.

If you are building dry-stone walls, you will need a home-made device called a batter frame to act as a guide. This consists of four lengths of wood nailed together in a gently-tapered A-shape, with its dimensions selected to match the wall height and its projected thickness at the base and top. It carries movable string-lines that are raised as the wall is built up to keep the wall faces on line.

When it comes to levelling sites, an ordinary spirit level (see BEDDING TOOLS below) is of little use. More versatile is a water level, a length of hosepipe with pieces of clear plastic tube inserted into the ends. The hose is filled with water and corked at each end. Then the tubes are tied to pegs driven into the ground and the corks are removed; the water level in the tubes indicates the true horizontal at each end of the hose.

BEDDING TOOLS

You will need a bricklaying trowel if you are working with mortar, whether bedding stones in a wall or laying slabs in a mortar bed. You can use its handle for tamping blocks and slabs into place, but you will find a club hammer better at this; it is also needed for cutting and shaping blocks and slabs, in conjunction with your cutting tools (see below).

The other essential tool for this stage of the work is a spirit level, to ensure that blocks and slabs are laid truly level. Choose a long metal level for accuracy, and make sure it has end vials to indicate true vertical as well.

CUTTING TOOLS

The basic tool for cutting blocks and slabs is the brick chisel or bolster. It is made of steel, measures about 180 mm (7 in) long overall, and has a cutting edge 55 to 100 mm (2½ to 4 in) wide which is ground on both edges. It is held at right angles to the material being cut, and is struck with a club hammer.

The latter, sometimes known as the lump hammer, is a scaled-down relative of the sledgehammer, and has a similar squared-off head weighing up to 1.8 kg (4 lb). It is used for driving carving tools (see below) as well.

An alternative to the club hammer for driving masonry chisels and bolsters is the brick hammer. This has a slightly curved head with a square driving face at one end, and a sharp chisel blade at the other, which is useful for hand-trimming cut edges after the block or slab has been cut.

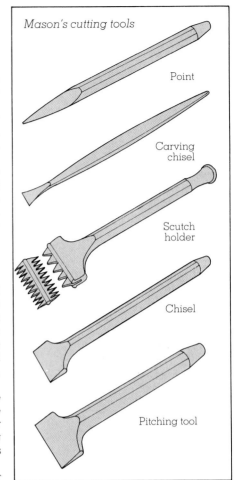

Mason's cutting tools

Point

Carving chisel

Scutch holder

Chisel

Pitching tool

CARVING TOOLS

For carving stone as opposed to just cutting it, you will need some special mason's carving tools (and a club hammer to drive them). The basic cutting and shaping tool is a chisel, an all-steel construction with a hexagonal cross-section and a square-ended cutting blade; it is available in sizes ranging from 12 to 50 mm (½ to 2 in) wide. The point chisel or punch, as its name implies, has a pointed cutting tip, and is used to concentrate the force of the hammer on a small area of the stone during the initial roughing-out of the workpiece. The pitching tool has a wide single-ground blade, and is used for removing larger amounts of stone when trimming a workpiece down to the required size.

For carving recesses, the most versatile tool of all is a mason's scutch holder, a special chisel-like tool with a replaceable cutting edge known as a scutch. This is double-sided, and may have plain or toothed edges. It is used after the initial roughing-out, and the toothed version leaves a series of furrows in the stone which can either be left as the final finish or can be smoothed off using either the plain mason's chisel or the wider mason's bolster.

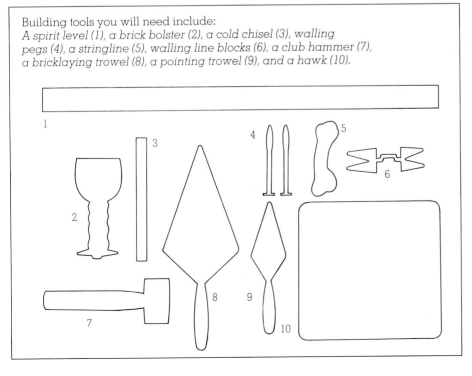

Building tools you will need include:
A spirit level (1), a brick bolster (2), a cold chisel (3), walling pegs (4), a stringline (5), walling line blocks (6), a club hammer (7), a bricklaying trowel (8), a pointing trowel (9), and a hawk (10).

Natural stone

The main stones used for outdoor projects fall into one of three classes: igneous, sedimentary and metamorphic. Igneous rocks were formed by the cooling of molten magma, while sedimentary stones were created either by the wearing down of older rocks or from accumulations of organic origin.

Metamorphic stones are stones that have been changed structurally from their original form by immense heat and pressure.

Granite is the commonest igneous stone. It is extremely dense and hard (and therefore expensive to quarry and cut), highly resistant to attack by pollution, and is almost impervious to water penetration. This makes it ideal for use as a paving material – usually in the form of small blocks called setts – and for areas getting heavy wear, such as steps and kerbs. Most granites are grey or black, but there are also varieties with green, red, pink or blue colouring, caused by the inclusion of felspar or other minerals.

The sedimentary stones are by far the most widely used for outdoor stonework projects. They fall into two broad groups, the sandstones and the limestones. Sandstones consist mainly of particles of quartz, bound together by other minerals such as silica and carbonates and often contain iron ores which help to give the stone its attractive colouring. This can range from almost white to red, brown and even blue-grey. The best sandstones are very durable, but as a type they tend to weather less attractively than the limestones and some can quickly become soiled by atmospheric pollution. Their most popular use is as split flagstones.

Limestones consist mainly of calcium carbonate (calcite), and were formed in one of three ways. Most of the building limestones are known as oolitic stones,

Top: *If you are lucky enough to live near a quarry, this will prove an invaluable source of supplies for your projects.*

Left: *Otherwise, you will have to rely on the smaller stocks of stone held by many builders' merchants and garden centres.*

and were formed by the accretion of calcite round small grains of sand or shell, these then being cemented together by more calcite. Limestones were also formed by deposition – the accumulation of organic remains such as shells and other animal or plant remains – or by crystallization from solution (stalactites and stalagmites, for example). They vary widely in hardness, although as a group they are generally softer and easier to work than sandstones, making them ideal for carving as well as for more general building work. They are, however, attacked by acid rain which initially makes the surface self-cleaning but which in the longer term can cause rapid decay of the softer types. Colours range from creamy white (Portland-stone, for example) to light brown.

Since both sandstones and limestones were formed in layers, they have distinct bedding planes which should be reproduced in any structure built with them; they will gradually delaminate if laid with the bedding plane parallel to an exposed face of a wall, for example.

The most common metamorphic stone is slate, formed from heated and compressed clay – a process that turned limestone into marble and sandstone into quartzite. This process resulted in a stone that has distinct planes of cleavage, often almost at right angles to the original bedding planes, along which the stone can be split to form slabs of varying thickness. It is strong in tension and compression and has good resistance to moisture penetration, although some types are attacked by acidic pollution, and can be used in blocks as well as slabs for a variety of end uses.

As mentioned earlier in the book, your choice of stone for garden projects is likely to depend on what local suppliers stock unless you live close to quarries and can specify your requirements more precisely. You will also be in your supplier's hands as far as selecting stone in the size, shape and finish you want. Stone surfaces are classified according to the degree of finish they have been subjected to. The most common terms, in increasing order of

Below: *Examples of the wide range of colour and surface texture available, especially in the sandstones and lmestones that are the most popular materials for most stonework projects. If possible, choose stone that matches existing features in your garden.*

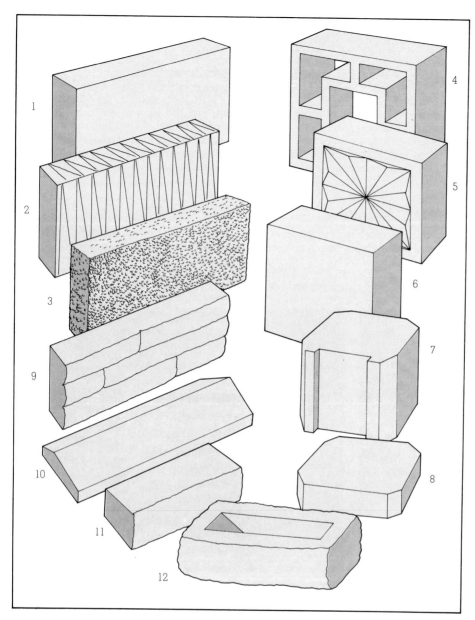

– an actual size of 290 mm (11⅜ in) square and about 90 mm (3½ in) thick, giving a work size of 300 mm (11¾ in) square. You need 11 blocks per square metre of wall. Coping stones, if available, usually come in 610 mm (2 ft) lengths – long enough to bridge two of the walling blocks and three 10 mm (⅜ in) mortar joints. The special hollow pier blocks that some manufacturers make as part of their screen walling block range are about 200 mm (8 in) square and 190 mm (7½ in) tall. Allowing for a 10 mm mortar joint, this means that three pier blocks build up to the same height – 600 mm or just under 2 ft – as two walling blocks.

PAVING SLABS AND BLOCKS

Reconstituted stone paving slabs are mostly squares or rectangles, and come in a range of sizes based on a 225 mm, 250 mm, 300 mm or 500 mm (9, 10, 12 or 20 in) module. The largest manageable size is 675 x 450 mm (27 x 18 in). To estimate roughly how many slabs will be needed for a particular project, divide the area to be paved by the area of an individual slab. In practice, however, it is better to design paved areas if possible so they are a whole number of slabs wide and long, to minimise the need for cutting slabs. Then you can count how many rows there are and how many slabs are needed in each row, and multiply the two figures. If you are laying mixed slabs of different sizes, draw a scale plan on squared paper and count how many of each size will be required.

Some paving ranges also include hexagonal and circular slabs. The former are usually 400 mm (16 in) wide, measured between two opposite parallel sides, and come with matching straight-sided half slabs to allow you to pave square or rectangular areas with them. You will need 55 x 400 mm hexagonal slabs to pave an area of 10sq m (108sq ft). Circular slabs come in several diameters from 300 mm (12 in) upwards, and are intended to be laid as individual stepping stones.

Cast concrete slabs – the cheapest type – are usually 50 mm (2 in) thick, while the more expensive reconstituted stone types are generally 40 mm (1⅝ in) thick. They are surprisingly heavy – a 450 mm (18 in) sq slab weighs around 16 kg (36 lbs) – so lift them with care.

Block pavers are generally rectangular, although there are some made in

---

smoothness, are: rockfaced; rough picked; fair picked; axed; fine axed; split (riven); sawn or ribbed; sanded; gritted; honed or rubbed; polished (unlikely to be required in the garden). As far as quantities are concerned, give as much detail of the project you are tackling as possible and take your supplier's advice.

MAN-MADE WALL BLOCKS

Reconstituted stone blocks, made to imitate natural stone, come in a wide range of sizes. The most common measure from 200 to 325 mm (8¼ to 12¾ in) long, 75 to 150 mm (3¼ to 5¾ in) wide and 65 to 150 mm (2¾ to 5¾ in) high – the same height as a standard brick. Others in the range are usually multiples of this, which allows you to lay the blocks in a wide range of decorative bonds.

In some countries you may also find larger blocks which have their outer face moulded so they resemble a number of smaller, randomly-shaped blocks. The moulded joints are deeply recessed, and each block may have projecting units at each end to allow a stretcher-style bond to be achieved between neighbouring blocks. The result is a stronger wall than could be built with simple stack bonding.

To estimate the quantities you will need for a particular project, first select the block you want to work with and then use its actual size as a guide. To work out how many blocks will be required for one square metre (11sq ft) of single-thickness masonry, add 10 mm (⅜ in) to the actual block length and height (in mm) to allow for the thickness of the mortar joint, multiply the two figures together, and divide the result into 1,000,000 (the number of sq mm in a sq m). So, for a 440 x 65 mm block, the sum is: 450 x 75 = 33,750 sq mm, then 1,000,000 divided by 33,750 = 29.63, which means you need 30 blocks per sq m.

Perforated decorative screen walling blocks are made in just one standard size

inter-locking shapes to give a less regular look to the surface of the paved area. The standard block size is 200 x 100 mm (8 x 4 in) so estimating coverage is easy; you need 50 per sq m (42 per sq yd). Some are as thick as 65 mm (2½ in) or even 80 mm (3¼ in); other light-duty blocks are only 50 or 60 mm (2 or 2⅜ in) thick, and are intended for use as paths and patios rather than for driveways.

MORTAR AND CONCRETE

The raw materials used to make mortar and concrete are cement, aggregate of one kind or another, and various additives that improve the performance or ease of handling of the mix. It can be difficult to estimate materials accurately since they have to be ordered in large quantities for all but the smallest jobs, and waste costs money.

Cement is widely sold only in 50 kg (112 lb) bags, although some DIY superstores stock smaller and more manageable 25 or 40 kg (55 or 88 lb) packs. The mortar and concrete mix formulae below are based on the use of standard 50 kg bags.

Sand, both soft (for building or bricklaying) and sharp (for concreting) varieties, are sold either in bags or by volume. Bags – either 40 or 50 kg – are convenient for small jobs, but work out extremely expensive for large projects such as laying patios or concrete slabs. For these it is best to order by volume from a builders' supplier or transport company. The smallest quantity most will deliver is half a cubic metre, or about three-quarters of a ton. Remember that a cubic metre is some 30 per cent bigger than a cubic yard.

Aggregate is also sold bagged or loose by volume, and is graded according to the size of the particles they contain – fine if it will pass through a 5 mm (¼ in) sieve, and coarse otherwise. Coarse aggregates for concreting usually have a maximum stone diameter of 20 mm (⅞ in), although you can get 10 mm (⅜ in) aggregate for use in fine concrete. A cubic metre weighs nearly two tons, and is a surprisingly large heap when delivered.

DRY MIXED MATERIALS

DIY superstores and hardware stores stock small bags of dry, ready-mixed mortar and concrete – usually 25 or 40 kg sizes, occasionally in smaller packs down to 10 kg in size. The usual varieties include bricklaying mortar, rendering mix, and fine and coarse concrete. Use them where the scale of the job or where their convenience outweighs their comparatively high cost.

READY-MIXED CONCRETE

When ordering ready-mixed concrete, be sure to specify the volume of material you need, what it will be used for, when you want it, how you will handle the delivery and whether there is easy access to the delivery site. The supplier will then ensure that the appropriate

---

Below: *Split sandstone is a durable material and ideal for paving projects.*

mix for the job is delivered. To help you assess whether access is possible, most mixer trucks are up to 8 m (26 ft) long and 3 m (10 ft) wide, and can discharge their contents via a shute within about 3 m (10 ft) of the back of the truck.

M<small>ORTAR</small> AND CONCRETE MIXES

For mortar, use table 1 to select the mix you need according to the job you are tackling, then use the formula for the mix as detailed under Mix types. For concrete, use table 2. The figures in column 3 of the concrete table are the amounts needed to make 1 cu m of concrete. Note that all mixes should be carefully proportioned by volume, using a bucket.

1: M<small>ORTAR</small> MIXES

Use	Exposure	Mix
Walling	Moderate	Mix B soft
	Severe	Mix A soft
Pointing	Moderate	Mix A soft
	Severe	Mix C soft

M<small>IX</small> TYPES

Mix A
1:½:4 cement:lime:soft sand, or
1:3-4 cement:soft sand plus plasticiser, or
1:2½-3½ masonry cement:soft sand

Mix B
1:1:6 cement:lime:soft sand, or
1:5-6 cement:soft sand plus plasticiser, or
1:4-5 masonry cement:soft sand

Mix C
1:3 cement:soft sand

1 Mix the ingredients dry.

2 Form a central crater.

3 Pour in some water.

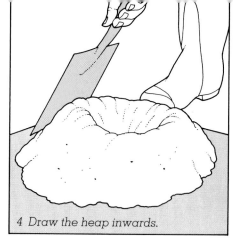
4 Draw the heap inwards.

5 Turn the mix thoroughly.

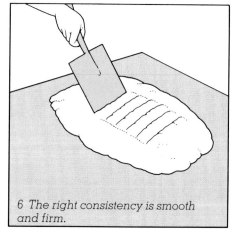
6 The right consistency is smooth and firm.

2: C<small>ONCRETE</small> MIXES

Use	Proportion by volume		Amount per cu m	Yield per 50 kg bag of cement
GENERAL PURPOSE Most uses except foundations and exposed paving	Cement	1	6.4 bags	0.15 cu m
	Sharp sand	2	680 kg/0.45 cu m	
	20 mm aggregate	3	1,175 kg/0.67 cu m	
	OR All-in aggregate	4	1,855 kg/0.98 cu m	
FOUNDATIONS Strips, slabs and bases for precast paving	Cement	1	5.6 bags	0.18 cu m
	Sharp sand	2½	720 kg/0.5 cu m	
	20 mm aggregate	3½	1,165 kg/0.67 cu m	
	OR All-in aggregate	5	1,885 kg/1 cu m	
PAVING All exposed surfaces, all driveways	Cement	1	8 bags	0.12 cu m
	Sharp sand	1½	600 kg/0.42 cu m	
	20 mm aggregate	2½	1,200 kg/0.7 cu m	
	OR All-in aggregate	3	1,800 kg/0.95 cu m	

W<small>ORKING</small> WITH CONCRETE

You may be using concrete to form foundation strips for garden walls, or to create a slab as a base for a garden structure. Start by clearing the site of surface vegetation – shrubs, weeds and the like. Then mark out the trench or slab shape with pegs and string, rope or hosepipe as appropriate, positioning your guidelines about 150 mm (6 in) away to allow you adequate room to position the formwork if this is needed to contain the concrete.

Next, excavate the site to the required depth. If you can re-use the soil elsewhere in the garden – as the base for a rockery, for example – pile it up neatly. Otherwise dump it in a skip.

You can now set the pegs that will

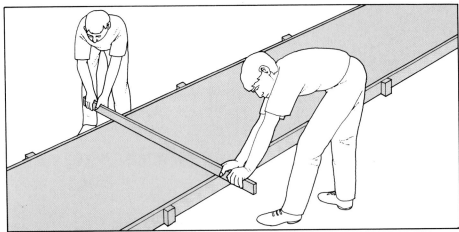

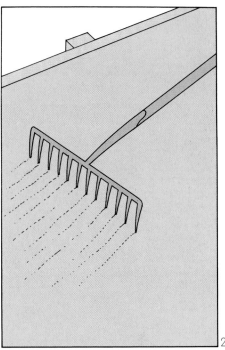

support the formwork in position. Use substantial timber – 50 mm (2 in) sq is ideal – and taper one end of the pegs to make them easier to drive in. Hammer them well into the subsoil, and use your spirit level or a water level to set their tops at the desired level for the foundation surface. Then nail the formwork planks to the pegs, and check that you have not disturbed them.

The next step is to put down a level of hardcore. Shovel it out evenly over the base of the excavation to a depth of around 100 mm (4 in) and tread or tamp it down thoroughly – a length of old fence post is an ideal tamping tool. Fill obvious gaps and hollows with smaller bits of broken brick or handfuls of aggregate.

You are now ready to lay the concrete. Simply tip it in (1), rake it out level (2) and, with a helper, tamp it down well with a stout beam long enough to span opposite sides of the formwork (3). Use a chopping action first of all to compact the concrete thoroughly, adding more concrete to any hollows that develop. Pay particular attention to the edges, tamping the concrete down firmly against the formwork. Then finish off with a sawing motion of the beam.

This will leave the concrete with a slightly rippled finish. If you want a smoother surface, you can work over the surface with a soft broom, the back of a clean shovel or a wooden plasterer's float. On large slabs this will mean forming a movable bridge from which you can reach all parts of the surface.

Left: *For ambitious projects, like this rock garden, you may need to hire some mechanical help to place the stones.*

The simplest way of making one is to use a ladder with planks laid on the rungs; rest the ladder on piles of bricks outside the formwork so the slight sagging as you kneel on it will not touch the fresh concrete surface.

Finally, as soon as the slab surface is hard enough not to be marked, cover it with polythene sheeting to prevent it from drying out too quickly (it will crack if it does). Weight the polythene down at the edges, and sprinkle sand across it to prevent it ballooning up and down in the breeze. Leave it on for about three days in colder climates; then remove it, and knock away the formwork. You can walk on it at this point, but you should wait a further five to seven days for the concrete to develop its full strength before starting building on it.

If you are laying a slab more than about 4 m (13 ft) across, you will have to include expansion joints to prevent the slab from cracking. You can incorporate these joints in one of two ways; whichever you choose depends on whether you are using ready-mixed

Below: *It is always worthwhile dry-laying paving stones before starting work in order to check where the cuts (right) will be needed.*

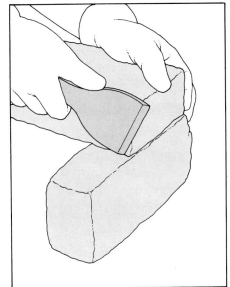

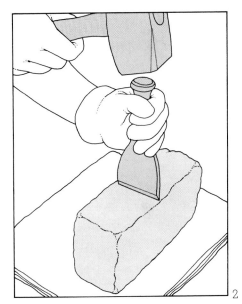

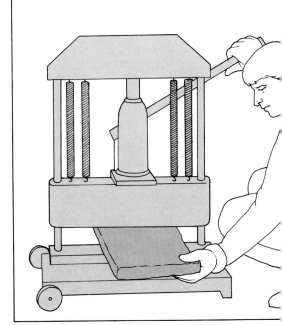

concrete or not. Aim to divide the slab up into two or three equal-sized bays, depending on its size.

If you are laying ready-mixed concrete, use hardboard filler strips running the full width and depth of the slab and held in place with blobs of concrete. The strips should finish level with the top of the formwork, and will remain in place once the slab is cast. If you are mixing your own concrete, simply create the bays with more formwork. Concrete one bay (or the two side bays if you have three) and leave to set; then remove the dividing formwork and fill the remaining bay, simply butting the new concrete up against the edge of the existing bays.

CUTTING BLOCKS AND SLABS

Whatever you are constructing, you are sure to need to cut blocks and slabs at some stage of the job. You need a sharp brick chisel or bolster and a club hammer for most cutting work; an angle grinder can be useful for making cut-outs in paving slabs, and a hydraulic splitter will make light work of cutting block pavers, which can be hard to cut by hand.

To cut a natural or man-made stone block, lay it on a thin bed of sand or soil. Score it all round the desired cutting line with the tip of the chisel (1), then hold the blade upright on the cutting line and strike the chisel firmly with your club hammer (2). Repeat if necessary to split the block.

Use a similar technique to cut paving slabs, first scoring a line across the slab surface and then using the chisel and hammer to deepen the cut until the slab splits.

To operate a splitter, mark the desired cutting line on the face of the slab or block, place it on the base of the machine with the marked line beneath the blade, and pull down on the lever handle to 'guillotine' the block in two (3).

95

WOODWORK

INTRODUCTION

IF YOU WANT TO TURN YOUR GARDEN FROM A FLAT PLOT OF LAND INTO A LANDSCAPE WITH SOME PHYSICAL FEATURES, WOOD IS THE OBVIOUS CHOICE OF BUILDING MATERIAL FOR EVERYTHING FROM FENCES TO SUMMERHOUSES. BECAUSE WOOD IS SUCH A VERSATILE MATERIAL, THERE IS VIRTUALLY NO LIMIT TO WHAT YOU CAN DO WITH IT. THE ONLY POSSIBLE RESTRICTION WILL BE YOUR OWN LEVEL OF WOODWORKING SKILLS, BUT EVEN AMATEUR CARPENTERS WITH TEN THUMBS CAN BUILD PERFECTLY ACCEPTABLE STRUCTURES OUT OF DOORS WHERE THE EYE IS LESS CRITICAL OF SLIGHTLY OUT-OF-SQUARE JOINTS OR A LESS-THAN-IMMACULATE FINISH ON WHATEVER YOU DECIDE TO TURN YOUR HAND TO.

Using wood in the garden adds a wonderfully natural feel to the surrounding area. Wooden structures are easy to construct, relatively cheap to make and, using a range of timbers and styles, incredibly diverse. There is also a large selection of wooden furniture and other projects available in kit form from DIY stores, which are simple to assemble and make stylish additions to your garden area.

The woodworking projects in this section range from simple items, such as a bird table or a window box, to more complex structures such as garden buildings and children's play equipment. Information on fences and gates deals with all the most commonly used types, and tells you everything you need to know about choosing and erecting them, plus tips on keeping them in good working order.

There are also details about building pergolas and walkways in a range of styles and materials over which you can train your climbing plants, plus how to use trellis to best advantage.

Your garden is sure to need paths and steps, plus somewhere to sit out when the lawn is wet or soft, so this section also looks at using wood for natural-looking path and step surfaces, and building timber decks, and goes on to deal with erecting gazebos and summerhouses that will enable you to form the perfect centrepiece for your garden design.

While you are busy relaxing, children expect to be entertained, and the play equipment information and projects cover everything a child could want, from swings, seesaws and slides to sand pits, climbing frames and tree houses. There is even a design for a colourful and highly unusual garden aviary.

Finally, there is a selection of small weekend projects for you to tackle, followed by a comprehensive reference section covering the tools and materials you will need to use and the basic techniques you will be employing repeatedly as you work.

Throughout, the colour photographs and detailed illustrations show how everything is put together. The accompanying text and captions take you through every stage of each project from estimating and buying materials to constructing and finishing whatever you have chosen to make. It even encourages you to try out variations on the themes, to help you create a range of unique and personalized garden features and structures.

Above: *Even the simplest structures such as a rustic pergola and a timber seat can provide a focal point in the garden.*

Left: *Timber is the perfect material for the more formal features of your property, such as boundary fences and gates.*

Right: *Every garden needs somewhere cool and shady, and a trellised arbor is a stylish and practical way of providing it.*

Below: *A tree house is every child's idea of the perfect hiding place, and is easy to construct from scrap timber.*

FENCES

FENCES ARE THE MOST POPULAR BOUNDARY MARKERS AROUND. THEY ARE WIDELY AVAILABLE, COME IN A RANGE OF TYPES, ARE EASY TO PUT UP AND MAINTAIN, AND NEED NOT COST THE EARTH. OF THE MAIN ALTERNATIVES, WALLS ARE OF COURSE MORE DURABLE, BUT TAKE TIME AND EFFORT TO BUILD AND WILL COST A GREAT DEAL MORE THAN A FENCE, WHILE HEDGES ARE FINE IF YOU CAN AFFORD TO WAIT FOR THEM TO GROW AND ARE PREPARED TO LOOK AFTER THEM REGULARLY TO ENSURE THAT THEY REMAIN FIT AND HEALTHY. BUT IF MONEY AND TIME ARE BOTH IN SHORT SUPPLY, A FENCE IS THE ANSWER.

Whether you are putting up a new fence where none exists, or replacing an existing fence because it is dilapidated, you need to do some homework before you start. There are three main areas you should think about.

Firstly, what sort of fence do you want? Looks are important, and you may need privacy or a barrier to keep children and pets in (or out); alternatively, you may want to hide garden eyesores like the compost heap, or provide an attractive backdrop for your display of plants.

Secondly, how much are you prepared to pay? Many people are surprised at how long their boundaries are (and hence at the likely cost, especially of the more expensive fencing types available).

Thirdly, are there any legal complications? Apart from the possibility of a dispute with your neighbours over ownership and boundary lines, there may be other legal restrictions on the way you fence in your property. See Legal considerations on page 102 for more details.

WHICH TYPE TO CHOOSE?

Most people think of timber when choosing a new fence, since there is a bigger choice in timber than in other materials. All timber fences are the same in principle. You put up a line of posts along the boundary line, and then fill the gaps in between with rails or panels.

The simplest type has one or more horizontal rails between the posts – known as **post-and-rail fencing**, or **ranch fencing** if the rails are flat boards. This type is fine as a boundary marker, but not much good at keeping pets or

children in (or out). You can make the fence a better barrier by adding vertical timbers to the horizontal rails; if you leave spaces between the verticals you get a **picket fence**, which is see-through but child and petproof, while overlapping them creates a **close-boarded** fence with complete privacy.

A variation on the ranch fencing idea has horizontal planks fixed to both sides of the posts so that the planks on one side coincide with the gaps on the other – this is known as **interference fencing**. There is a similar variation on picket fencing, with vertical timbers on both sides of the horizontal rails; this is generally called **interlap fencing**.

Panel fences differ from post-and-rail types in having made-up panels of various types fixed between the posts. These may be simple rustic affairs –

Right: Shaped pickets make a highly distinctive and decorative fence, while painted wood makes a contrasting formal planter.

agenda, whether it is to screen a patio or shelter tender plants. The same 'solid' fences that provide excellent privacy are one answer, but you must be sure that posts and panels are securely fixed to resist the buffeting the fence will receive from high winds. An alternative where total privacy is not so important is interference or interlap fencing, which allows air to pass between the opposed slats and so does not form such an impenetrable barrier to the wind as solid fences do.

Family security – keeping children and pets in or out – is another factor. The types already mentioned in this section will do a good job here, but if privacy is not important you could consider a high picket fence, chestnut palings or even open trelliswork. All will restrain small children and fat pets, but low types can be climbed fairly easily.

If you want to use your fence to **train climbing plants**, open trelliswork is the best, since eventually the plants will create a boundary with a completely natural look. Trellis also has the advantage of allowing light and water to reach the roots of the plants unhindered; solid fences sited to provide shelter may deprive plants on the leeward side of water and, depending on their orientation, sunlight too. If you use trellis, you must make sure that it is

Left: The ultimate in simple garden wood-work – rustic poles for the fence and a reclaimed railway sleeper for a seat.

Below: Second-hand timber can also be put to use for more substantial structures.

woven **willow hurdles**, for example, or stout wires carrying split **chestnut palings** or more elaborate (and more expensive) framed panels with **horizontal slats** (often rough-edged), **vertical boards** (similar in appearance to a traditional close-boarded fence, but minus the horizontal rails), **interwoven slats** of thin timber or even open **trelliswork**. These panels are generally made in a range of standard sizes; most are 1.8m (6ft) long, while heights range from a lowly 610mm (2ft) up to a more lofty 1.8m (6ft) tall.

POINTS TO PONDER

Apart from thinking purely about fence styles, there are other factors to consider when choosing your new fencing.

For most people, **privacy** is the most important. If you want to exclude prying eyes completely, you need a fence that is at least 1.8m (6ft) high, and your choice of types is restricted to vertical closeboarded types or solid panels.

Providing **shelter from prevailing winds** may also come high on the

FENCES

made from durable timber such as cedar, and that it is treated with preservative to keep rot at bay; future maintenance will be difficult once the plants have become established.

If all you want to do is mark a boundary, any type of fencing can be used. Probably the cheapest is a row of posts connected by either a single rail or lengths of ornamental chain.

Lastly, looks may matter, especially if you want your fencing to be unobtrusive. For example, high solid panel fences, unless softened by plants, can make a long, narrow garden look like a wood-panelled corridor, and white pickets and ranch-style fencing are very difficult to disguise – they are actually a strong garden feature in their own right.

Low fences tend to be less obtrusive, and the use of rustic poles and trellis helps to soften the effect still further. Remember, too, that leaving fences to weather to a natural grey colour can help them blend unobtrusively into the surroundings.

LEGAL CONSIDERATIONS

If you are replacing an existing fence, the first thing to do is to establish who owns it. The title deeds to your property may show this (on new developments, a T-mark on the site plans against a boundary lies on the property responsible for maintaining it). The old 'rule' that posts and rails are always on the owner's side is by no means infallible.

If you cannot establish ownership, try to come to a written and signed agreement with your neighbour, and keep it safe for future reference. If a dilapidated fence is his and he will not agree to repair or replace it, there is nothing to stop you from erecting a new fence on your side of the boundary line. Remember that you will need planning

permission in the UK to erect a fence over 2m (6ft 6in) high, except where the boundary faces a highway; then the height limit above which permission must be sought drops to 1m (3ft 3in). Hedges are not subject to planning permission. The Highways Acts may require you to lower a fence or hedge if it obstructs the view of motorists (usually only applicable on corner sites).

Lastly, your own deeds may contain restrictive covenants which curtail your right to erect certain types of fencing. For other countries, check your local regulations before proceeding.

BUYING FENCING

Fence prices vary widely from supplier to supplier, so the best advice is to shop around. The obvious places to buy fencing are from local fencing contractors, garden centres, builders' merchants or, for a restricted choice of the more popular types, do-it-yourself superstores. You will get the best choice from a fencing supplier. Remember that delivery may be extra, especially on

Above: Pickets cut to a profile that matches the elegant post tops and set on a gravel board cut a dashingly formal look.

Right: More pickets, this time marching smartly up hill and down dale to create an unusual formal boundary fence.

Top right: A simple post-and-rail fence makes an economical boundary marker where security is not an important factor.

Far right: Prefabricated panels provide the simplest and quickest way of putting up a fence.

small orders, and many 'trade' outlets quote prices without VAT. If you are in any doubt, ask.

When you are buying timber fences, check the wood quality carefully and try to avoid posts, rails and panels with splits or large numbers of knots. Make sure that all timber components have been preservative-treated either by pressure or vacuum impregnation, and that metal fittings have been galvanized or sherardised so they will not rust too quickly. Make sure that panel types have capping rails to shed rainwater, and buy caps for all the posts too.

PUTTING UP A TIMBER FENCE

The traditional way of putting up a fence is to set the posts in holes in the ground, and then to erect the rails, panels or whatever between them. The general rule of thumb is to bury one quarter of the post length in the ground, so for fencing 1.8m (6ft) high a post 2.4m (8ft) long is needed. You will find more detailed information about erecting posts on pages 180-181.

Above: *A horizontal closeboarded fence makes a sturdy peep-proof wind-break. The boards can have square or rough (untrimmed, often bark-covered) edges.*

LOOKING AFTER FENCES

The biggest enemy of timber fencing is neglect. Wind loosens posts and strains fixings; physical damage breaks rails and splits panels; rot attacks exposed endgrain and post bottoms. Regular treatment of all surfaces with wood preservative will help to keep rot at bay (see page 184), and regular inspection especially after periods of rough weather will help to pinpoint weakened fixings and loose posts before total collapse results.

Fix loose boards and panels by driving extra fixing nails into the rails or posts. Reinforce loose posts either by excavating round them and forming a concrete collar, or if rot has set in by fitting a concrete fence spur or a fence spike. See page 185 for more details.

CLOSE-BOARDED FENCES

The close-boarded fence is probably the finest fence you can build. It combines great strength with impressive good looks, and if carefully erected will give years of service. Its main drawback is that it uses a lot of solid wood, so tends to be more expensive than other types. However, one advantage that close-boarded fence has over other 'solid' fence types is that it can be built to follow a slope; you simply set out the

posts, add the rails parallel to the slope and nail the boards to them.

Its basic structure is quite simple: a line of posts connected by two or three arris rails depending on the fence height, with overlapping feather-edged boards nailed to the rails to complete the fence. In good quality work the arris rails are set in mortises cut in the posts, but nowadays galvanized metal brackets are more commonly used to secure the rails to the posts. The lower ends of the fence should rest on horizontal gravel boards which, as their name implies, prevent soil or gravel from being washed under the fence. They also stop rot from attacking the lower ends of the fence boards, which would otherwise be in contact with the ground. It is cheaper to replace a single rotten gravel board than a whole row of boards.

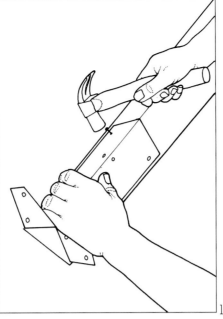

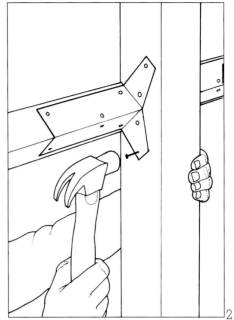

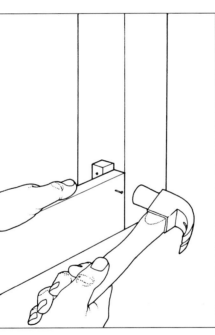

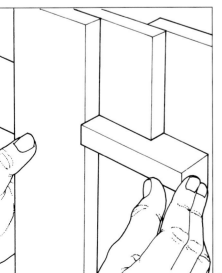

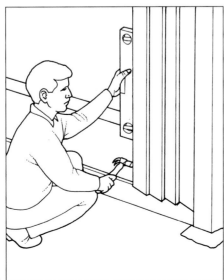

Erecting the fence

1 Once you have set out and erected the line of fence posts (see pages 180-181), measure the lengths of the arris rails needed to fit between each pair of posts and cut them to size. Nail an arris rail bracket to each end of the rails.

2 With a helper supporting the other end of the rail, drive nails through the angled flanges of the bracket to fix it to the fence. Fit all the rails, checking that they are parallel with the ground and, on three-rail fences, equally spaced.

3 Nail small cleats to the sides of each post to support the gravel rail with its face flush with the face of the post. Cut the gravel boards to length and then nail each one to its cleats. Set up a string line between the posts to help you get the tops of the boards level, about 75mm (3in) below the post tops. Cut the first board to length, set its lower end on the gravel board with its thicker edge against the post and check that its top is aligned with the string, then nail it to the upper rail by driving a nail through the board close to its thicker edge. Nail the board to the lower rail, and to the center rail too if one is fitted. Nail on the second board so its thicker edge overlaps the thinner edge of the first board by about 12mm (1/2in). Drive the nails so they penetrate both boards.

4 Use a notched piece of scrap wood as a gauge to ensure a consistent overlap between adjacent boards.

5 Continue nailing up boards, checking after every four or five boards that they are truly vertical using a spirit level. When you reach the next post, reverse the last board so its thicker edge is against the post and nail it in place. Complete the remaining bays of the fence in the same way, then add the post caps. Give the boards protection by fitting a bevelled capping strip.

FENCES

Right: *Prefabricated panels can be made with overlapping rough-edged boards or thin interwoven strips.*

PANEL FENCES

By comparison with the relative complexities of the close-boarded fence, a panel fence is simplicity itself. You simply nail prefabricated fence panels to the posts and finish off by adding the post caps. The result is not as sturdy as a boarded fence, since the panels are made from relatively thin wood with light-duty framing timbers. However, they are very quick to erect and are relatively inexpensive by comparison.

There are two points to remember when erecting panel fences. The first is that the post spacings must be very accurately matched to the panel width if gaps or buckled panels are to be avoided. The second is that they obviously cannot be used on sloping ground unless they top a wall that can follow the ground slope in a series of steps.

1 Since fence panels are a standard width, it is vital that the posts are accurately spaced to match the panel size. Use a batten cut to match the panel width as an aid to positioning the posts to precisely the right separation.
2 With the posts set in place, position the first panel between its posts, resting on bricks or timber offcuts to lift the panel just clear of the ground. Drive fixing nails at 300mm (12in) intervals.
3 Alternatively, use galvanized panel brackets – two per side on low fences, three on high ones.
4 Slot the panel into place and drive nails in through the bracket holes.
5 If you need a narrow panel to fill in the last section of the fence run, pry off the outer frame battens and reposition them to form a panel of the required width. Drive fixing nails through the upper batten so they pass through the lower one and hammer their points flat. Cut down the panel alongside the repositioned battens, then test its fit and nail it into place between its posts.

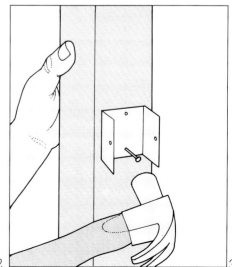

PICKET FENCING

The picket fence, with its closely-spaced row of vertical timbers, is perfectly redolent of the thatched country cottage with roses around the door. It is a style traditionally used for low fences, often with a hedge planted immediately inside it, and looks especially effective against dark foliage if painted white. The tops of the individual pickets are usually rounded or arrowheaded, but there is nothing to stop you from being more artistically creative and cutting spade or club shapes, forming pierced cutouts and so on, if you have the time. Pigmented wood stains are a better finish than paint if you want to avoid regular tedious redecorating.

Once you have decided on the post spacing and set up the posts, cut the rails to length so you can work out how many pickets you will need for each bay. Cut all the pickets to length and shape.

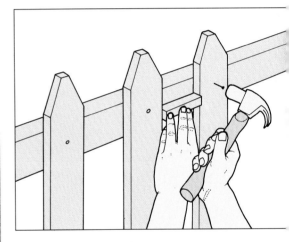

1 Nail the pickets to the rails using an offcut of wood as a spacer to ensure that the gaps are uniform

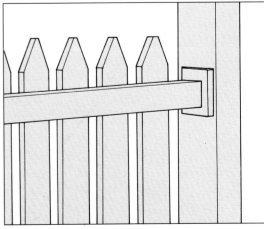

2 Use wooden cleats to secure the rails to the posts. Screw them to the post sides first, then screw through the rails into the cleats.

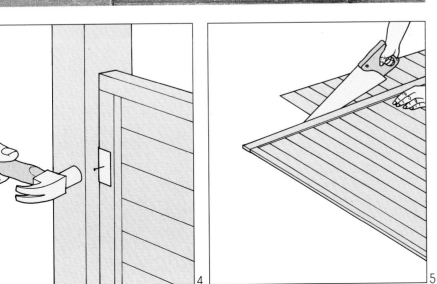

Fences

Post-and-rail fences

Post-and-rail fences, as their name implies, consist of a row of posts linked by horizontal rails with gaps between them. They can be made from sawed or planed timber, which gives them a sleek appearance suitable for a modern house with a neatly regimented garden, or from rustic poles which look more natural and suit the rambling style of a more well-established garden. However, unless the rails are closely spaced the fence is not particularly secure, and all types can be easily climbed so they are perhaps best avoided when you want to keep inquisitive children in. With rustic poles, you can embellish the fence and improve security a little by using shorter pieces to create infill panels between the posts.

If economy and boundary marking are all you require of a fence, chestnut palings could be the best choice. These are slim split poles linked together by strands of galvanized wire to form a 'fence on a roll'. All you have to do is to unroll it, cut it to length and secure the wires to your fence posts with stout staples or bent-over nails.

Above: Closely spaced rustic poles form a natural looking, yet very secure fence.

1 With your posts in position, start by nailing the lowest rail to the posts.
2 Use offcuts as spacers when nailing on the second and subsequent rails to ensure uniform gaps between them.
3 On level ground, use a spirit level to check that the rails are truly horizontal and parallel with each other. To create interference fencing, nail more rails to the other side of the posts in line with the gaps on this side.

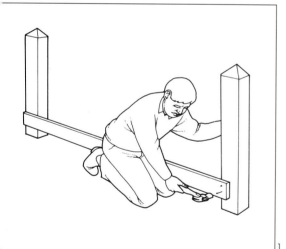

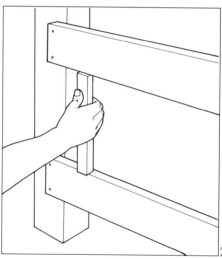

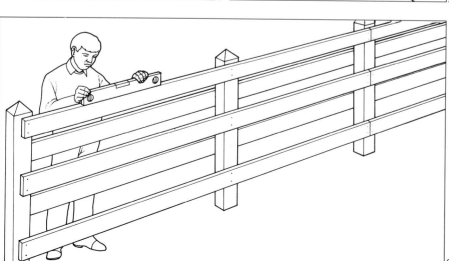

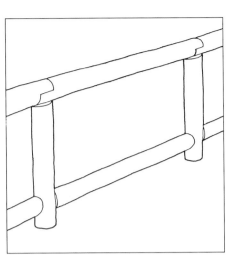

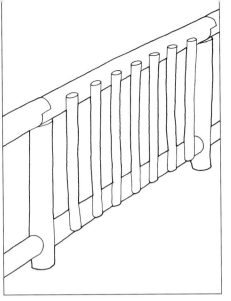

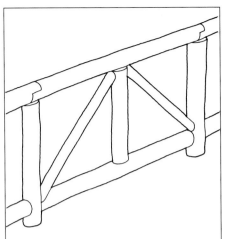

1 Start by nailing stout poles to the tops and sides of the posts to form the main horizontal rails of the fence. Drive the nails in at opposing angles.

2 If you want a relatively solid fence, nail closely-spaced slimmer poles to the rails. Support these from behind as you drive the fixing nails.

3 To create a decorative effect, use short lengths of slim pole cut with angled ends to form geometrical designs between the posts and the main rails.

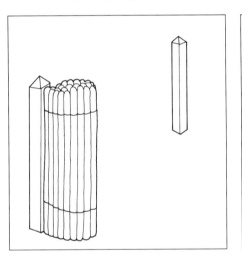

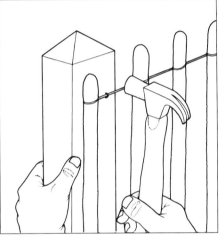

1 Set out the fence posts at the required spacing, then unroll the paling bundle along the fence run. Check that all the poles are securely held by the wires.

2 Stand the fencing up against the posts and secure one end of the length to the first post using stout galvanized wire staples hammered well into the post.

3 Go to the next post and pull the length taut, then secure it to the post. Continue along the run, removing any unwanted section with wire cutters.

Left: *Horizontal rails nailed to posts look smart, but can be climbed very easily. Add wire mesh for extra security.*

Above: *Chestnut paling makes an excellent temporary boundary and is easy to put up and take down.*

GATES

GATES CAN MARK THE ENTRANCE TO YOUR PROPERTY, DETER
PROWLERS FROM ENTERING YOUR BACK GARDEN OR KEEP CHILDREN
IN AND STRAY ANIMALS OUT. THEY COME IN A WIDE RANGE OF
STYLES, MATERIALS AND SIZES, RANGING FROM A LOW BARRIER SET
IN A FRONT FENCE TO IMPOSING ENTRANCE GATES, OFTEN HUNG IN
PAIRS, FOR VEHICLES. THE MOST POPULAR MATERIAL IS WITHOUT
DOUBT TIMBER, AND THE GATE IS OFTEN MADE TO MATCH THE STYLE
OF ANY ADJACENT FENCING.

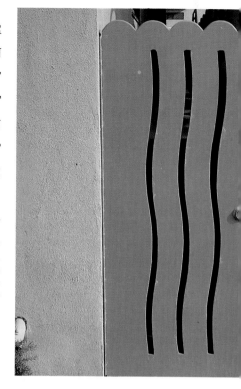

The most important part of any gate is the gate posts, which must be strong enough to carry the gate's weight without allowing it to sag. You can hang your gate from timber posts, often available from the gate supplier, or you can build more permanent brick piers at each side of the opening.

You are likely to choose a gate for one of three positions: as a pedestrian entrance gate at the front of your property, as a side gate to bar access round the house to the back garden, or as a vehicle entrance to a driveway. Front gates – whether for pedestrians or cars – are generally around 1m (3ft 3in) high (you may need planning permission for a higher gate and fence on a boundary fronting a road). Widths range from about 1m for single front gates up to about 4m (13ft) for single barred field gates. Double gates can span drives as narrow as 2m (6ft 6in) and openings as wide as 6m (20ft). Side gates are usually 2m (6ft 6in) high and 1m wide.

CHOOSING MATERIALS

Most wooden gates are made of softwood – usually larch – which has been pretreated with preservative to keep rot at bay. More expensive gates in woods like oak and cedar have better resistance to rot and insect attack, but are more expensive.

Timber gate posts are also either preservative-treated softwood or oak (the latter are preferable, though they

Above: *A gate can be as individual as its owner, and will certainly help callers to recognise where you live!*

Below: *Nothing looks smarter than crisp white paint on a front gate, especially when it matches the house paintwork.*

cost more). Choose 100mm (4in) posts for low single gates, and 125 or 150mm (5 or 6in) posts for high side gates and wide drive gates. As far as post length is concerned, you need to bury about 450mm (18in) of post in the ground for a single gate 1m high, and 600mm (2ft) for a gate 2m high. For double gates, increase the buried depth to a minimum depth of 750mm (2ft 6in).

Many gates are hung between brick piers, either standing alone or as part of a boundary wall. They should be at least one brick (215mm) square for 1m-high gates, and 1½ bricks (330mm) square for higher or wider gates, and must be built on firm foundations. If you are building the piers up before hanging the gate, you can build in the hinge supports as the pier rises; alternatively, you can attach face-fixing plates direct to the brickwork, or even fit timber battens to the piers to carry the fixings. This last method is a useful way of making a standard width gate fit an opening that is a little too wide for it.

FOUNDATIONS

Good foundations are essential to keep gate posts upright and secure, or to support brick piers. It is best to set posts for side and narrow entrance gates in a continuous foundation, with the concrete securing the two posts linked by a strip of concrete about 200mm (8in) thick across the opening. This prevents the hinge post from being pulled inward by the gate's movement. Each post should be set in a concrete collar about 150mm (6in) deep, in a hole around 300mm (12in) across and deep enough to accept the necessary buried length of the gate post.

Brick piers should be built on a concrete pad twice the size of the pier for low gates, three times the size for high ones. It should be at least 150mm (6in) thick. Use a 1:2:3 sand:cement:aggregate mix for the footings, and leave to set for at least seven days before building the piers.

Above: *You can echo your house's colour scheme on your front fence and entrance gate too.*

HANGING A GATE

The most important stage is working out how far apart the posts should be, and to do this you should lay the gate and the posts flat on the ground (with the gate supported on battens to raise it level with the rear face of the post to which the hinges will be attached). Then lay the hinges and catch in position, and adjust the gap between gate and posts to give adequate clearance. Mark a depth line across each post about 75mm (3in) below the bottom of the gate to act as a guide when setting them in the ground.

Check with a tape measure to ensure that the posts are parallel, and then pin three battens (two at right angles, one diagonal) to the posts to hold them the right distance apart.

GATES

Next, mark the gate post positions on the ground, and dig out a hole for each post to about 50mm (2in) more than the required depth. Link the two holes with a trench about 200mm (8in) deep if the posts are 1m or less apart. Lay some gravel or well-broken hardcore in the base of each hole, and set the linked posts in place. Tap them down until the depth marks coincide with ground level; then pin angled struts to each post to hold it precisely vertical, by checking with your spirit level.

You can now pack in more hardcore to within about 150mm (6in) of the surface, and pour in the concrete (a fairly dry mix of 1 part cement to 5 parts combined aggregate). Tamp this down well to form a collar round the posts,

Right: Even the simplest gate can be the focal point of the façade, if treated to a splash of colour.

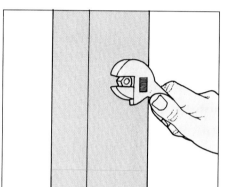

1 Fix wooden spacer to pier.

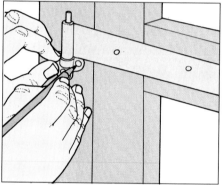

4 Fit upper hinge and hinge cup.

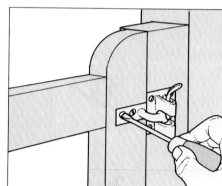

5 Fit latch to gate and post.

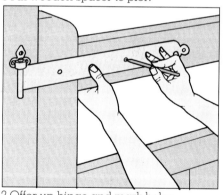

2 Offer up hinge and mark holes.

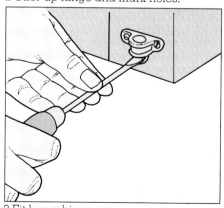

3 Fit lower hinge cups.

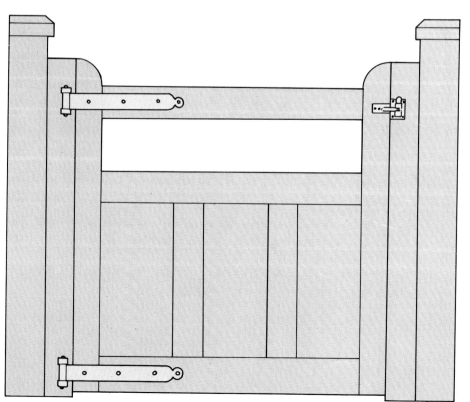

taking care not to knock them off line, and slope the surface away from the post faces to aid drainage. Then lay more concrete in the trench between the post holes to consolidate the whole setting. Leave the concrete to harden around the posts for 48 hours before removing the struts and braces.

Prop the gate between the posts on bricks or timber offcuts, and use timber wedges to center it between them. For flush hinges, set the gate's inner face flush with the rear of the posts; for pintype fittings, center the gate between the front and rear faces of the posts.

Now hold each fitting in place against the gate and mark the positions of the fixing screws. Most gates are hung with tee or reversible hinges; make sure that the strap of the hinge is centered on the gate's horizontal rails, and if the gate has a diagonal brace make sure that it runs up from the hinged edge, not down towards it. Drill

pilot holes and attach the fittings – initially with just a couple of screws, so you can test the gate's operation before driving in the rest. Make sure that catches and automatic latches work easily, and reposition them slightly if they do not.

Heavy, wide timber gates are usually hung on strap hinges and suspended from pins that are bolted through the post for extra strength. Fit the pins to the posts first, then prop up the gate so you can mark the strap positions.

You can add a range of 'optional extras' to your gate to make it more convenient to use. These include self-closing springs and automatic latches, hold-backs (to hold the gate in the open position) and bolts for additional security. These can engage in keepers mounted on the gate posts or, for double gates across a driveway, in a stop block set in the ground. You can add padlocks or locking chains for extra security.

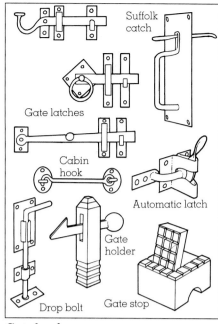

Gate hardware

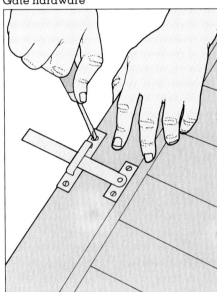
4 Attach the latch to the gate.

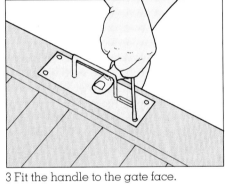
3 Fit the handle to the gate face.

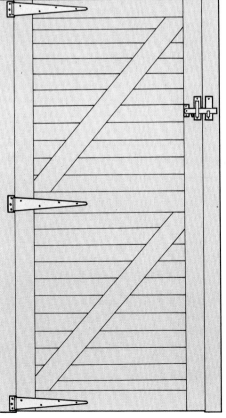

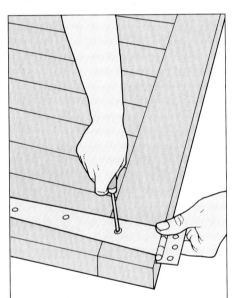
1 Attach the hinges to the gate.

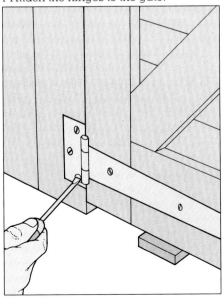
2 Prop the gate and attach the hinges.

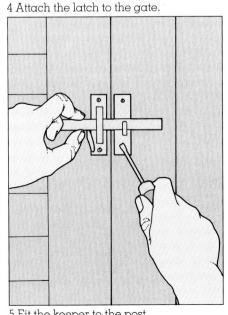
5 Fit the keeper to the post.

Pergolas and Walkways

Free-standing arches form an attractive feature of any garden, especially where there are distinct zones – lawn and vegetable garden for example – and can be built easily in a variety of materials to provide a sturdy framework for plants such as climbing roses. Pergolas are just a series of linked arches built to create a pleasant walkway – down the side of the garden, for example, or across it to shade a patio or sitting-out area – which offer more scope for displaying climbing and trailing plants to good effect.

The most popular material used for garden arches and pergolas is the rustic pole – the trimmed stem of a slender sapling (usually pine) up to about 75mm (3in) in diameter, with or without its bark – but you can build these structures equally well using sawn or planed timber, perhaps in conjunction with brick piers, or by using metal hoops (homemade or prefabricated). Individual plant supports can be provided by incorporating guide wires or by adding sections of trelliswork to the structure.

Arches and pergolas are available in kit form – the perfect answer for the gardener in a hurry – but the big advantage of building your own is the control you have over size, shape and style. The job is pleasingly simple, especially if you go for an all-timber construction, and the end result will be an attractive addition to your garden. Either way, you have the pleasure of designing the support and choosing and training the plants that will make it your own.

Left: *Planed and stained timber makes the perfect pergola for this walled patio.*

Choosing the Size

Overall size matters relatively little where arches and pergolas are concerned, although you obviously want to keep some sense of scale. A huge pergola could spoil the proportions of a small garden, while a puny little arch in the middle of an acre of lawn would appear quite ridiculous. It is a good idea to have a close look at what friends and neighbors have achieved in their gardens before finalizing your own plans.

There are some practical minimum dimensions to bear in mind as far as width and height are concerned, however. You need enough clearance between the uprights of arches and pergolas not only to allow you to walk easily, but also to allow you to push a wheelbarrow through without the foliage snagging clothes or skin. For an

PERGOLAS AND WALKWAYS

Left: *This sturdy hardwood pergola, left to weather naturally, blends in with its surroundings perfectly.*

Below: *A painted pergola-style arch adds a touch of grandeur to this pathway.*

arch, around 1.2m (4ft) between the uprights is usually adequate, while a pergola can be much wider if you wish. As far as height is concerned, 2.1m (7ft) is a sensible minimum for both arches and pergolas, and you should increase this to 2.4m (8ft) if you plan to grow trailing plants over them.

DESIGN FEATURES

The actual design of your arch or pergola is entirely up to you. Rustic poles are generally formed into simple rectangular frames with diagonal cross-braces, while sawn or planed timber looks best with the roof members projecting over the 'walls', since this allows trailing plants to hang freely without obstructing the walkway. For a pergola, aim to have an upright post every 1m (3ft 3in) or thereabouts.

PREPARING THE SITE

Wherever you plan to site your arch or pergola, the first step is to ensure that there are no overhead obstructions –

tree branches are the most obvious candidate for trimming. Next, clear away unwanted vegetation from each side of the opening if you are building an arch, and around each post position for a pergola.

If the site is covered with loose-laid paving slabs or bricks, lift units to allow you to position your uprights; they can be cut to size and replaced later. With concrete and mortared-in paving (crazy paving, for example), either chip holes in the surface so you can sink your posts or use surface-mounted sockets to support them.

CHOOSING MATERIALS

If you are planning an all-timber construction, your choice lies between rustic poles and sawn or planed timber.

Rustic poles look best in an informal cottage-style garden. Choose poles with a base diameter of around 75mm (3in) for posts, plus some slimmer poles for cross-braces and infill members. Most are sold with the bark on, but you can easily strip this off if you prefer a 'bare'

look (the weather will remove the dead bark anyway in time). Garden centres are the best source of supply, although in rural areas local farmers and even the Forestry Commission may be worth contacting too.

Sawn and planed timber creates a more formal effect, although you can still make your constructions blend in unobtrusively if you can find some well-weathered wood to use. For arches, posts should be of 75mm (3in) square timber, while pergola uprights should be 100mm (4in) square for extra strength, and main side bearers should be 100 x 50mm (4 x 2in). Other arch rails and braces can be of 50mm (2in) square wood, while pergola 'joists' can be 75 x 50mm (3 x 2in) or even 75 x 38mm (3 x 1¹/₂in), set on edge. All wood should be pre-treated with preservative, unless you are using a naturally rot-resistant wood such as cedar, so fencing suppliers or specialist timber merchants are probably the best source of materials.

Apart from the wood, you will also need some concrete (or metal fence spikes for square posts) to set the uprights in place, plus 100mm (4in) long galvanized nails to secure the joints and some extra preservative to treat cut ends. For pergolas with brick piers, add some galvanized angle brackets plus fixing screws and wallplugs for securing the main bearers to the masonry.

If you are planning to set your pergola on masonry piers rather than on timber posts, you can choose brick, reconstituted stone walling blocks or even the pilaster blocks sold with pierced screen block walling (which could itself be laid between the piers). Brick is the cheapest material to use, especially if you can get hold of some well-weathered second-hand ones, but you need a reasonable level of brick-laying skill to get good results.

Right: *This simply constructed walkway has become a feature of the garden thanks to a clever planting scheme.*

Below right: *Rustic poles are used to good effect to create this simple archway between two garden zones.*

Below: *This elegant pergola has been designed to span the whole of the garden, with planting beds between the formally laid paths.*

Reconstituted stone walling blocks are easier to handle for ham-fisted bricklayers, since even jointing is not so critical, but they are more expensive than bricks. Screen wall pilaster blocks with hollow centers are the easiest of all to build up, but the pier must be built around a steel reinforcing rod set in the pier foundation and the center of the column must be filled with concrete. Whichever material you choose, builders' merchants are likely to be the best (and cheapest) source of supply.

Brick-and-wood pergolas

If you plan to have masonry piers to support your pergola, you must first of all lay concrete foundation pads at each pier position. These should be about 450mm (18in) square and at least 100mm (4in) thick, laid over 75mm (3in) of well-rammed hardcore. If the piers will rise off an existing concrete or rigidly-paved surface, no further foun-

Above: A pergola that is well-clad with foliage can also create the ideal shaded sitting-out area for hot sunny days.

dation will be needed, but slabs and pavers laid on sand are not a strong enough base and must be lifted so a foundation pad can be laid. Where pilaster blocks are being used, set an L-shaped starter bar of 16mm (⁵/₈in) diameter deformed steel (available from builders' merchants) in the foundation and then tie more steel bar or 50mm (2in) angle iron to it with a 500mm (20in) overlap using galvanized wire.

Build up brick and block piers 1¹/₂ units square; with bricks this gives a pier 330mm (13in) square, while the size of a block pier will depend on the basic block size.

When the piers reach the desired height, set the main 100 x 50mm (4 x 2in) wall plates in place on top and secure them with galvanized angle brackets screwed to drilled and plugged holes in the pier tops. Then measure the span across the pergola and notch the cross rails so they fit over the main wall plates at each end, and secure them in place

with nails driven in at an angle. Finish off by treating all the woodwork with a coat of non-toxic preservative.

PLANED TIMBER PERGOLAS

Whatever design you choose for a timber pergola of this sort, you should start by setting the uprights in position. Post spacing isn't critical – a 1m (3ft 3in) gap is about right, but you could increase this to 1.2m (4ft) if you prefer.

On open ground, you can either set the posts in concrete or use metal fence spikes (quicker to use, but less sturdy with tall posts). If you are using concrete, you need to set at least 450mm (18in) of post in the ground, so make sure you can get posts long enough.

If you are using fence spikes, you simply drive them into the ground with an offcut of post timber placed in the socket to protect it; then discard the offcut, set the post in the socket and secure it with nails or screws. Although these spikes offer a quick fixing, it can be difficult to get the spikes truly vertical, especially in stony soil.

On existing concrete and rigid paved surfaces, it is probably easier to secure

the posts with special post shoes which are fixed in place with masonry bolts.

Once the posts are in place, let the concrete set. Then either notch the tops of the posts to accept the main bearer rails at each side of the pergola, or simply nail them to the faces of the posts. Finally, add the cross rails as described earlier for a brick-and-timber pergola. See pages 121-123 for more details on pergola construction.

RUSTIC PERGOLAS

It is much easier to build arches and pergolas using rustic poles than it is using masonry and sawn or planed timber, because you do not have to take so much care over the assembly; many of the joints are simply overlapped and nailed together, and any genuine joints are only half-laps.

You can build a rustic arch in two ways – either by setting the posts in place first and then adding the cross-rails, braces and arch head as shown on pages 118-119, or by making up the side and top panels first and then setting each side panel in place as one unit before adding the top panel.

Pergolas and Walkways

If you plan some pre-assembly, select your uprights and lay them flat on the ground. Then position the main cross-rails and braces across the posts, marking the joint positions with tape when you are happy with them. To form the joints, either saw down the sides of each cut-out and chisel out the waste to form halving joints, or else make a rounded cut-out in one member to accept the rounded surface of the other. Apply a liberal dose of preservative to all cut surfaces before final assembly. Then secure the joints with galvanized nails driven in at opposing angles for extra strength.

You can now position each side frame, setting the two posts in concrete and bracing each side panel upright while the concrete sets. When it has, nail or screw the arch head sections into place to complete the construction.

1 Start by marking the positions of the pergola uprights on the ground – a handful of sand makes an ideal marker – and check that you are starting out with everything square by measuring the diagonals between the corner posts. They will be equal if the base layout is square or rectangular.

Then dig out the holes to a depth of about 450mm (18in). You can check on progress by standing the post in the hole, laying a cane across it at ground level and marking this level on the post. Dig down a further 75mm (3in) or so and set a brick in the base of the hole on which to stand the pole when you come to set it in place.

You can secure the posts either by surrounding them with a collar of concrete, as though you were putting up fence posts, or by sinking short sections of clay drain pipe in the ground to act as post sockets (the posts are later wedged firmly into the sockets by trickling sand

into the pipes around the posts). The advantage of the latter method over direct concreting is that you can more easily replace a rotten post if necessary in the future.

If you go for direct concreting, stand the post upright on its brick and brace it in position with two lengths of scrap wood nailed to the post at about 45° to the ground and set at right angles to each other. Their other ends simply rest on the ground or can be weighted with bricks on paved surfaces.

Next, mix up the concrete to a dryish consistency, shovel it in around the base of the post and tamp it down with a post offcut. Finish the concrete about 75mm (3in) below the surrounding ground level. This allows soil or turf to be replaced around the post when the construction is completed.

If you prefer the socket method, use the same technique as for concreting posts to set the socket in the ground. Here the top of the socket should be at ground level, with the concrete stopping about 75mm (3in) below it.

With sockets, put a post in and check with a spirit level that it is standing truly vertical before you finish concreting in the socket. Use pressure on the post to change the position of the socket slightly if necessary.

Complete the groundwork by placing and concreting all the other sockets or posts, and leave them overnight for the concrete to harden. Do not remove the braces until it has done so.
2 Next, mark the height you want the pergola to be on the uprights, and saw them to length. It is better to fit slightly over-long posts to begin with and cut

them to size than to try to install cut-to-length posts precisely the same depth in the ground. One will always finish up a little shorter than its neighbors.

Before proceeding with the rest of the pergola structure, treat the cut ends of the posts with preservative to provide some additional protection against rot. Also treat all cuts and joints you make in the other components of the pergola with preservative as you cut them.

Use a bowsaw and chisel to shape simple joints in the cross-rails. You can either use the saw on its own to make roughly semi-circular cut-outs which will accept the rounded surface of the adjacent frame member, or else use a broad chisel as well to cut square

4

6

right angles to the first, again shaping simple joints first and then nailing down through the joint into the rail below. Make sure that the second lot of nails miss those securing the lower rail to the post top.

At this stage you can also add intermediate cross rails to give the structure a 'roof' if you want plants to climb across the pergola as well as up it.

Next, hold up shorter poles for use as struts so you can mark the post and rail angles on them. They look best set at 45° angles to the posts, but you can fit them at other angles if you prefer.

Saw or chisel the ends of the struts to the required angles. If you make the cut concave across the width of the pole, it will fit more positively against the posts and rails and the joint will look more natural than it will if the cuts are made squarely.

6 Check each strut for fit, and trim the length or alter the angle if necessary to get a good fit against the adjacent posts and rails.

Drive the fixing nails partway through each end of the strut, then hold it up and use an offcut of pole to knock it into place before hammering the nails fully home. Do not place the nails too close to the angled ends of the struts or they may split as you fix them in place.

You can also add horizontal braces between the top rails at the corners of the pergola to increase its rigidity and to provide additional support for climbing plants.

5

halving joints in each component so that they interlock. The latter makes for a stronger structure, but takes a little longer.
3 Fix the first set of rails to the posts by nailing down through the joint. Here a semi-circular cut-out in the top of each post creates a positive location for the rail. Use galvanized nails for all the fixings so they will not rust away. If any nail points completely penetrate the rails, hammer them over so they cannot

injure anyone (this is called clench nailing, and actually strengthens the structure because the hooked nail cannot be pulled out by high winds).
4 If the rails are not long enough to span the whole structure from side to side, cut them long enough to reach about 50mm (2in) past the next post. Then use your bowsaw again to make simple spliced joints above the post and nail down through the joint into the post top.
5 Add the second set of cross-rails at

Above: *Rustic poles make a natural support framework for climbing roses along a walkway leading to the rose garden itself.*

With the structure of the pergola complete, go around and check that all the joints are securely nailed, that no nail points are protruding anywhere and that all joints and cut ends have been treated with at least two coats of wood preservative.

Next, backfill around concreted posts and clay pipe sockets with soil, and trickle sand into the sockets to lock the posts securely into position inside them.

Finally, staple lengths of galvanized training wires across the structure to provide additional support for climbing plants. Alternatively, you can fix up pieces of trellis – ideal if you want one side of the pergola to be relatively peep proof once it is clothed in vegetation. Make sure that the panels are securely fixed to support the weight of the foliage.

PREFABRICATED KITS

If all this do-it-yourself activity is too much for you, you may prefer to opt for a pergola or arch in kit form. Some are of timber, closely resembling the types discussed here, but most kits have metal frame members which are simply set in place – either by driving the uprights into the ground directly, or by setting them in concrete as for DIY types. Assembly is quite straightforward.

PERGOLAS AND WALKWAYS

Left: A pergola in its infancy, waiting for nature to catch up. Now is the time for thorough preservative treatment.

BUILDING A PLANED TIMBER PERGOLA

The step-by-step construction shown here covers all the basic steps involved in building a pergola using standard off-the-peg sawn timber. Follow them carefully whether you wish to copy this particular design or decide to experiment with one of your own. The resulting structure will be sturdy enough to support even the most luxuriant plant cover, yet is relatively unobtrusive as a garden feature.

If you do want to build a variation on this theme, it is a simple matter to alter the proportions of the pergola shown to make it longer – to serve as a walkway along a path, for example – or wider. In the former case, increase the depth of the cross rails by 25 or 50mm (1 or 2in) to prevent them from sagging over a wider span; in the latter, simply add on extra bays – additional pairs of posts, extended side rails and a further set of cross rails – to the length you want.

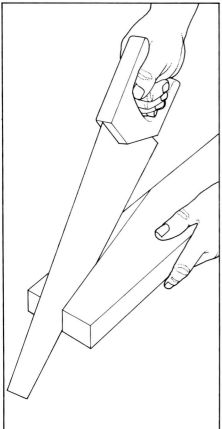

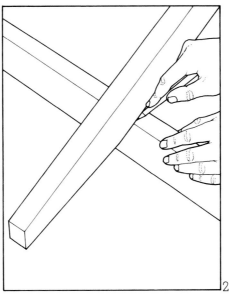

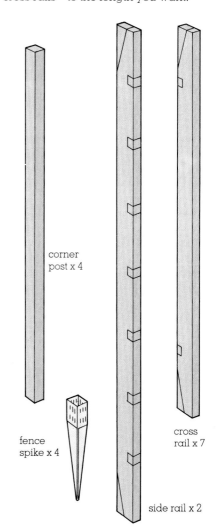

1 Cut the side and cross rails to length, then use a panel or rip saw to make the sloping cuts at each end of the rails.
2 Lay the side rails and two cross rails on the ground with a 300mm (12in) overhang at each corner. Measure the diagonals to ensure that the frame is square. Mark the positions of the cross rails on the top edges of the side rails at each corner, ready for the halving joints to be cut in each component.

corner post x 4

fence spike x 4

cross rail x 7

side rail x 2

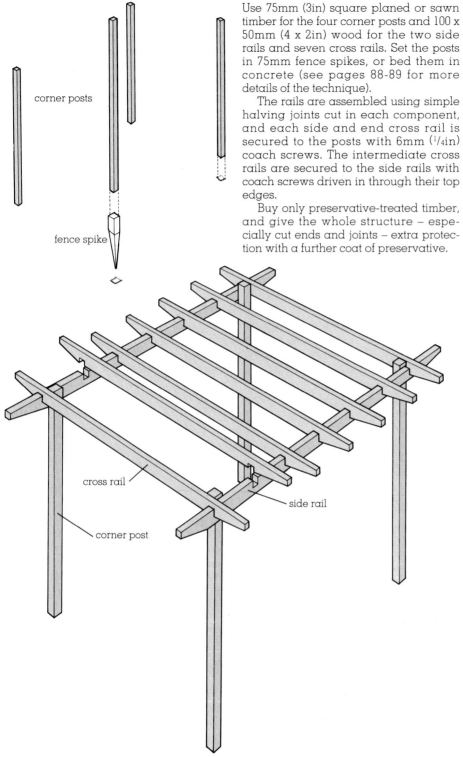

corner posts

fence spike

cross rail

side rail

corner post

Use 75mm (3in) square planed or sawn timber for the four corner posts and 100 x 50mm (4 x 2in) wood for the two side rails and seven cross rails. Set the posts in 75mm fence spikes, or bed them in concrete (see pages 88-89 for more details of the technique).

The rails are assembled using simple halving joints cut in each component, and each side and end cross rail is secured to the posts with 6mm ($\frac{1}{4}$in) coach screws. The intermediate cross rails are secured to the side rails with coach screws driven in through their top edges.

Buy only preservative-treated timber, and give the whole structure – especially cut ends and joints – extra protection with a further coat of preservative.

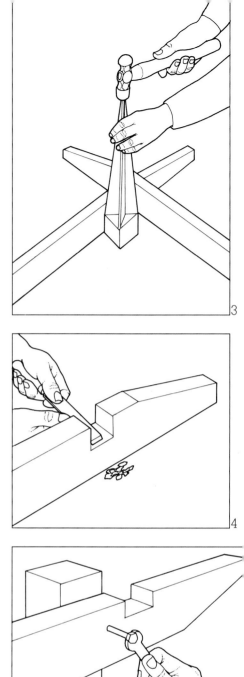

3 Hold a post offcut or an inverted fence spike in each corner of the frame and strike it with a hammer to mark the post positions on the ground. If you are using fence spikes, drive them in at the marked positions using a mallet, with an offcut of post timber in the socket to protect it. If you are using concrete, excavate each hole and put some hardcore in the bottom. Brace the posts upright, check their positions and tamp in the concrete.
4 Mark out the halving joints on the rails

by squaring lines down their sides to their midpoints and adding a depth line. Cut the sides of each joint with a tenon saw down to the depth line, then chisel out the waste to leave a slot.
5 Drill 6mm ($\frac{1}{4}$in) pilot holes through each rail 38mm from the halving joints. Use 6mm coach screws to secure the side and end cross rails to the posts.
6 Drill holes through each cross rail, and screw them to the posts. Check that everything is square and tighten up the screws with a spanner.

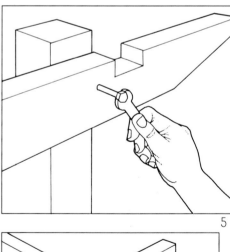

Right: *A simple patio pergola can be made to seem like an extension to the building if decorated to match the house colour scheme.*

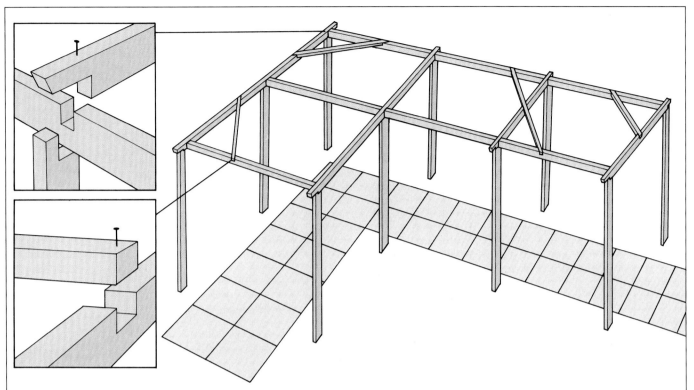

It is a simple matter to extend the basic pergola structure shown on page 122 to create a walkway that can run along a path and even turn corners. The diagonal roof braces are an alternative means of stiffening the structure if trellis or training wires are to be used to support the plants instead of roof slats. The details show how the tops of the posts are cut away to provide a positive location for the side rails, which are in turn notched to accept the transverse rails. Simple nailed joints like these also help give the structure additional rigidity.

Pergolas and Walkways

Roofing a Pergola

The natural cladding for a pergola is of course climbing plants, and if you add cross rails, training wires or trellis panels to the structure you will soon encourage them to form a natural roof. However, if you want quicker results or you need a structure that provides a greater degree of shade and shelter, there are a couple of other 'roofing' options you could consider.

The first is to provide a roof that keeps off the rain but lets in the light, and for this rigid plastic sheet is the best answer

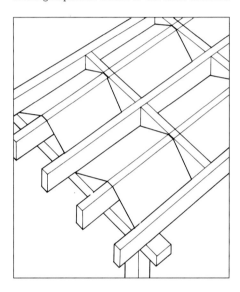

Above: *You can add temporary shading to a pergola simply by draping opaque fabric over and under the joists and tacking or stapling it into place.*

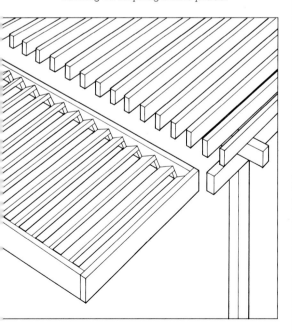

Above: *Closely-spaced slats provide some shade when the sun is not directly overhead. You can create more shade by angling the slats like louvers.*

- not the flimsy and ugly corrugated type, but so-called twin-wall polycarbonate sheeting which is widely used nowadays as a low-cost alternative to safety glass for conservatory roofs. Obviously you cannot use this successfully with a rustic pergola because of the uneven nature of the individual poles, but it is ideal for pergolas constructed with sawed or planed timber.

To support the individual panes, nail 25mm (1in) square battens to the inner sides of the roof beams so they slope slightly downwards. Then cut the panes to size with a fine-toothed saw and lay them in place on the battens. If you want the roof to be waterproof, pipe a bead of non-setting mastic along the top edge of all the battens first and press the sheet down into it to seal the edges. Then nail on more square battens to the roof beams above the panes to sandwich them securely in place. Repeat the process for the other bays of the roof.

The second option provides temporary shade from the sun, but not a waterproof shelter. It involves using roller blinds in an unconventional way, running them horizontally between the beams that make up the roof of the pergola rather than in their more usual vertical mode of operation. Remember that it is essential to use waterproofed awning material for this, not interior blind fabric which will soon become waterlogged and will then rot.

The blind is made up to suit the width of each bay of the roof, and is fixed in position by screwing the standard roller support brackets to the inner face of one of the side beams. To support it when it is extended lengths of plant-training

Below: *This ingenious arrangement of horizontal roller blinds provides shade for the patio when it is needed and can be rolled back when it is not.*

wire are fixed between the transverse beams, just below the blind roller position. To extend the blind, a cord is fitted to the draw bar and runs across the bay to the opposite side, where it is taken over a pulley and drops to a cleat on one of the pergola posts. The cord is freed from its cleat and pulled down to extend the blind, which runs out across its supporting wire as far as is needed to shade the area below; the cord is then tied off to the cleat. When you want to retract the blind again, you simply release the cord from the cleat and allow the roller spring to pull the blind back onto its roller again.

Right: *Here a basic pergola structure has been fitted with a glazed roof to provide a covered but well-lit walkway.*

Below: *Roofing your pergola with trellis-work creates attractive shadows.*

TRELLIS

TRELLISWORK, USUALLY IN THE FORM OF AN OPEN LATTICE MADE FROM SLIM TIMBER LATHS, IS ONE OF THE MOST VERSATILE AND INEXPENSIVE OF GARDEN FEATURES. IT IS MOST COMMONLY USED AS A SUPPORT FOR CLIMBING PLANTS, BUT CAN BE A SIMPLE VISUAL SCREEN IN ITS OWN RIGHT, ESPECIALLY IN ITS MORE ORNATE DECORATIVE FORMS. IT CAN BE FIXED TO WALLS AS A WAY OF SCREENING UGLY FEATURES OF A BUILDING, OR SUPPORTED ON POSTS TO FORM A TRELLIS FENCE. IT CAN EVEN BE USED TO FORM THE WALLS AND ROOFS OF GARDEN BUILDINGS, WHERE ITS OPEN STRUCTURE ALLOWS SUNLIGHT TO FORM INTERESTING PATTERNS OF LIGHT AND SHADE ON THE FLOOR SURFACE INSIDE.

Trelliswork offers almost endless variety to the creative gardener. In its most basic form it consists of a square or diamond-shaped grid of slim wooden laths nailed or stapled together and sometimes fitted with a perimeter frame to hold the lattice in its formation and to make it easier to handle and mount.

The grid size can vary too; most ready-made trellis panels have a 100mm (4in) grid repeat, but if you are making up your own trellis it can be smaller or larger than this. Remember that the smaller the grid size, the more rigid the trellis will be. A small grid will

also appear more 'solid' and visually intrusive than will a larger size....but this may well be the effect you want to achieve anyway.

The basic trellis format is of course open to all sorts of design adaptations. The simplest is to use single pins to secure the overlapping laths, allowing the square grid to be deformed into a diamond shape. This is essential if you want to use trellis on a sloping site – atop a boarded fence, for example, or to screen a flight of steps. As you make up the grid, you can mix large and small squares, set some as lozenge shapes

enough when you first put it up, but once plants have grown up the trellis it may have to support a considerable weight of foliage and must be fixed securely enough to withstand high winds without collapsing. Since the fixings between individual laths are not particularly strong, the combination of framing and good support is essential.

There are two other factors to bear in mind when making and fitting trellis. The first is that once it is in position and plants have started to grow up it you will have great difficulty in maintaining or decorating it. To get round this potential problem, either use wood such as cedar which is naturally resistant to decay or buy preservative-treated wood and treat it liberally with more preservative after making the trellis panels up; pay special attention to the cut ends, leaving them standing in preservative overnight after cutting but before final assembly so the liquid can penetrate deep into the end grain. If you want your trellis coloured rather than *au naturel*, use pigmented wood stains or microporous paint rather than conventional outdoor paints, which will soon begin to crack, peel and look generally unsightly behind the foliage.

The second problem concerns not the trellis, but any wall against which you decide to fix it. As with the point made earlier about maintenance, a fully clothed trellis will effectively prevent you from reaching the masonry behind. Brickwork should not need any remedial work anyway so long as its pointing is in good condition, but if the wall

Above: *Trellis makes a stunning fencing material in its own right.*

Left: *Trellis lines the walls of this courtyard, and has also been used to surround the flower beds.*

Right: *Another example of trellis used as a design feature, here to form a frame behind a statue.*

within outer squares, and add diagonals and other details as you wish. There is no reason why you should not use laths of different thicknesses for different areas of the design. You can even create curves if the laths you use are thin enough to be bent without splitting (soak them in water first to make them more pliable).

You do not need a perimeter frame round the trellis if it is being fixed to a wall, unless you want the look of a framed panel; the fixings will hold the lattice in formation. However, a freestanding trellis will need a frame unless it is well supported by fence posts or the framing members of a garden building. Remember that it may look strong

surface is painted you will not be able to repaint it in the future unless you think about the problem now. The best solution is to position the bottom edge of the trellis panel 600mm (2ft) or so above ground level, and to hinge its lower edge to a wall-mounted batten. It will then be possible – with care – to release the other wall fixings and let the trellis fall away from the wall at an angle so you can paint behind it. The flexibility of the plant stems, allied to the generous ground clearance, should allow this movement of the support without damaging the plants themselves.

TROMPE L'OEIL TRELLIS

There is no limit to the visual effects you can achieve with trellis...except your ingenuity. In the picture above, the rear wall of an already stunning loggia has been fitted with three panels of hand-made trelliswork to give the appearance of three apses framed by classical columns. The effect is almost perfect, thanks to the extremely skillful use of perspective in positioning the various converging and diverging lines.

A matching panel of traditional trellis fills in the garden side of the loggia, and even the roof support columns are constructed as tubes of trelliswork. The entire creation is finished with white microporous paint to minimize the need for future redecoration, a job even the most avid housepainter would approach with some trepidation.

If you are mounting trellis on wooden supports, you can simply nail it in place. Use round wire nails with flat heads, rather than oval nails or panel pins, to provide a secure fixing that will resist the trellis pulling free under heavy wind loadings. Drill small pilot holes before driving in the nails, so you do not split the slim laths. Better still, use screws; they are more time-consuming to fix, but are more secure in the long run.

To mount trellis on a wall, it may be tempting to use masonry nails. Don't. They will be almost impossible to remove in the future if you want to replace the trellis. In any case, you want a gap between trellis and wall to allow

---

Below: Green painted trellis follows the line of this lower ground floor entrance. It adds style and privacy, whilst supporting flowering climbers.

plants to twine around it, and nails will pull it flat against the wall surface. Instead, use screws driven into wallplugs; again, drill pilot holes in the trellis first. When mounting the trellis, slip a short spacer cut from small-diameter copper or rigid plastic pipe over the screw before driving it into its wallplug. Use rust-proof screws wherever possible for all the fixings.

Fixing shallow trellis panels on top of a boarded fence is a popular way of gaining extra privacy once plants have become established. If you do this, stiffen the panels by adding a perimeter frame which can be secured to the top of the fence boards as well as to the posts themselves. Trellis panels do not, of course, have to be flat. Thanks to the flexibility of the laths, panels can be bent into gentle curves, allowing you to use them for making structures such as trellis arches and roofed walkways; you

could even construct a cylindrical arbour. The thinner the laths used and the larger the trellis grid, the more flexible the panel will be. However, do not expect to achieve a radius of curvature much smaller than about 500mm (20in) without splitting of the laths occurring.

Once your trellis is fixed in place, you can begin to train plants to climb it. As they spread, tuck the growing shoots in and out of the latticework so they get a good grip on the structure, and do not be afraid to add extra ties to the trellis at intervals to provide additional support – essential if you are growing fruit-bearing species, for example. As the plants spread, you can always add extra sections of trellis to support them; all you have to do is to match the existing trellis size and style when making up the new section.

FITTING TRELLIS TO A WALL

Installing a run of trellis along the top of a garden wall is a good way of gaining extra privacy as well as providing a support for climbing plants (1). Start by deciding on the length of post you require; this will be the height of the trellis plus about 600mm (2ft) to allow for fixing to the wall surface. Then cut the posts to length.

Hold each post against the wall, checking that it is vertical with a level, and mark the positions for two fixing screws in line with brick centres, not with the mortar joints. Then drill clearance holes in the posts.

Reposition the post against the wall and mark the positions of the clearance holes on the wall surface. Switch to a masonry drill bit and hammer action to drill the holes in the bricks, then insert wall plugs and screw the post into place. Next, offer up the first trellis panel to the

side of the post and drill clearance holes through its side frame members. Screw it to the post so it can act as a spacer for the next post.

Hold the second post in place against the other end of the panel, check that it is vertical and repeat the post fixing process (2). Then screw the trellis panel to the second post.

An alternative to driving screws into a previously-placed wallplug is to use a frame plug – a long wallplug complete with screw which you simply hammer in after drilling the post and wall holes (3).

With the second post in place, screw on the next section of trellis (4) and position and fix the next post. Continue in this way until the run is completed (5).

Above: *Open trelliswork and a simple arch form an attractive divider between the patio and the garden beyond.*

You can use trellis in a variety of ways to create a screen across the garden – perhaps to divide off a vegetable garden, to create a visual centerpiece, to hide an eyesore or gain extra privacy for when you are sitting out in the garden. You can incorporate an arch in the structure to form a walkway, either fitting a simple flat head or constructing a more elaborate curved design – the ideal support for climbing roses, for example. The screen can be left to weather naturally, or can be painted. White looks especially good against dark green foliage.

For a straight screen containing a central arch, set up one of the arch posts first (see pages 180-181 for details) to give you a point of reference from which to work. Then set up a stringline across the screen site to act as a guide to positioning the remaining posts (1).

Use a trellis panel as a spacer to gauge the required post separation, and install the other posts (2).

Stand the first panel up against the posts, resting its bottom edge on offcuts of wood so it stands squarely. Tap it sideways to line it up with the face of the post. Note that here the trellis is being fixed to the face of the posts instead of fitting between adjacent posts (3). Use this technique if you find that your post separation has altered while you were installing them and the panels no longer fit between them.

Nail the trellis to the top of the post. As a precaution against splitting the laths, drill pilot holes through the trellis before driving in the fixing nails.

Drive in another nail at the bottom of the post, and add intermediate fixings at roughly 300mm (12in) intervals.

Fit the other trellis panels in the same way, then nail an offcut of fence post across the top of the opening (4).

Finish the job by re-laying any turf you lifted earlier, and add climbing plants along the foot of the screen.

3

4

Decking, Paths and Steps

Sitting-out areas, garden paths and steps do not have to be paved or concreted. Wood makes an unusual and practical alternative that suits any garden, since its colour and texture will blend in naturally with its surroundings as it weathers, and the surface is a sympathetic one to walk or sit on. It dries quickly after rain, and will last for years if durable timber species are chosen and the wood is well treated with preservative before being placed in position. Lastly, it is a far easier material to work with than concrete or stone, although rather more expensive.

Above: *Baulks of heavy timber make a level sitting area in this attractively cobbled town garden.*

Right: *Carefully laid timber decking makes a stunning outdoor surface, especially when used on several levels.*

The first thing to think about is where you want your decking to go. The obvious site is at the back of the house, but you may prefer to site it elsewhere in the garden to take full advantage of the sun and the view or to gain greater privacy from your neighbours.

Next, examine the lie of the land. If it is basically level, you can build up your decking on bricks or low sleeper walls, aiming to keep the final surface of the deck about 150mm (6in) below the level of the damp proof course (dpc) in the house wall so that rain falling on the decking cannot splash back above the dpc and lead to damp penetration. If the land slopes, it is a simple matter to support the decking on posts, allowing you to create a level sitting area far more easily than with conventional building methods.

Thirdly, think about shape and size. Using timber gives you total flexibility as far as shape is concerned, while the size should take into account the likely use to which the decking will be put. Allow ample space round chairs and tables, both for access and to allow through traffic to cross the decking easily between house and garden.

Lastly, remember the safety angle. Decking more than about 450mm (18in) above the surrounding ground level should be fitted with handrails, and steps should be provided to link the decking to the garden. If you have small children, it is wise to have a balustrade with no more than 100mm (4in) gaps between the posts to stop heads getting trapped, and to design it so it is not readily climbable. A gate at the garden steps would then convert the decking into a full size outdoor playpen, perfect for toddlers. Gaps between the deck planking should be kept to no more than about 6mm (¼in), to allow easy surface drainage without letting chair legs slip into them.

CHOOSING MATERIALS

The obvious enemy of wood is rot, so the ideal types of timber to choose for a decking are rot resistant species such as Western red cedar or teak. However, the expense of these woods is likely to mean that most people will use ordinary softwood; this is fine so long as it is treated with preservative – ideally at the timber yard, using pressure or vacuum impregnation to ensure that the preservative penetrates deep into the wood.

Most of the structure can be built using sawn wood, with planed timber for the decking itself and for handrails and balustrades if these are required. The sizes needed will depend on the dimensions of the decking, and on whether it is built substantially above ground level or not. As a rough size guide, 100 x 50mm (4 x 2in) joists need

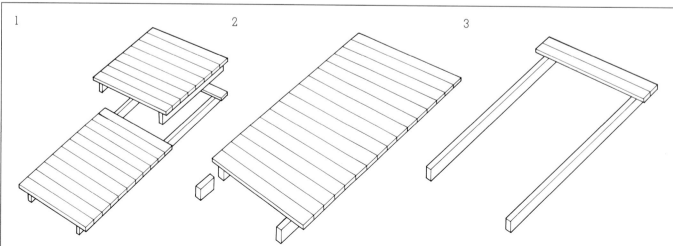

The decking in the picture above consists of a series of smaller modules laid side by side to cover the required area. Make them up by laying two bearers side by side and nailing slats across them with a slight gap between them for drainage (1). When the module reaches the desired length, trim off the bearers (2). Make steps up as shorter modules which can be skew-nailed into place on top of an unboarded section of a full-sized module (3).

Left: Timber decking provides the perfect link between house and garden, and can be used for flights of steps too.

supporting every 1.5m (5ft), while 150 x 50mm (6 x 2in) joists can span up to around 3m (10ft). Both are laid at 600mm (24in) centres, and are covered with 100 x 19mm or 150 x 19mm (4 x ³/₄in or 6 x ³/₄in) planks. Posts for supporting raised decking should be 100mm (4in) square, up to a maximum height of around 1.8m (6ft). For structures higher than this, professional advice should be sought to ensure that the components of the decking are correctly sited and are strong enough; the consequences of a collapse could be serious.

For low level decking, the joists can simply be set on individual bricks, garden walling blocks or paving slabs over an area of cleared vegetation, or can be placed directly on an existing area of concrete (see page 137). Low brick walls on concrete strip foundations will be needed if the ground clearance is to be more than a few inches. With raised platforms, the support posts will have to be set in concrete, or else must be bolted to fence spurs set in a concrete footing.

Most of the fixings can be made with galvanized nails, although coach bolts should be used to assemble the main framework with raised decks. You may need some masonry bolts if the decking adjoins the house and is to be suspended from a wall plate on the house wall. Lastly, have some wood preservative handy so you can treat all cut ends, joints and the like as you assemble the decking.

LOW LEVEL DECKING

If your decking will be just above existing ground level on a flat site, you can support the joists in several ways, as mentioned earlier. Mark out the position of the decking and clear the site of vegetation; then level and compact the surface. Set one corner brick or paver on a bed of sand, check that it is level and position other supports using this first one as a datum point. The sand bed makes it easy to bed the supports down to the required height. Space them to match the spans mentioned in the previous section.

Next, put a strip of roofing felt or dpc material on top of each support; a dab of bituminous mastic will help to keep it in place. Rest the joists on top of the supports, butt-joining lengths over the centre of each one if necessary, and then cover the ground beneath the decking with 2mm black polyethylene sheet and then weight it down with a 100-150mm (4-6in) layer of gravel to discourage weed growth.

Now you can start nailing or screwing on the decking planks to tie the whole structure together. Use a plywood offcut as a spacer to ensure an even gap between the planks. Remember that you do not have to lay the planks floorboard fashion; you can experiment with diagonal layouts and chevron patterns if you prefer.

At the edges of the decking, lay the boards so that their ends finish flush with the side joists; overhangs can be a trip hazard. If you wish, finish off the edges with a 50 x 25mm (2 x 1in) batten nailed in place level to the board ends, with the decking surface.

If you want to build a more substantial structure or need more ground clearance, build sleeper walls up to the required height in stretcher bond on concrete strip foundations 100mm (4in) thick. Space them to suit the joist dimensions, and incorporate a dpc in the wall two courses above ground level to keep the masonry dry.

With this type of construction built next to the house, it is often best to attach the house edge of the decking to the house wall; this saves having to build a sleeper wall here. You can do this in one of two ways. Either fix a timber wall plate to the wall with masonry bolts and skew nail the joists to this, or use galvanised steel joist hangers fixed to the wall to support the individual joist ends.

RAISED DECKING

Life becomes a little more complicated on steeply sloping sites, where the decking has to be supported by vertical posts. Start by marking out the site, indicating the positions of post holes with pegs. Then clear the site as before, and

Below: Decking fixed wall-to-wall transforms this tiny back yard into an attractive outdoor living space.

Above: Heavy blocks of wood on a fine gravel base make a striking path.

dig out the holes to a depth equal to one quarter of the post height and about 300mm (12in) across. Then set the posts in position (see pages 180-183) and concrete them in.

An alternative approach, suitable for decks up to about 1.2m (4ft) above ground level, is to set concrete fence spurs in the ground as described for wooden posts, and then to bolt the posts to the spurs. This avoids having timber buried in the ground where it may be attacked by rot.

Bolt the main cross bearers to the posts, checking that they are level as you attach them. Then trim off the post tops if necessary, and start screwing or bolting the joists to the cross bearers. Finally, fit the decking planks as before. With a raised deck of this sort, a guard rail is essential. Screw or bolt 50mm (2in) sq uprights to the joists all round the perimeter of the decking, and add handrails (and balusters if you wish). Then build up steps down to the garden or up to the house if the design calls for them. Make the treads at least 300mm (12in) deep from front to back, with a rise of no more than about 150mm (6in) per step. Fit a handrail at each side if the flight has more than three steps.

SPLIT LEVEL DECKING

There is no reason why you should not have several areas of decking at different levels, and this can look particularly attractive on a sloping site. It will also make the construction easier, since you may be able to build several low level decks running into each other with steps between them instead of having to use posts to cope with the slope.

MAINTAINING DECKING

So long as the timber you used for your decking was preservative-treated, the only maintenance you will need to carry out will be an annual scrub-down in the spring to remove algae which will have grown during the winter, and regular inspections for splinters along board edges which could injure bare feet. Cut away any you find and sand the board edge smooth, giving it a slight chamfer to prevent further splitting.

If you want to spruce up the looks of your decking and maintain its defences against rot, brush on a generous coat of clear or pigmented preservative once every couple of years.

PATHS AND STEPS

There is no reason why you should not use timber to create paths and steps elsewhere in the garden too. Paths can be constructed in two ways; with planks or with roundels cut across the log and laid like small circular pavers. The former works only on virtually straight paths, while the latter can form either straight or curved paths with ease.

If you decide to use the plank method, use sawn timber with a fairly substantial cross section – say 150 x 50mm (6 x 2in) – and ensure that it has been pre-treated with preservative. Whether you lay the planks lengthwise, parallel with the path direction, or crosswise depends on how the ground slopes.

If you prefer to use roundels, simply saw logs of various sizes into cylinders about 100mm (4in) long; anything shorter will split. A mixture of sizes not only makes an attractive path; you will also get a closer fit between adjacent roundels.

The best way of laying a planked path is to excavate the site to a depth of about 100mm (4in) and to put down a 50mm (2in) layer of fine gravel. This not only makes it easy to bed and level the

Left: *Roundels set in concrete make an unusual surface for garden paths.*

Below: *Stout planks laid edge to edge allow the path to cope with gradients, and can even be built into steps (bottom).*

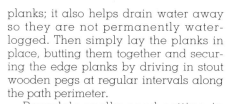

planks; it also helps drain water away so they are not permanently water-logged. Then simply lay the planks in place, butting them together and securing the edge planks by driving in stout wooden pegs at regular intervals along the path perimeter.

Roundels really need setting in concrete to stop them working loose in use and becoming a trip hazard. Excavate to a depth of about 150mm this time, again put down a gravel bed and then tamp the roundels into position, butted together and levelled with their neighbours. Then fill the gaps between them with a dryish concrete mix to lock them all in position.

Use planks or roundels for making steps too, simply setting them in place to follow the slope of the ground. Mark out the position of the flight on the bank, and excavate step shapes in it. If you are using planks, again choose fairly substantial timber and cut the planks to the step width you require. Peg a vertical riser in place at the back of each step first, then lay the treads. Check that each plank is set level across its width and has a slight slope towards the front edge of the step, then secure the front plank of each step to the bank with long wooden pegs hammered into position.

If you are using roundels, you will have to cut the steps in the bank deep enough to accept units cut to a length of between 150 and 200mm (6 to 8in). Peg vertical planks in place first to form the front edge of each step, then place and concrete in the roundels that form the tread of the step.

137

GARDEN FURNITURE

GARDEN FURNITURE IS A FINE INVENTION, AND CAREFULLY CHOSEN PIECES CAN TRANSFORM YOUR PATIO OR GARDEN. GOOD-QUALITY ITEMS ARE EXPENSIVE TO BUY, BUT BY MAKING YOUR OWN YOU CAN SAVE MONEY AND CREATE FURNITURE THAT CAN STAY OUT COME RAIN OR SHINE, AND IF THEY ARE WELL BUILT IN THE FIRST PLACE THEY WILL NEED NO MAINTENANCE FOR MANY YEARS APART FROM AN OCCASIONAL WIPE OVER WHEN THE BIRDS HAVE BEEN EATING TOO MANY BERRIES. ABOVE ALL, BY CHOOSING DESIGNS AND MATE-RIALS CAREFULLY YOU CAN CREATE SEATING THAT LOOKS AS THOUGH IT BELONGS IN THE GARDEN INSTEAD OF JUST BEING PLANTED THERE.

Begin by thinking carefully about what you actually need. Is it simply a rustic bench where you can sit occasionally and admire the view? Or do you want furniture you can sunbathe on in comfort? If you will be eating out of doors, how many will you be catering for? Do you want individual seats or benches? What about an all-in-one picnic table-cum-bench? Do you need to provide shade? Answers to these questions will give you a basic shopping list – three sun loungers, a bench and two upright chairs, a table with an integral parasol and so on.

Next, think about how the furniture will be used. Working this out will help you define the *type* of furniture you want to make. For example, you may want to leave some items out all year round, so they will have to be durable and heavy enough not to blow away in high winds. Others will only be taken out when they are actually needed – typically items such as sunbeds and parasols. In between come things like upholstered seats and loungers, where just the cush-ions will be stored indoors when they are not in use. Think about this storage question now as well; if things are to be stored indoors, designing them to fold up means they will take up less space than 'solid' ones.

The last factor to consider is what the furniture will be made of, how well it will stand up to the elements and to everyday wear and tear, how easy it will be to carry about, and most impor-tantly, how comfortable and practical it will be to use.

Wood's advantages are that it suits its environment, especially if left to weather naturally, and it wears well so long as a durable species is chosen or regular preservative treatment is applied. It is also warm to the touch and relatively easy to repair if damaged. Its draw-backs are that smaller items are light enough to be blown about in high winds, and larger ones tend to be heavy and decidedly non-portable. Wood also takes a while to dry out after rain. However, for traditional furniture in a traditional setting it is hard to beat.

Above: *It takes little to make the simplest garden seat: just a baulk of timber set on two stout logs.*

Left: *Take a simple bench and paint it in a bold colour to create an eye-catching feature against the garden's foliage.*

Ordinary softwood will soon deteriorate and begin to rot if used out of doors, so you must ensure that any wood you use is thoroughly impregnated with preservative – ideally by vacuum or pressure treatment carried out by your supplier. Some hardwoods require similar treatment, but there are several species that can be used out of doors without the need for extra protection. Some are softwoods, of which Western red cedar is the least expensive and most widely available. Others are hardwoods – either the tropical species from Africa, South America and Southeast Asia, or the temperate ones from areas such as Europe and North America.

From the first group of hardwoods comes teak – arguably the best wood of all for outdoor use. Its natural oiliness gives it more or less permanent resistance to moisture, and if it is left untreated it weathers to an attractive silvery grey colour. Other suitable tropical hardwoods include afrormosia, iroko and utile, but all are expensive.

American white or European oak is the best choice among temperate hardwoods. The Japanese and American red varieties are more prone to decay. Chestnut is a good runner up.

Man-made boards are of little use to the maker of outdoor furniture, with one exception: marine plywood. This is made from veneers that are either naturally weatherproof or have been treated with preservative, and the adhesive used to bond the veneers together is waterproof too. Avoid other grades even if labelled as suitable for exterior use; the adhesive may be up to the job, but the veneers are not unless completely protected from the weather by paint or

varnish. In any case, plywood seldom blends in well in the garden because it is man-made; natural timber simply looks more natural.

It is important to think about how you will assemble your garden furniture. The trouble with nails and screws is that steel rusts. Worse still, being out of doors the wood will swell and shrink as the seasons change, and this will put considerable strain on any fixings you use. The best solution is to rely on simple but sturdy woodworking joints – mainly variations on the mortise and tenon joint, with the occasional halving joint used where necessary. Tenons can then be locked in place with pegs or wedges so that the joint stays tight even without the use of adhesive. The best framing joint of all is the projecting wedged tenon (also known as the tusk tenon), where the projecting end of the tenon is itself mortised to accept a tapered wedge which can simply be driven in a little further whenever the joint shows any sign of movement.

Garden Furniture

Adhesives are generally of little use for assembling garden furniture; only the urea-formaldehyde (UF) and epoxy types are totally weatherproof. Unfortunately the oiliness that protects the best outdoor timbers such as teak from the weather also stops water-based UF adhesive from bonding well. Interlocking joints really are the best solution for outdoor furniture.

The way you design your furniture has a bearing on how well it performs too. For example, avoid wide pieces which will shrink and swell proportionately more than narrow ones. In addition, their exposed surfaces will tend to cup curl up at the edges on the side furthest from the centre of the tree from which they were cut. Narrow pieces also help to shed rainwater more easily, which is why slatted designs are so widely used for seats and table tops.

Endgrain will absorb moisture much more readily than side grain, so try to design your furniture so that as much endgrain as possible is concealed. Where it is exposed, seal it with a thin solution of UF adhesive, bevel or round off the end of the component so water runs off it easily, or cap it otherwise.

Lastly, remember that garden furniture often has to stand on uneven ground, so pieces should be designed to stand on legs or feet rather than on the edges of boards. Remember that furniture with three legs is the perfect solution: it never wobbles!

Above: *A table built round a specimen tree makes an unusual garden centre-piece with its own built-in shade.*

Left: *If garden furniture is made from a durable species, it can be left to weather naturally to an attractive silvery grey colour.*

Below: *Restrict the use of paint to furniture that is normally kept indoors.*

MAKING A SLATTED TABLE

This table incorporates all the principles mentioned earlier. It is made from Western red cedar; however, the cross-sectional sizes given correspond to the usual finished dimensions of other softwoods which may be more readily available than cedar.

The long rails which support the slats are bridle-jointed to the tops of the legs, while the cross rails are pegged into mortises. The slats are, with two exceptions, secured by screws driven up from beneath the table, and are positioned so they conceal and protect the vulnerable end grain on the tops of the legs. The ends of the long rails have optional curved detailing, while the taper and groove at the foot of each leg is also an option; they can be left plain and square if this is preferred.

Start by cutting the four legs over-long; their final length will be 725mm (28in). Then mark the open mortises for the bridle joints as shown in (1) overleaf. They should be about 40mm (1¹/₂in) wide and 10mm (³/₈in) shorter than the width of the long rail, which is cut from 75 x 50mm (3 x 2in) wood. Cut them out with a tenon saw and coping saw.

Mark the mortises for the cross rails on the inner face of each leg (1 overleaf) and chisel them out to a depth of about 50mm (2in) ready to accept the tenoned ends of the cross-rails. This minimizes the exposure of their end grain.

Now mark the bridles on the long rails, starting with the shoulder on the under side which should be kept shallow to preserve the strength of the rail while providing a positive lock to the leg when the joint is assembled. Then mark the shoulders on the rail's thickness with your marking gauge so its reduced width matches the size of the bridles on the top of the legs. Remove the waste wood with a fine tenon saw and broad chisel (2). Finish the rails by marking and cutting the decorative end curves if required.

Use the shoulders cut on the long rails as a guide to marking the tenon positions on the cross rails, then use a marking gauge to set the tenon width so it matches that of the mortise in the legs. Cut the tenons, leaving a 10mm (³/₈in) shoulder on the underside.

Cut the tapers on the legs at this stage if you want them, using a tenon saw, and add the grooves on their inner faces with a carving gouge or a router (3).

Drill right through each leg where the center of the cross-rail tenon will be, using a bit to match the size of your pegging dowel. Push the tenon in and use the bit again to mark the hole position on it. Remove the tenon and make another mark 1.5mm (¹/₁₆in) closer to the shoulder than the one made by the bit. Drill through the tenon at this second mark, and reinsert it in its mortise.

Taper the end of a length of dowel and hammer it home right through the joint. It will automatically pull the joint

tight. Trim and plane the ends of the dowel off flush with the leg. Repeat the process for the other three joints to complete the two H-shaped leg assemblies. If you are using softwood other than cedar, apply a liberal coat of clear wood preservative to all exposed areas of end-grain.

Drop the long rails into their bridles on top of the legs to assemble the table frame. Leave these joints unglued so the table top can be easily removed for storage; so long as you cut the bridle joints carefully earlier, they should be a perfect fit – tight enough to lock the whole structure rigidly togther, yet easy to knock apart with a mallet if you want to dismantle the table for storage. Then glue the 25mm (1in) square battens through which the slats will be screwed to the inner faces of the long rails. Note that you must fit one long length of batten between the legs and a short length to the inner face of the projecting ends of each rail.

Loose-lay the slats on the frame, with the center one over a carefully-marked center line. Space them out so that the middle slat of each group of five to the left and right of the center slat fits precisely over the top of the legs. Mark the slat positions on the rails; they

Below: *This garden table and bench are made from Western red cedar. The unusual curve in the seat slats gives the set an oriental feel.*

should end up about 15mm (⅝in) apart. Drill clearance holes through the 25mm (1in) square batten in line with the slat centers, and counter sink them on the underside.

Cut the center slat to length, saw both ends to a double 60° splay, and drive its brass fixing screws up through the holes drilled in the batten and into the underside of the slat. Check the

length of screw you use to ensure that it penetrates the slat as far as possible without its point breaking through the slat surface.

Cut a single 60° splay on one end of the next slat, but leave the other end over-long. Lay it in position, with spacers to keep the correct separation between it and the center batten, and align the splayed ends using an offcut of

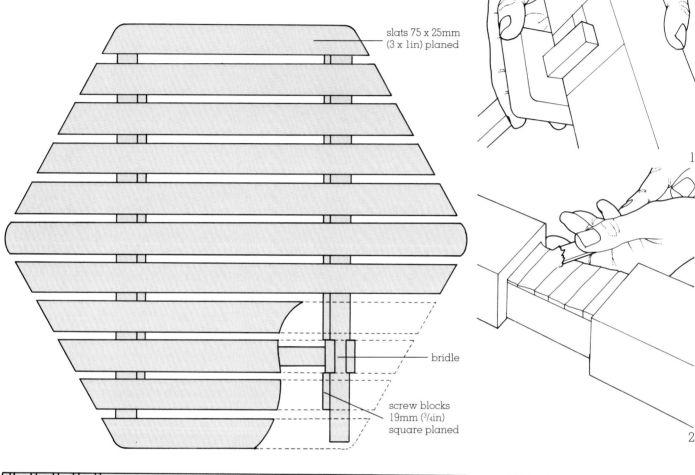

slats 75 x 25mm
(3 x 1in) planed

bridle

screw blocks
19mm (¾in)
square planed

1

2

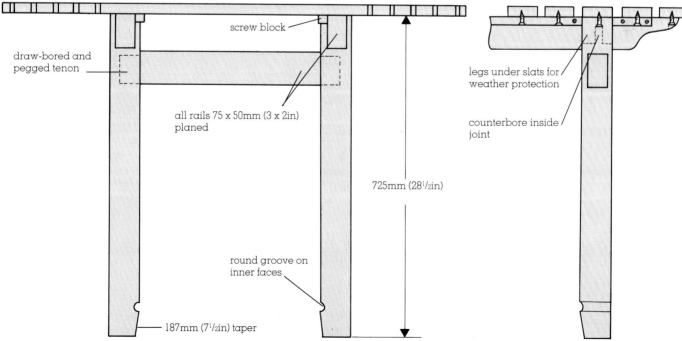

draw-bored and
pegged tenon

screw block

all rails 75 x 50mm (3 x 2in)
planed

725mm (28½in)

round groove on
inner faces

187mm (7½in) taper

legs under slats for
weather protection

counterbore inside
joint

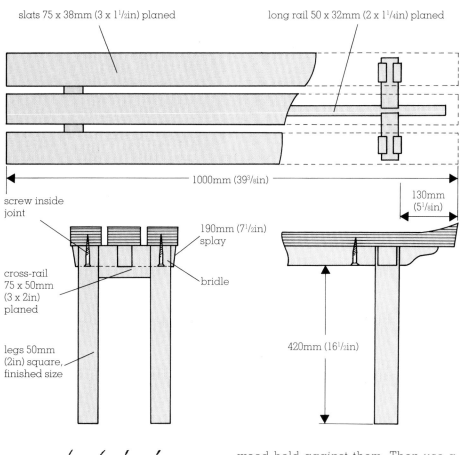

slats 75 x 38mm (3 x 1½in) planed

long rail 50 x 32mm (2 x 1¼in) planed

1000mm (39⅜in)

screw inside joint

190mm (7½in) splay

130mm (5⅛in)

cross-rail 75 x 50mm (3 x 2in) planed

bridle

legs 50mm (2in) square, finished size

420mm (16½in)

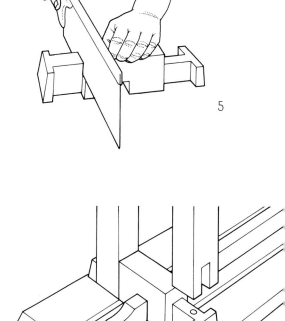

5

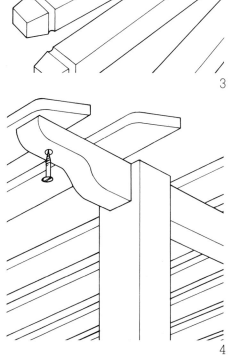

6

3

4

wood held against them. Then use a sliding bevel to mark the position of the splay on the other end of the slat, cut it to length and screw the slat in place. Repeat this process to cut and fit the other slats, with the exception of the two that will cover the tops of the legs. Note too that the outermost slats are fixed by driving screws up through holes drilled in the ends of the long rails (4).

Lift the table top off, turn it upside down and drill counterbores and clearance holes in the undersides of the bridles in the long rails. Position the two missing slats carefully and drive screws through the counterbores into their undersides to secure them to the rails. Replace the table top to complete the assembly.

Finish off the table by treating all exposed surfaces either with teak oil or with a clear wood preservative. Rub oil in with a rag, wiping off any excess after leaving it to soak in for a while. Brush preservative on, flooding end grain thoroughly for maximum protection.

MAKING A MATCHING BENCH

The slatted bench consists of four legs, two short cross rails that link each pair together, and a long centre rail that links the two cross-rails. Set out the joints for both cross-rails on one piece of wood for ease of handling, with the open mortises for the long rail centred on the upper edge of the piece between the two pairs

of bridle joints (5). Then cut the joints and separate the two rails, which slot into matching open mortises cut in the tops of the legs.

Flare the ends of the slats by driving wedges into three parallel saw cuts, or shape them from solid timber, then attach them to the leg assembly. Fix the two outer slats with screws driven up through the bridle joints (6), and attach the centre one via a counterbore in the underside of the centre rail. Finish it like the table.

SITING SEATS

The final step is to decide where you want to sit. You may be lucky enough to enjoy a magnificent view from a particular spot in the garden – a perfect choice. On the other hand, the view may be not worth looking at, so you should look for a site that lets you enjoy individual features of your own garden – a pool, rockery or specimen tree, for example. Try to find a site that is in the sun as much as possible (unless you prefer to sit in the shade, of course), and is also well sheltered from the prevailing winds on breezy days.

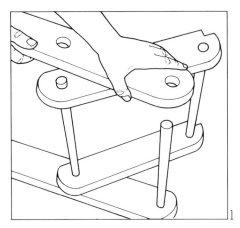

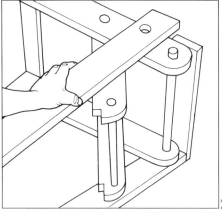

Foldaway furniture

The attractive slatted-top table and its matching benches have one major advantage over most other items of garden furniture; the table can be folded flat for ease of transportation and storage, yet can be set up quickly wherever you want it. It is extremely simple to make, since only butt joints (glued and nailed or screwed together) are used in its construction. The table is made mainly from 100 x 25mm (4 x 1in) wood, while the matching benches use 75 x 25mm (3 x 1in) wood throughout. Full details of all the parts you will need are given in the cutting list below.

Cutting list

The table
From 100 x 25mm (4 x 1in) wood cut:
15 top slats 750mm (29^1/$_2$in) long
2 side rails 1495mm (58^7/$_8$in) long
2 top end rails 706mm (27^3/$_4$in) long
2 bottom end rails 704mm (27^3/$_4$in) long
4 legs 765mm (30^7/$_8$in) long
4 leg braces 456mm (18in) long

From 25mm (1in) diameter dowel cut
2 top leg bars 750mm (29^1/$_2$in) long
2 brace bars 704mm (27^3/$_4$in) long
2 brace bars 658mm (26in) long

In addition you will need
2 125mm (5in) lengths of 75 x 50mm
   (3 x 2in) wood and
2 125mm (5in) lengths 75 x 38mm
   (2 x 1^1/$_2$in) wood for the leg clamps
2 100mm (4in) long coach bolts 6mm
   (^{1}/$_4$in) in diameter, plus matching wing
   nuts and washers
8 50mm (2in) No 8 rustproof counter-
   sunk woodscrews

The bench
From 75 x 25mm (3 x 1in) wood cut:
15 top slats 400mm (15^3/$_4$in) long
2 side rails 1195mm (47in) long
2 top end rails 356mm (14in) long
2 bottom end rails 400mm (15^3/$_4$in) long
4 legs 702mm (27^5/$_8$in) long
4 leg braces 410mm (16^1/$_8$in) long

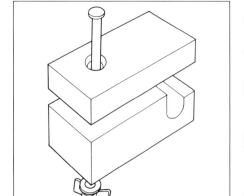

For both pieces you will need 19mm (^{3}/$_4$in) and 38mm (1^1/$_2$in) rustproof (sherardized) oval wire nails, some waterproof urea formaldehyde (UF) wood glue and some clear or pigmented wood preservative.

Start by marking out and cutting all the components to length, with the exception of the table legs and leg braces which should be cut slightly overlong so their ends can be rounded off driving assembly.

Clamp the table side rails together and drill a 25mm (1in) diameter hole through each end of both rails, 71mm (2^3/$_4$in) from their ends.

Draw a centre line along one face of each leg and mark off along it at 48, 53 and 268mm (1^7/$_8$, 2^1/$_8$in and 10^1/$_2$in) intervals. Set a compass point on the 53mm (2^1/$_8$in) mark and scribe an arc from one edge of the leg to the other to draw the shape of the top of the leg. Measure 715mm (18^1/$_8$in) along the centre line from the top of the arc and square a line across the leg. This is the bottom of the leg. Measure back 50mm (2in) from this line and square a second line across the leg. Stand the end of an offcut of 100 x 25mm (4 x 1in) wood on the face of the leg so one narrow edge is aligned with this second line and draw round it to mark the cut out for the bottom end rails. Mark out the other three legs identically, then cut them to length, round off their tops with a coping saw or jig saw, remove the marked cut outs and drill

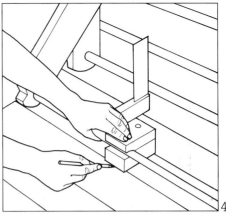

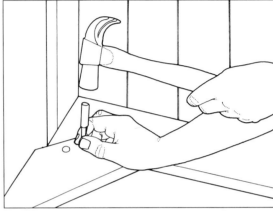

25mm (1in) diameter holes through each leg at the 48 and 268mm (1^7/$_8$ and 10^1/$_2$in) marks made earlier.

To make up the folding leg braces, first cut the four 456mm (18in) long pieces that form their sides, mark a centre line along each one and make a mark on this 53mm (2^1/$_8$in) from one end. Draw an arc and round off one end of each brace. Make a second mark on the centre line, 311mm (12^1/$_4$in) from the first mark, and draw a similar arc here, then round off this end too and drill 25mm (1in) diameter holes through the braces at both marks. Finally use a tenon saw to cut a 35 x 22mm (1^3/$_8$ x ^{7}/$_8$in) notch in one end of each brace; this fits round the table's bottom end rail when the legs are folded.

To assemble the table, glue together the leg braces first, checking that the longer bar protrudes by an equal amount at each side. Then slot these protruding ends into the holes in two of the table legs (1), check that they swivel freely and link the two legs with a bottom end rail (glued and nailed in place) and a top leg bar (glued), again checking that the latter protrudes by the same amount through each leg. Repeat the process to assemble the other end of the table, then link the two end frames with the two long side rails and the top end rails after checking that the leg rotates freely (2), and complete the assembly by nailing and gluing on the top slats.

145

GARDEN FURNITURE

Make up the clamps as shown (3). Fit the bolt through the thinner block, then fit the clamp round the leg bar using the washer and wing nut (4). With the leg at 90° to the table top, mark the block position on the underside of the table. Undo the clamp and screw the thinner block to the underside of the table top. The clamp will then secure the leg in both the open and closed positions.

To assemble the bench, link the side and top end rails first, then add the slats before attaching the legs, the bottom end rails and finally the angled braces (5). Finish both pieces with a generous coat of wood preservative.

MAKING A PATIO SET

This colourful set of patio furniture could not be easier to make. The table top and bench seats are simply planks of wood, set on sturdy X-frame legs to form a solid structure that is heavy enough to stay put even in high winds. They are finished in microporous paint, which allows water vapour to pass through the paint film without causing the inevitable cracking and peeling that occurs with ordinary paints. This type weathers by erosion, so redecorating is simply a case of washing down the existing paintwork and applying a fresh coat over the top.

Make up the table top first, to whatever size you need for your patio. The table illustrated has a top consisting of eight pieces of 150 x 38mm (6 x 1½in) wood, screwed to two 50 x 38mm (2 x 1½in) transverse bearers with a narrow gap between each plank to allow rainwater to drain off easily. Countersink the screw holes deeply and fill the recesses with exterior-quality wood filler to remove any risk of rust showing through the paint finish. Make up the bench seats in exactly the same way.

Next, make up the legs from two pieces of 100 x 38mm (4 x 1½in) wood, joined with a cross-halving joint at an angle of 60°. If you do not have a protractor and a sliding bevel to help you set out the angles, remember that all three sides of a triangle with 60° corner angles measure the same length, and use this to set the pieces at the correct angle. Cut the halving joints with a tenon saw and chisel, check their fit, then drill through the joint and secure it with a coach bolt.

Screw each leg assembly to the outer face of a transverse bearer beneath the table top or seat. Then screw a short length of 50 x 38mm (2 x 1½in) wood to the under-side of the top/seats, at right angles to each bearer, to which the diagonal leg braces will be attached. Measure up the required length for each pair of braces, cut their ends at 45° angles, drill deep counterbores for the fixing screws and fix them in position. Finally, sand and paint each item.

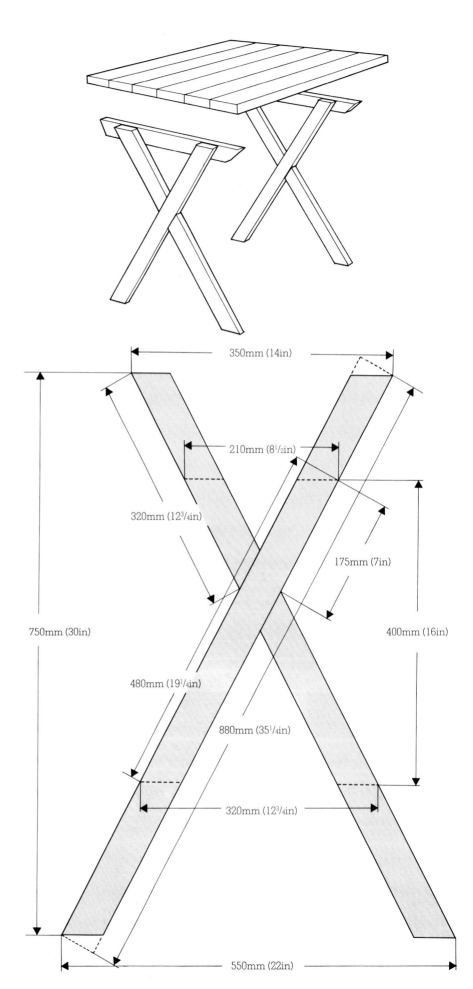

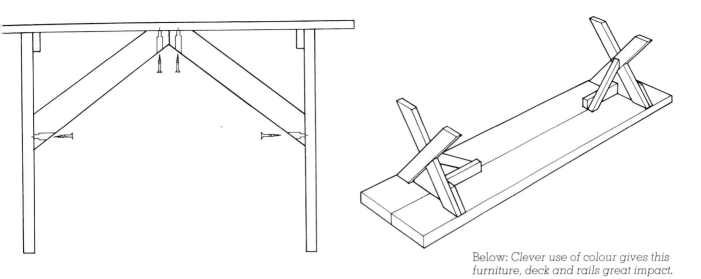

Below: Clever use of colour gives this
furniture, deck and rails great impact.

Garden buildings

THE FEATURES THAT ARE LIKELY TO MAKE THE BIGGEST VISUAL IMPACT ON YOUR GARDEN ARE ANY BUILDINGS YOU CHOOSE TO PUT IN IT, SIMPLY BY VIRTUE OF THEIR LIKELY SIZE. MOST GARDENS BOAST A SHED OF ONE SORT OR ANOTHER, USUALLY UNTIDILY FULL OF GARDENING TOOLS, MATERIALS AND BROKEN DECKCHAIRS, BUT SUCH A FUNCTIONAL BUILDING IS RARELY A VISUAL DELIGHT AND USUALLY ENDS UP HIDDEN AT THE BOTTOM OF THE GARDEN. MORE EYECATCHING ARE BUILDINGS CONSTRUCTED FOR LEISURE USE, SUCH AS A GAZEBO OR SUMMERHOUSE.

Garden buildings have a long and fascinating history. Ever since man has cultivated his garden as a thing of beauty rather than a source of food, he has graced it with buildings of one sort or another. Some were included as part of the overall design, perhaps providing a visual centerpiece to the scheme of things as well as offering a pleasant place to sit and admire the garden layout. Many were built as follies – architectural jokes and oddities with a certain curiosity value.

Below: *A well-kept summerhouse in the style of a Swiss chalet makes an attractive feature in any garden.*

Left: *Open trelliswork can be used to good effect to make a garden arbour, and blends in well with the greenery if left to weather naturally. This one has apparently turned into a fern house.*

Below: *Trellis walls and a shingle covered roof turn this miniature band-stand into an eye catching garden building that is also a shady retreat.*

Other buildings were sited to take advantage of a view, either of the surrounding scenery or of the house itself – the belvedere or gazebo. The storage shed, on the other hand, is really a necessary but visually uninspiring garden feature unless it is carefully designed and sited and is kept in good condition. Few are.

The manufacturers of sectional garden buildings offer a comprehensive range of prefabricated summerhouses, sheds and greenhouses, and if you can wield a spanner and a screwdriver you can build one in an afternoon. However, you will be stuck with the maker's design, shape and size, and unless you are happy with that you will have far greater flexibility if you design and construct your own garden buildings.

There are several factors you need to take into account if you decide to take this route. The first is the raw material you will use. This is likely to be softwood, on grounds of cost as much as anything else, and it is essential to buy wood that has been pre-treated with preservative.

The second is the type of roof and roof covering you want. As far as roof type is concerned, your choice lies between having a ridged roof or a flat one (in fact, usually sloping at between 5° and 10°). Ridged roofs always look more attractive, even if they are a little more difficult to construct. As far as roof coverings are concerned, you must first decide whether the structure is to be weatherproof or not. Most prefabricated garden buildings have a boarded roof covered with roofing felt, and although this is really your only choice for a flat roof it never blends in very well with the garden. Better choices for ridged roofs are wooden shingles or, if the building is substantial enough, small clay tiles. If the roof is decorative rather than functional, you can use open slats or trellis and then train plants over it if you wish.

The third factor to consider is the wall finish, and here too what you choose depends on whether or not the structure must be weatherproof. If it must, timber cladding or shingles are the obvious choice. If not, then you can again use trellis....or simply leave the structure with open sides.

Lastly, does the building need a floor, or will it simply stand directly on a concrete or paved base? If you decide to have a floor, you need to make some provision for keeping rising damp from rotting it away by setting it clear of the ground or placing a damp proofing layer underneath it. Strips of roofing felt laid beneath the floor joists are one solution to the problem.

When you have made these choices about the building's function, you can turn your mind to its design. You can borrow your inspiration from prefabricated buildings, from magazine illustrations, even from history books if you want a miniature Parthenon down the garden. If the building is to be open to the elements you have a virtually free hand, but summerhouses and garden sheds are likely to draw on at least some prefabricated components such as doors and windows, and the styles and sizes available will have some bearing on the final design of the building.

Think too about the building's decorative finish, especially as far as ease of future maintenance is concerned. Avoid traditional paint and varnish, which will eventually crack and flake; go instead for microporous paints or wood stains (both easy to re-coat when necessary) if you want colour, and use clear wood preservative if you prefer a natural finish. Lastly, think about security for summerhouses and storage sheds. They often contain valuable tools and furniture, and so should be securely locked.

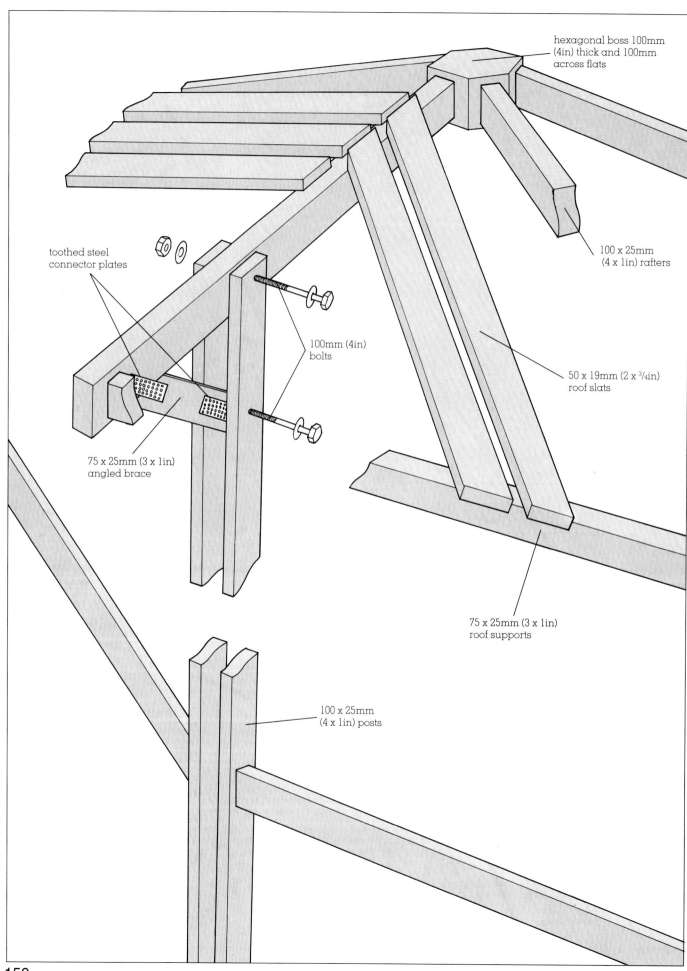

hexagonal boss 100mm (4in) thick and 100mm across flats

100 x 25mm (4 x 1in) rafters

50 x 19mm (2 x ¾in) roof slats

toothed steel connector plates

100mm (4in) bolts

75 x 25mm (3 x 1in) angled brace

75 x 25mm (3 x 1in) roof supports

100 x 25mm (4 x 1in) posts

MAKING AN OPEN GAZEBO

This unusual hexagonal building provides an attractive centrepiece for any garden, with its open sides and slatted roof offering the prospect of pleasantly cool shade within. Its main frame consists of six pairs of uprights linked on five sides by rails at waist height. Each pair of posts sandwiches a rafter and an angled support brace, and the projecting ends of the rafters are linked by perimeter roof support members. Each roof panel has two further roof supports, fixed parallel to the perimeter ones at intervals equal to one-third and two-thirds of the rafter length respectively. The rafters meet at the apex of the roof, which consists of a hexagonal centre boss, and each of the six roof panels is covered with spaced battens cut and fixed so that adjacent pairs of roof slopes have an attractive chevron pattern.

The posts and rafters are all cut from 100 x 25mm (4 x 1in) wood. The roof supports and angled braces are 75 x 25mm (3 x 1in) wood, and the roof slats are 50 x 19mm (2 x ¾in) in size, spaced about 25mm (1in) apart. The hexagonal central roof boss is cut out of a block of wood 100mm (4in) thick and is about 100mm (4in) wide, measured across opposite 'flats'. Glue two pieces of 100 x 50mm (4 x 2in) wood together to make it if you cannot easily obtain wood 100mm (4in) thick.

Above right: The open slatted roof of this unusual hexagonal arbour has a carefully matched chevron pattern on each of the roof sections.

Below: The roof provides varying amounts of shade as the sun moves.

Start by marking out the site accurately. Since a hexagon consists of six adjacent triangles, each with a 60° angle at each corner, the simplest way of setting the post positions is to start at the centre of the structure. Set up a string line passing through this point, and measure along it in each direction out from the centre a distance X equal to half the overall width of the building to mark the positions of one pair of opposite posts.

Next, take one string line of length X from the centre point and one of the same length from one post position. where they meet is the next post position. Repeat this exercise all the way round to position the six sets of posts.

Build the structure by making up the six post/brace/rafter assemblies first, using bolts and steel connecting plates as shown in the drawing. Then, with the aid of a helper, erect opposite pairs in turn, screwing them to the centre boss with pre-drilled metal strips. Brace them all in position while the concrete sets round the posts, then add the rails and roof supports. Finally cut the roof slats and nail them in place.

Making a lean-to

Shelter

This striking garden shelter would be an attractive and practical addition to any garden, and can be built up against a perimeter wall or fence, or against the house itself. It is also extremely simple to construct. The four corner posts are set in concrete to provide a solid framework for the building, and an additional post in the middle of the back wall provides extra support for the waney-edged timber cladding which helps give the building its rustic appearance. The roof is supported on two sturdy bearers that

link the corner posts at the front and back; these are bridged by rafters secured at their top and bottom ends by birdsmouth joints at 600mm (2ft) centres.

Tiling battens run across the rafters, and are spaced to match the size of the second-hand clay tiles used for the roof. Any ordinary roof tiles can be used; you may want to match the roof of the house, especially if the building is against the house wall. Second-hand tiles, if you can find them, help give the building a 'ready aged' look.

To prevent any risk of high winds lifting the topmost row of tiles, lead flashing is secured to the top of the rear wall and is dressed down over the ridge and onto the face of the tiles.

Above: *Naturally weathered timber and old second-hand tiles combine to create a garden shelter with a rustic look.*

With the main frame erected and the roof structure in place, the cladding and trellis panels are fixed in position to battens which are themselves nailed to the inner faces of the corner posts. The finishing touches are provided by adding a fascia board (which could be given a decorative edging) and making the two curved brackets that fill in the front corners of the open structure. These are made by gluing two pieces of 100mm (4in) square timber together with waterproof urea-formaldehyde adhe-

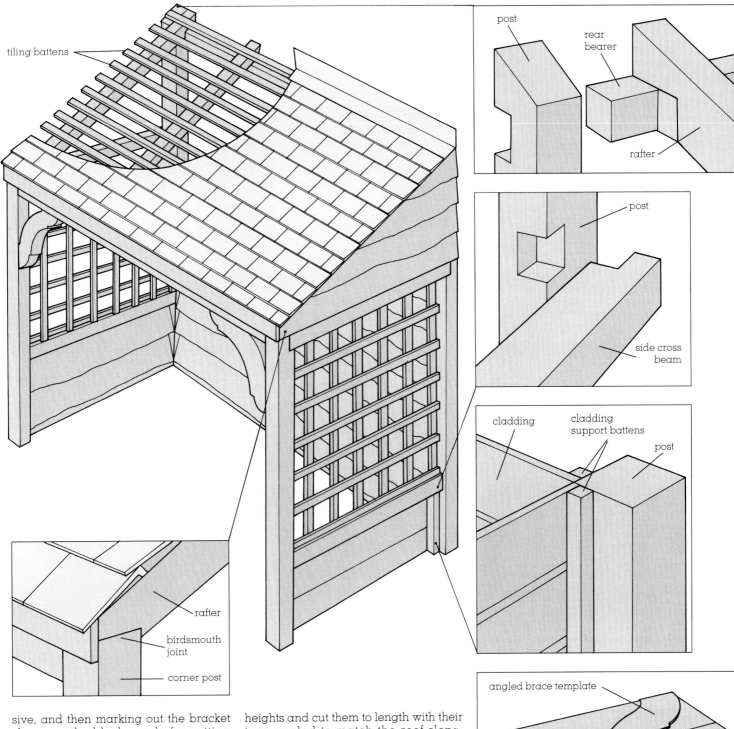

tiling battens

post

rear bearer

rafter

post

side cross beam

cladding

cladding support battens

post

rafter

birdsmouth joint

corner post

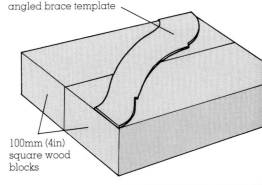

angled brace template

100mm (4in) square wood blocks

sive, and then marking out the bracket shape on the block, ready for cutting and fitting.

Finish the building with a generous coat or two of preservative stain.

You can tailor the size of the shelter to suit the space available in your garden. This building is about 3.6m (12ft) wide and 1.5m (5ft) deep from front to back, but you can vary both width and depth as necessary. The overall height is about 2.75m (9ft) at the ridge and 2m (6ft 6in) at the eaves. If you do alter the building's dimensions, aim to keep the roof slope the same as here – a gradient of about 1 in 2.

Cut the posts slightly over-long and set them in place, then mark their

heights and cut them to length with their tops angled to match the roof slope. Next, mark out and cut the recesses in the posts to accept the ends of the main cross-bearers. and nail these in place.

Add the rafters at 600mm (2ft) centers, with the outermost pair set against the sides of the corner posts. Cut birdsmouth joints in each rafter so it sits neatly over the bearers at the top and bottom of the roof slope. Fix the tiling battens at spacings to suit the tiles you are using.

Add the side cross beams and the battens to support the cladding and trellis. Then fit the lead flashing, add the fascia board and make and fit the decorative corner brackets.

Above: *The details to the main drawing show how the various frame members fit together, how the tiling and cladding are fixed and how the angled braces are marked out for cutting to shape.*

OTHER GARDEN BUILDINGS

Unless you are fortunate enough to have a garage large enough to provide storage space as well as room for the car, you are sure to need a garden shed of some description in which to keep your lawnmower, your other gardening tools, bags of fertiliser, bottles of weed-killer and all the other paraphernalia the average gardener always collects. Such a building might do double duty as a workshop or potting shed, and could also store foldaway garden furniture and even things like a mobile barbecue. Think carefully about exactly what you will expect it to cope with before deciding on how big a shed you will need. If in doubt, add a metre (3ft) to the length and width you first thought of; you will soon fill up the additional space.

As with other garden buildings, you have the choice between buying something prefabricated or building it yourself. With the cost of wood being relatively high nowadays, you will have difficulty matching the cost of a prefabri-

cated shed if you decide on the do-it-yourself route, but you will at least be able to design and construct a building that precisely matches your requirements. You will also be able to pay more attention to its looks; most prefabricated sheds do tend to have a somewhat utilitarian appearance.

Unlike other garden buildings, a shed really needs a floor. Without one, its contents will be permanently damp: tools will rust and dry materials such as fertiliser will rapidly turn into a useless solid lump. A simple boarded floor on preservative treated battens is all that is required; set the battens on strips of roofing felt or similar material, laid on the concrete base under the building, to keep the floor dry.

Incorporate windows only if you intend to use the building as a workshop. Would-be burglars are likely to find a selection of useful housebreaking tools in a shed, and can easily break a

---

Below: *A garden shed need not be hidden at the bottom of the garden if it is well designed and well maintained.*

window to gain access, especially if the shed is sited away from the house. If you do need windows, consider fitting them with wired glass or, better still, a plastic glazing material such as polycarbonate sheeting which is almost unbreakable. Make sure that the door is secure too, ideally with a padlocked hasp and staple at the top and bottom of the door in addition to any existing lock or latch. Even if you are not the target of a housebreaker, there is a busy trade these days in expensive garden equipment such as lawnmowers. It is well worth keeping yours securely under lock and key.

If you plan to use the shed as a workshop, especially in the winter months, it pays to insulate it. Cover the floor with 25mm (1in) thick rigid polystyrene board and lay tongued-and-grooved boards over it to form a floating floor. Cut pieces of the same insulating board to fit between the wall framing timbers, then line the walls with oil tempered hardboard (more damp-resistant than the ordinary grade) or thin plywood. Use the same technique to insulate the underside of the roof too. You could even double-glaze the window and draughtstrip the door.

Lastly, you will find an electricity supply invaluable, both for supplying light and power to the workshop and also for powering electrical equipment such as hedgetrimmers. Make sure that the circuit complies with local wiring regulations.

Above: *The traditional potting shed, with its wall to wall windows facing the sun, is the perfect retreat for the gardener who likes to raise everything from seed or from carefully potted cuttings.*

Left: *Timber cladding is the perfect wall surface for all sorts of garden buildings, especially when the wood is left to weather naturally.*

1

2

3

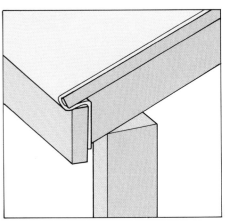

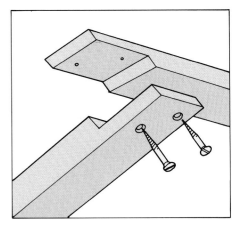

Building a timber shed

If you decide to construct a garden shed from scratch, you have the opportunity to use good-quality materials and a high standard of joinery to produce a building that will last for years, especially if you make sure that all the wood you use has been pre-treated with preservative.

Begin by making up the floor, using 75 x 50mm (3 x 2in) joists set at about 300mm (12in) centers for extra rigidity. Notch the joist ends to accept 50 x 25mm (2 x 1in) cross battens that will keep the joists square while you add the floor decking. This can be tongued-and-grooved boards, plywood or roofing-grade chipboard, nailed to the joists. Set the completed frame in place on its base, with strips of roofing felt under the joists to keep the damp at bay.

Next, make up the four wall panels to the required dimensions, again using 75 x 50mm (3 x 2in) timber with vertical studs at about 450mm (18in) centers and a horizontal rail halfway up each panel for extra strength. All the joints are simple halving joints, glued and screwed together. Position door and window frame members to suit the sizes of the off-the-shelf door and window. The end walls have integral gables, with the angled rafters notched into tops of the wall studs.

When the wall frames are complete, stand two adjacent frames in position on the edge of the floor and cramp them together. Drill two holes right through both the corner posts, about one-third and two-thirds of the way up, then bolt the two frames together with carriage bolts. Repeat the process with the other panels to complete the shed frame (1).

Next, fix the remaining rafters, which are simply nailed to the tops of the side wall frames, and start attaching the wall cladding. Cover the end walls first, working from the bottom upwards and cutting the pieces so they finish flush with the face of the side wall frames. Clad these next, letting the cladding overlap the cut ends of the cladding on the end walls to protect its vulnerable end grain from water penetration. Treat the end grain of the side wall cladding with preservative once it is in position.

You can now turn your attention to the roof. Cut and fit two panels of exterior-grade plywood or chipboard, screwing each panel to the rafters at 300mm (12in) intervals (2). Lay the first strip of roofing felt in position, taking it over the ridge of the roof if it is wide enough, and fix it with galvanized clout nails. Lay the second strip on the other side of the roof slope, again bringing it over the ridge so it overlaps the first piece. On wider roofs the felt will not reach from eaves to ridge; in this situation, lay a third strip along the ridge so it overlaps the two lengths lower down the roof slopes. Cut the felt at the corners of the roof, and fold and tack the overlaps down neatly. Turn the lower edges of the felt over the edges of the roof boards, tack them and fit a fascia board. Fit a gable end cut from wide board or exterior-grade plywood (3), then finish off by glazing the window, hanging the door and applying an overall coat of preservative (4).

4

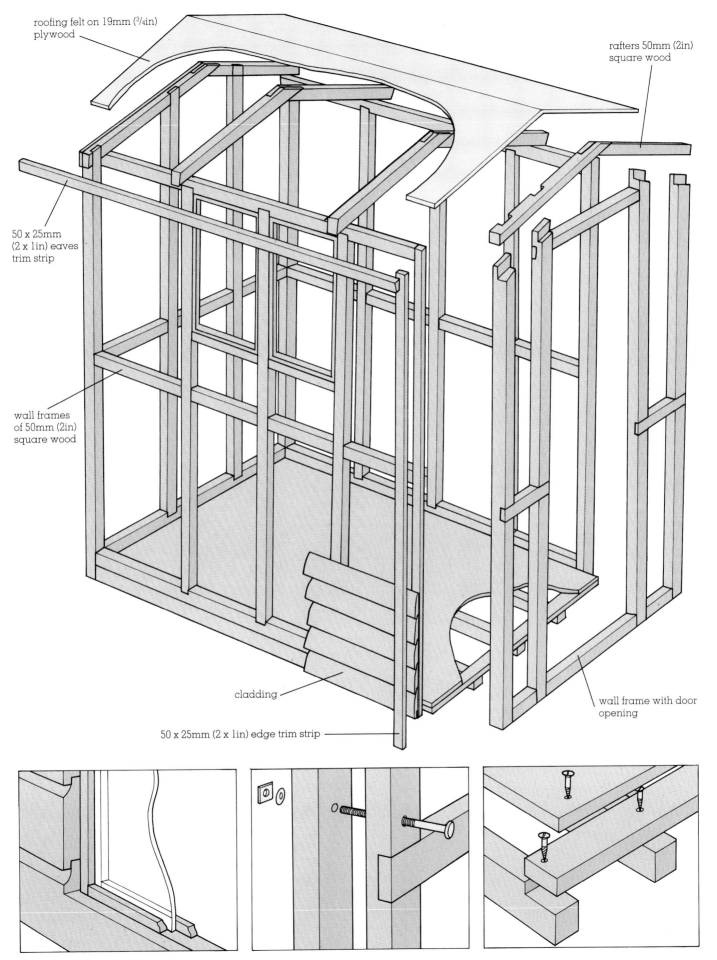

roofing felt on 19mm (³/₄in) plywood

rafters 50mm (2in) square wood

50 x 25mm (2 x 1in) eaves trim strip

wall frames of 50mm (2in) square wood

cladding

wall frame with door opening

50 x 25mm (2 x 1in) edge trim strip

PLAY EQUIPMENT

ALL CHILDREN ENJOY PLAYING OUT OF DOORS, ESPECIALLY IF THE GARDEN CONTAINS SOME SPECIAL PLAY EQUIPMENT ROUND WHICH THEY CAN DEVELOP THEIR OWN GAMES. WOOD IS AN EXCELLENT MATERIAL TO USE FOR EQUIPPING A PLAY AREA, WHETHER YOU ARE MAKING JUST A SIMPLE SANDPIT OR A MORE ELABORATE CONSTRUCTION SUCH AS A CLIMBING FRAME OR TREE HOUSE. IT IS STRONG, EASY TO FIX, CLEAN AND ABOVE ALL SAFE IN USE, SO LONG AS YOU TAKE CARE TO SMOOTH ALL SURFACES AND ROUND OFF ALL EDGES SO THEY ARE SPLINTER-FREE. YOU MUST ALSO TAKE STEPS TO ENSURE THAT WHATEVER YOU MAKE IS SECURELY ANCHORED TO THE GROUND SO IT CANNOT MOVE OR TOPPLE OVER.

BUILDING A SANDPIT

As every family knows, children love the seaside – especially a sandy beach, where they can dig and build to their heart's content. The trouble is that for most families the seaside is too far away for more than the occasional trip. The answer is to provide a bit of beach in your back garden, in the form of a sandpit, where they can play whenever they want.

Building a permanent sandpit in the garden is a perfect do-it-yourself job, and a good opportunity to practise your woodworking skills on a relatively simple project. It can be raised or sunken (the latter is even easier to construct than the former), and can be turned into an ornamental pond or planter once the children outgrow it.

SITING A SANDPIT

There are two points to take into consideration when you are deciding where to put your sandpit. The first is safety: you really need to be able to keep an eye on its occupants from the house, so having it in view from the kitchen window is the ideal answer. The second is tidiness; sandpits have a habit of spreading their contents over a fairly wide area, so surrounding the pit with a hard surface such as paving or giving it a wide seat all round will make it easier to sweep up straying sand at the end of the day. Try to avoid putting it under a tree, where resin and bird droppings could fall on its occupants in summer (autumn leaves are not such a problem – the season is not so popular for outdoor games anyway).

DESIGNING A SANDPIT

If you plan a raised pit, aim to make the sides about 380mm (15in) high so even tiny tots can climb in on their own. Similarly, a sunken pit needs about the same depth of sand. As far as other dimensions go, it really depends on the size of your garden, but a practical minimum is about 1.2m (4ft) square. Make it bigger if you can.

CHOOSING MATERIALS

You can surround a sandpit in several ways, two of which are illustrated here. One is to set logs on end in the ground, butting them closely together to form a palisade round the pit area. The other is to use planed timber to build a purpose-made pit in the form of a timber box with

Left: *A generous allocation of space for play will take pressure off the rest of the garden.*

extended sides that help to stop the sand straying and also act as a seat.

As far as sand is concerned, the best type is washed silver sand, which is available from builders' merchants. On no account use bricklaying or concreting sand, which will stain clothes and hands horribly. If you live near the seaside, you may be tempted to 'borrow' some sackfuls of your local beach sand; this is also not recommended since it will have a high salt content which can make little hands sticky and sore. You need enough sand to fill the pit to a depth of about 225mm (9in): if it's any deeper, a lot more will find its way out of the pit over the sides. So for a pit 1.2m square you'll need about a third of a cubic metre (yard) of sand. Scale the figure up accordingly for larger pits. The last items on your materials list are designed to stop the sandpit from turning into a bog in wet weather, and to prevent local pets from using it as a toilet (with potentially unpleasant consequences for your children's health). To allow rainwater to drain through the sand bed, fill the base of the pit with about 50mm (2in) of gravel, topped with a sheet of heavy-

Above: *Designed with a young family in mind, this town garden provides a safe play area for all ages.*

duty polyethylene that you have perforated with small holes every 100mm (4in) or so (a small electrician's screwdriver is ideal for this). The polyethylene layer also discourages would-be human moles from digging too deep. To cover the pit at night and to keep animals from using it as a toilet, make a matching wooden cover which can simply be lifted into place.

Play Equipment

Building a sunken pit

Pick your site and mark out the extent of the excavation with pegs and string lines. Excavate the pit to a depth of about 300mm (12in), cutting the sides neatly and keeping them as vertical as possible. Look out for buried services as you dig, and reposition the pit if you find any. To line the walls of the pit area, you can drive in sharpened log stakes, butting them closely together to keep the sand in place and to stop the surrounding soil from collapsing into the pit, Alternatively, drive wooden stakes into the ground round the edge of the pit at, say, 900mm (3ft) intervals, then cut a sheet of exterior-quality plywood into strips, and nail them to the stakes to form a box with its top edge just below ground level. Smooth off and tamp down the base of the hole, then lay 50mm (2in) gravel covered by your poly-ethylene sheet. Finally shovel in the sand to the required depth.

Building a matching pit and tree seat

1 Choose your site, and strip away any turf or other vegetation first. Then mark out the site with string lines and pegs.
2 Next, drive in a fence spike at each corner of the construction, using an offcut of wood in the socket to protect it as you hammer it in. For the sandpit, add four more spikes at the corners of the pit area itself.

3 Cut the halving joint in the top of each 100mm (4in) square post as shown in the diagram, and secure it in its socket with nails or screws. Then prepare the main 100 x 50mm (4 x 2in) perimeter rails by cutting their ends at 45° and forming the halving joint cut-outs in two of them at roughly 450mm (18in) centres. Fit the perimeter rails, then cut the intermediate joists to length, form halvings on each end and nail them into place.
4 To fit the seat round a tree, add short trimmer joists at right angles to the main joists, then fit short joist sections as necessary to fill in the gap between the perimeter rails and the trimmer joists.

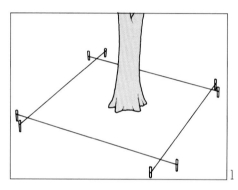

1

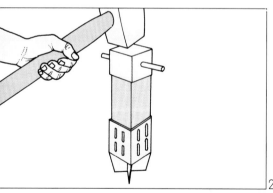

2

100 x 50mm (4 x 2in) rail

100 x 50mm (4 x 2in) joist

100 x 100mm (4 x 4in) post

3

Right: A matching tree seat, sandpit and swing – the perfect area in which the whole family can play or relax.

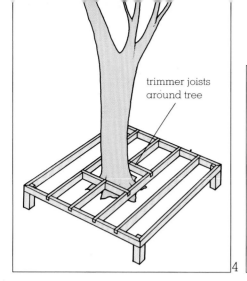

trimmer joists around tree

4

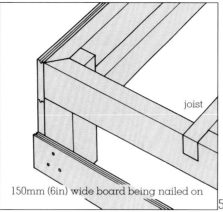

150mm (6in) wide board being nailed on

joist

5

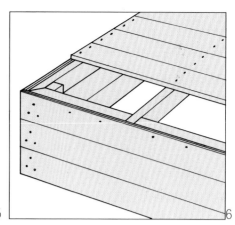

6

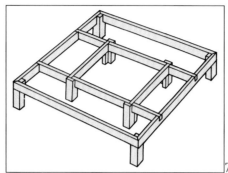

7

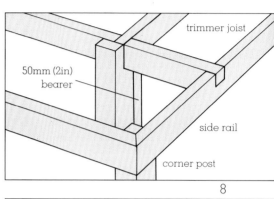

trimmer joist

50mm (2in) bearer

side rail

corner post

8

For the sandpit, add the rails round the pit area, and nail a 50mm (2in) square bearer to each post as shown in the diagrams (7, 8) to act as a fixing ground for the planks that will line the pit,

5 Now you can start nailing on the boards to form the sides of the structure and the pit, working from ground level upwards. Make sure that you recess the nail heads well using a punch.

6 Finish off by adding the boards forming the seat, nailing them to the perimeter rails and the joists. Finally lay gravel and a polythene sheet as for a sunken pit, fill with sand and fit a cover.

MAKING A COVER

Cut length of tongued-and-grooved timber cladding long enough to span the pit, assemble them and nail three 50 x 25mm (2 x 1in) battens across the back to hold them together and allow the completed cover to sit on the pit walls. Treat the wood with preservative to protect it from rot. Alternatively, use a piece of exterior-grade plywood, with battens pinned to it all round the underside to fit just within the pit walls. Again, treat it with preservative.

MAKING A SWING

The best place to site a swing is on the lawn; concrete and paved surfaces should be avoided at all costs, because of the risk of injuries resulting from a child falling from the swing itself.

This does mean, of course that the lawn will be badly worn immediately

main seat slats 375mm (15in) long ex 100 x 25mm (4 x 1in) wood

eye bolt x 4

washer x 4

wing nut x 4

block 200mm (8in) long ex 100 x 25mm (4 x 1in) wood

Swing

below the swing as time goes by, and for this reason it is a good idea to surround the swing with an area of soft material such as bark chippings to cushion any falls. The swing itself needs to be well anchored to prevent it lifting as energetic acrobats swing back and forth. The swing shown here has its 100 x 50mm (4 x 2in) posts set in concrete to a depth of about 600mm (2ft), and so should be able to withstand even the most energetic swinging. When the concrete has set (see page 151 for more details), fit the crossbar, securing it with screws rather than nails, then drill holes and insert two large eyebolts to take the swing ropes. Use nylon rope, which will not rot, and fuse the knots together so they cannot pull undone by heating them up gently with a hot air gun until the plastic just begins to soften.

PLAY EQUIPMENT

PLAY BUILDINGS

Most children, given a free choice of outdoor play equipment, opt unerringly for a home of their own. Adventurous types with a head for heights are likely to request a tree house (assuming there is a suitably-sized tree in the garden in which to build it) where they and their friends can get away from grown-ups and indulge themselves in Tarzan or commando-type fantasies to their heart's content. Others may prefer a more down-to-earth approach and choose a conventional play house. This can be anything from a perfectly-built scaled-down replica of a summerhouse or chalet to a much more ramshackle home-made structure, perhaps built by the children themselves with a little adult supervision. Not only will such a shared project help to while away the holidays; it will give the children an immense sense of satisfaction to have been involved in building their own

play equipment. It could also be a good way of using up all those leftovers from your own do-it-yourself projects which you could never bear to throw away.

Whatever type of building you decide to construct, remember that it must be a safe place for your children to play in. That means paying as much attention to its construction, finishing and security as you would to any other garden project.

CREATING A DRY BASE

For a start, anything built at ground level should have proper foundations – ideally a concrete slab, although with simple structures you might be able to get away with building 'direct to earth' as long as you can support the structure clear of the ground and so keep damp at bay. If you decide to lay concrete, you need a slab about 75mm (3in) thick, laid over 75-100mm (3-4in) of well-rammed rubble. Use a 1:2:3 cement:sand:aggregate mix (or 1:4 cement:combined

aggregates), and lay the concrete in formwork so the slab has neat square sides. This will then provide the perfect base for a timber floor off which the rest of the building can be constructed. For a more temporary structure, you can support the building's floor – tongue-and-grooved boards or exterior-grade plywood nailed to square joists – on rows of frostproof bricks, garden walling blocks or paving slabs. Tamp these down firmly into the soil, check that they are level with each other and then place a piece of something waterproof - roofing felt or plastic damp-course material – on top of each one. Before you lift the floor into position, it is a good idea to treat the ground underneath to keep weeds under control. Lay black polythene sheeting over the supports, then set the floor in place on top of this.

ASSEMBLING THE BUILDING

Probably the best way of building up the structure from here is to follow the principles used by the manufacturers of prefabricated garden buildings, and to make up the individual wall panels with a simple frame covered in cladding. Use at least 50 x 25mm (2 x 1in) wood for the frame, and space uprights at about 450mm (18in) centres between the top and bottom plates to give the panel a reasonable degree of rigidity when the cladding is added. Exterior-grade plywood is probably the best cladding material to use, but you can press anything from old floorboards to fencing timber into service if you have it available. Fit cross-rails to form window and door openings, and then pin beading round the inside of the openings so the window can be glazed and the door has a stop bead to close against. Use the same material as for the walls to make up a matching door, with ledging and bracing on the inside, and hinge it to the door post. Either fit a simple hook and eye inside and out to keep the door shut, or fit a surface mounted latch and door handles if the budget will run to it.

Glaze windows with unbreakable rigid plastic sheet, held in place with beading all round. Use PVC tape to simulate glazing bars. With an extra pair of hands to help you steady the panels, lift the first one onto the edge of the floor. Then place the next panel at right angles to the first and fix the two together by nailing through the end frame uprights. Repeat the process to fit the third and fourth panels, then nail the bottom plate of each wall panel securely to the floor.

THE FRAMEWORK

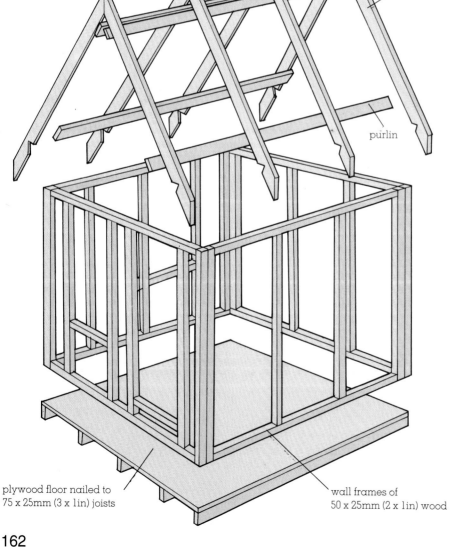

purlin

rafters

purlin

plywood floor nailed to
75 x 25mm (3 x 1in) joists

wall frames of
50 x 25mm (2 x 1in) wood

Right: A "Wendy House" will provide hours of entertainment. This one is large enough to become a wet-weather play area and den for older children.

ADDING THE ROOF

The simplest type of roof you can fit is a flat roof consisting of a rectangle of exterior-grade plywood, cut to overhang the walls by about 50mm (2in) all round. Give it a slight slope so rainwater drains off it. To do this, carefully saw a length of 100 x 50mm (4 x 2in) wood in half to form two matching strips tapering from 50mm (2in) thick at one end to nothing at the other. Nail one on top of each side wall, with the thicker ends at the front of the building, and add a length of 50mm (2in) square wood along the top of the front wall. Place the roof in position and nail it down all round. Then cover it with roofing felt, secured with galvanized

clout (roofing) nails. Turn the felt over the edge of the roof and tack it underneath the eaves. Make sure the nails do not protrude through the roof decking. If your building has a pitched roof, you can again use plywood but you really need to provide some support along the ridge line – few children can resist climbing on the roof of their 'castle' sooner or later. To avoid complex carpentry, the simplest solution is to form a home-made joist hanger from three offcuts of wood nailed in a U-shape to the inside of the apex on each side wall panel, and then to drop in a ridge board – length of 75 x 50mm (3 x 2in) or 100 x 50mm (4 x 2in) wood – so its top corners are level with the tops of the panels. Secure the board by driving a

100mm (4in) woodscrew through each side wall into the ends of the board, then position the roof panels and nail the top edge of each one to the ridge board, the other edges to the tops of the wall panels. Cover the roof with two strips of roofing felt, laid so each just extends over the ridge to give a double layer of waterproofing at the roof's weakest spot.

Right: *A good substitute for the ever popular treehouse, which requires a substantial and suitably-sited tree.*

Below: *This Scandinavian-style playhouse would make an attractive feature in any garden. Scaled up it would work equally well as a summerhouse.*

PLANTERS AND WINDOW BOXES

ALTHOUGH MOST GARDENERS' NATURAL INCLINATION IS TO PLANT THINGS DIRECTLY IN THE GROUND, THERE IS PLENTY OF SCOPE FOR AN ALTERNATIVE APPROACH — USING MAN-MADE PLANTERS ABOVE GROUND LEVEL AS A GARDEN FEATURE IN THEIR OWN RIGHT. WOOD IS A SPLENDID MATERIAL FOR THIS, SINCE IT GIVES YOU THE CHANCE TO DESIGN AND CONSTRUCT PLANT CONTAINERS IN ALL SORTS OF STYLES RUSTIC OR FORMAL AND IN WHATEVER SHAPE OR SIZE YOU WANT. YOU CAN LEAVE THE WOOD ITS NATURAL COLOUR, STAIN IT OR PAINT IT IF YOU PREFER; THE LATTER CHOICE IS PARTICULARLY POPULAR FOR WINDOW BOXES, WHERE YOU WANT THE CONTAINER TO MATCH THE HOUSE DÉCOR.

Above: *Wooden barrels make a wonderful show when planted with colourful annuals.*

Left: *This low wooden building has been much improved by the addition of white-painted boxes.*

You need little more than imagination and some very basic raw materials to create attractive and unusual planters for your garden. The basic requirements are to contain the planting medium soil or compost so rain does not wash it out, and to ensure that there is adequate drainage to prevent the planter from becoming waterlogged. Depending on the type of planter you are creating and any decorative finish you want to give it, you may also need to devise ways of keeping the wood out of contact with the soil by fitting some sort of liner inside the plant container.

Perhaps the simplest type of planter you can create uses 'raw' wood as a building material. For example, you could simply nail logs together into a trough shape, with short pieces filling in the ends, and stand the resulting container on two more logs to lift it clear of the ground, as shown in the picture above. Use fine gravel to fill the uneven joints between the logs, then firm in your planting medium ready for whatever you propose to grow.

An even simpler trick is to make use of ready made containers such as traditional wooden barrels cut in half – a favourite feature of many a cottage style garden, especially if they are painted white with a contrasting colour on the metal hoops as shown in the main picture. All you need to do to convert one into a planter is to drill some holes in the bottom of the barrel for drainage, then to line it with heavy duty black polyethylene sheeting held in place with staples to stop the wood being permanently saturated and therefore prone to rot. Pierce the sheeting where it covers the drainage holes, and fill the bottom of the barrel with a layer of gravel and small stones to prevent the planting medium from clogging the drainage holes. Then position the barrel clear of the ground on bricks, for example and fill it up with soil or compost ready for planting.

You can create more substantial garden planters by using large section sawn timbers, such as old fashioned wooden railway sleepers (ties), built up into retaining walls round flowerbeds or as free standing planters. Wood of this size is massive enough to need no fixings; its own weight will keep it in place. Old railway sleepers, if you can get hold of them, are ideal for this type of garden construction because they are heavily impregnated with wood preservative and so will not rot. Alternatively, contact local demolition contractors, who often save large section timber when knocking down old houses. Once you have positioned the lengths to create the structure you want with the aid of a helper (they are very

heavy), all you have to do is to fill it up with soil. Since they are sawn timber, they will fit together closely enough, so need no lining.

You can of course use your wood-working skills to make planting troughs in any shape and design you want (see page 169 for an example). One place where such planters can look particularly attractive is on window sills, if yours are wide enough to support a window box. Obviously, each window box has to be tailor made to suit its sill, but the basic construction can be very simple – just a long narrow box. The project overleaf shows you how you can make one.

The base of a window box can be solid wood or exterior-grade plywood, with holes drilled through it for drainage, or you can form a slatted bottom by spacing the pieces about 6mm (^{1}/4in) apart. Treat it thoroughly with clear wood preservative if you want to paint it, or with a coloured preservative wood stain otherwise, paying special attention to any exposed endgrain which is particularly prone to rot. Line the box with polyethylene sheeting, stapled into place, and pierce holes in it across the bottom before filling it with soil or compost. Alternatively, omit the lining; instead, simply plant out a number of square flower pots and stand them side by side in the trough.

Remember that all window boxes must be secured to the sill so they cannot fall or be knocked off accidentally. The simplest fixing is to use an L-shaped metal repair bracket at each side, screwed to the box and to the sill.

Left: *Rustic-style planter best constructed in situ and lifted off the ground to delay rot.*

Below: *Old railway sleepers have been used to form large, easily maintained, raised bed planters.*

MAKING A WINDOW BOX

You can make this simple yet stylish window box from natural timber or a suitable man-made board, 19mm (³/₄in) thick. The dimensions given in the cutting list are for a box 762mm (30in) long, 197mm (7³/₄in) high and 203mm (8in) from front to back, but you can vary the dimensions to suit any sill.

Cut the components to size, then cut 3mm (¹/₈in) deep housings across the inner face of the front and back pieces, 12mm (¹/₂in) from each end – a perfect job for a power router. The sides of the box will slot into these grooves when it is assembled. Cut another groove on these components along the bottom of the inner face, again 12mm (¹/₂in) from the edge. Finally, cut a similar groove along the bottom of the inner face of each end piece. These grooves will hold the bottom of the box.

Now you can start the assembly. Glue and pin the bottom into the groove in the back, then add the two ends and slot on the front, again gluing and pinning the joints to complete the basic box shape.

To finish the box off, cut the three sections that make up the top frame from 38 x 19mm (1¹/₂ x ³/₄in) wood, trim them to 45° and pin and glue them into place.

If the box is to contain soil rather than flower pots, drill drainage holes in the bottom and line it with polyethylene to keep the box free from rot.

CUTTING LIST

A: The box
Back 762 x 197 x 19mm (30 x 7³/₄ x ³/₄in)
Front 762 x 177 x 19mm (30 x 7 x ³/₄in)
Ends 172 x 177 x 19mm (6³/₄ x 7 x ³/₄in)
Base 705 x 172 x 19mm (27³/₄ x 6³/₄ x ³/₄in)

B: The frame
Front 762 x 38 x 19mm (30 x 1¹/₂ x ³/₄in)
Ends 193 x 38 x 19mm (7⁵/₈ x 1¹/₂ x ³/₄in)

Assemble the box using waterproof wood working adhesive and 38mm (1¹/₂in) pins.

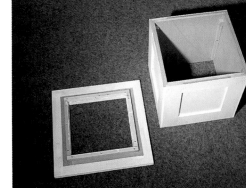

Left: *Finished planter painted white with small trees for formal effect.*

Left: *Painted bright red and planted for winter, the box makes a cheerful addition to an otherwise dull ledge.*

MAKING A PATIO PLANTER

This attractive patio planter is made from man-made board – exterior-grade plywood or medium-density fibreboard (MDF). It is basically a box with panelled sides, fitted with a removable top that neatly frames the planting area. The cutting list gives details of all the components; as with the window box, these can easily be varied to create a similar style planter of a different size.

Start by cutting all the components to size, and label them as per the cutting list. Then make up the four framed wall panels by gluing two rails and two stiles to each side. Note that opposite pairs of panels are slightly different sizes, denoted by A and B in the cutting list. Also note that the top and bottom rails fit flush with the edges of the side, while the stiles project by 12mm (1/2in). This forms strong overlapping corner joints when the four wall panels are pinned and glued together to form the basic box.

When you have assembled this, cut the base support battens to length and pin and glue them inside the box so they project below its bottom edge by about 10mm (3/4in). Cut the base panel to size and glue and pin it to the top surface of the support battens. Complete the box by fitting the four internal corner battens, and drill a series of 6mm (1/4in) diameter drainage holes in the base.

Make up the top by gluing and cramping the four sections of 25mm (1in) thick board together. Then add the locating battens to frame the underside of its opening.

Sand it all down, then prime it and finish it with two coats of paint inside and out.

CUTTING LIST

Cut	12mm (1/2in) board
2 Sides A	425 x 426 (17 x 17in)
4 Stiles A	425 x 100 (17 x 4in)
2 Sides B	425 x 402 (17 x16in)
4 Stiles B	425 x 88 (17 x 3 1/2in)
4 Top rails	250 x 75 (10 x 3in)
4 Bottom rails	250 x 100 (10 x 4in)
Cut	**25mm (1in) board**
1 Base panel	400 x 400 (16 x 16in)
2 Top pieces	550 x 100 (21 x 4in)
2 Top pieces	350 x 100 (13 x 4in)
Cut	**25 x 25mm (1 x 1in) timber**
4 Corner battens	360 (14in)
4 Base and top battens	400 (16in)
4 Base and top battens	350 (14in)

NOTE: Metric and Imperial dimensions are not interchangeable.

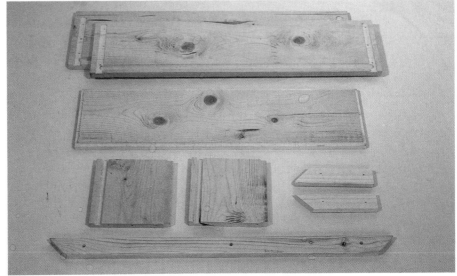

Small Weekend Projects

There are a lot of smaller-scale projects that the keen woodworker can tackle around the garden, from making feeding tables and nesting boxes, to building a cold frame that will give early planting a head start. These projects are ideal for the long winter evenings, since they can be built indoors and then moved outside when spring arrives. They are also ideal for children to tackle, with a little adult supervision.

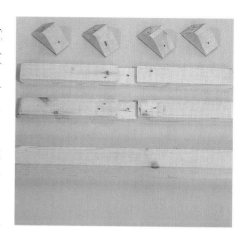

Making a bird feeding table

This unusual feeding table is easy to make from a few offcuts of softwood and exterior-grade plywood. It is basically a hopper that dispenses food – through openings in the sides. It is filled by removing the roof, and the pyramid inside ensures that gravity keeps the food flowing.

Start by cutting out the feeding table floor a 305mm (12in) square of 16 or 19mm (5/8 or 3/4in) thick plywood. Frame its edges by gluing and pinning on four neatly mitred 317mm (12½in) lengths of 30 x 6mm (1¼ x ¼in) beading, with their top edges flush with one face of the plywood.

Next, prepare the walls. Each is a 200 x 125mm (8 x 5in) piece of 12mm (½in)

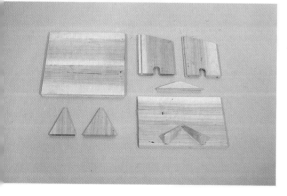

thick plywood, with a small door 35mm (1³/8in) high and 25mm (1in) wide cut into one edge with a coping saw. The top edges of each wall panel are cut away to an angle of 70° – a job for a protractor. Glue the four pieces together in sequence so that the face of one piece overlaps the edge of the next as you work round the square. Then glue the assembled walls to the table at a 45° angle to its edges.

Now you can turn your attention to the roof. Cut two pieces of 12mm (½in) plywood measuring 305 x 200mm (12 x 8in), and mark up and cut out the two gables – each a triangle with a base length of 175mm (6⁷/8in) and a height of 35mm (1³/8in), cut from 19mm (³/4in) plywood. Plane off one long edge of each roof section to an angle of 70° and test that the planed edges meet neatly when a gable end is held against their undersides. Glue the gable ends into place about 25mm (1in) from the edges of the roof. Then cut some scrap wood blocks and glue them to the underside of the roof to locate it in place. They should be a reasonably tight fit inside the walls.

Finally, make the pyramid to fit loosely inside the house, either by gluing four triangles of plywood together or by shaping it from a soild block. It measures 110mm (4³/8in) square.

The stand is made from a 1.4m (4ft 7in) length of 50mm (2in) square planed timber, and is located in a socket on the underside of the table formed with scrap wood. The feet are two 510mm (20in) lengths of 50 x 19mm (2 x ³/4in) wood, joined at right angles with a cross-halving joint. They are linked to the stand with four triangular braces cut from 75 x 50mm (3 x 2in) softwood, which are glued and screwed into place.

In windy locations, weight the feet down or dispense with them altogether and set the post in concrete or a fence post socket, instead.

Right: *Painted green and white, the bird feeding table will brighten up any winter garden.*

Left: This rustic-style bird table with shingle roof has been treated with wood preservative.

MAKING A NEST BOX AND FEEDING TABLE

This design combines an open feeding table with a nesting box – an essentially decorative touch, since only the least choosy birds will actually nest over a feeding table. Once again, begin with the table – a 305mm (12in) square of 16 or 19mm (⁵⁄₈ or ³⁄₄in) plywood, edged with mitred 317mm (12¹⁄₂in) lengths of 30 x 6mm (1¹⁄₄ x ¹⁄₄in) hardwood beading. Drill four 10mm (³⁄₈in) diameter holes in it at 200mm (8in) centres so you can dowel-joint the roof posts to it.

The four posts are 185mm (7¹⁄₄in) lengths of 30mm (1¹⁄₄in) square softwood. Drill a 10mm (³⁄₈in) diameter hole in one end of each post and glue in a length of 10mm (³⁄₈in) dowel so it projects by the thickness of the feeding table. At the other end, make a cut-out 15mm (⁵⁄₈in) square, and then cut the projecting stub off at an angle of 45° as shown in the components photograph. Glue the posts in their holes so that opposite pairs of cut-outs face inwards towards each other.

Next, cut out the nest box floor – a 230 x 200mm (9 x 7⁷⁄₈in) piece of 12mm (¹⁄₂in) plywood, and glue it into the notches in the tops of the posts.

Now you can start work on the roof. First mark up and cut out two gables. Each is a triangle with a base length of 232mm (9¹⁄₈in) and a height of 140mm (5¹⁄₂in), and has a 40mm (1⁵⁄₈in) diameter opening drilled in it about 25mm (1in) below the top of the triangle. One also has a dowel perch glued into a further

hole just below the opening. Cut a third triangle to the same shape but measuring 38mm (1¹⁄₂in) less across the bottom, to act as a divider between the nesting compartments, and glue it across the middle of the nest box floor.

The roof itself consists of tongued-and-grooved softwood boards, glued together and then cut into two panels measuring 320mm (12¹⁄₂in) wide and 260mm (10¹⁄₄in) high. After assembling them, bevel one long edge of each panel to 45°. Then cut a 267mm (10¹⁄₂in) length of 30mm (1¹⁄₄in) triangular moulding to act as the ridge board, and glue the roof panels, gables and ridge board together. Glue the wider face of a 280mm (11in) length of 19mm (³⁄₄in) triangle moulding to the underside of the roof slope at the point where the base of the gable meets the roof, and add similar pieces of 15mm (⁵⁄₈in) moulding to the edges of the nesting box floor between the roof posts as shown in the photographs. Finally, fit the roof. The post is the same as for the other feeding table described on this page.

Above: Painted blue and white, the feeding table makes an attractive and practical addition to any garden.

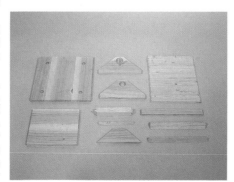

Small Weekend Projects

Making an aviary

If you keep caged birds such as budgerigars, you can add a touch of colour to your garden by making them a summer aviary such as the one featured here. It is designed as a mobile unit, so you can roll it into the sun or the shade as required, and also 'drive' it into the garage and close the door before you transfer the birds to their indoor cages.

The structure could not be simpler. It consists of four corner posts of 50mm (2in) square timber, linked at top, centre and bottom by four 50mm (2in) square rails. All the joints are simple halving joints, glued and screwed together. With the framework assembled, the next step is to glue and nail lengths of 50 x 25mm (2 x 1in) wood to the outer faces of the top, centre and bottom rails on three sides of the structure; leave the back unadorned, ready to be covered with a full-length panel of 12mm (1/2in) thick exterior-grade plywood, which is glued and nailed to the posts and rails all round. Another panel forms the floor, again simply glued and nailed into place to the underside of the four bottom rails.

The roof consists of two panels of plywood cut to overlap the eaves and gable ends by about 50mm (2in) all round. Use a power saw to cut some 50mm (2in) square wood lengthwise into right-angled triangles. Then glue and nail a length to the upper face of each top side rail to act as a roof support, and use another length as a ridge board to link the two roof panels at right angles to each other. Set the assembled roof panels in place on the aviary and nail through them into the triangular roof supports. Then cut two gable pieces to fit and nail them to the ends of the ridge board and the roof supports at the front and back of the structure.

The next job is to line the inside of the door opening with 38 x 25mm (1½ x 1in) wood all round, fitted flush with the front faces of the corner posts and horizontal rails, and then to make up the door to fit the opening. Use 38mm (1½in) square wood for this, using either halving or mitre joints at the corners, and hinge it to the lining at one side. Add a hasp and staple at the other side.

Now you can cut the mesh to size, but do not fit it until you have painted the structure inside and out. Once the paint has dried, staple the mesh into place. Note that the upper section is in one piece for security. Measure up the length of the three sides of the aviary internally, then cut the mesh to the length and height required and make the two 90° folds in it on your workbench. Then manoeuvre the section inside the aviary, and start fixing one end to one of the rear corner posts. Next, staple it to the horizontal side rails, working towards the adjacent corner post. Hold the first fold against the post and staple it there, then take the mesh across the front of the aviary to the other front corner post and finally back to the other rear corner post. Staple the top and bottom edges carefully to the top and centre rails.

Complete the mesh work by cutting panels to fit the two lower side wall sections and the door, and staple them in place too. Last of all, fit the castors, screwing them through the floor panel into the bottom ends of the corner posts.

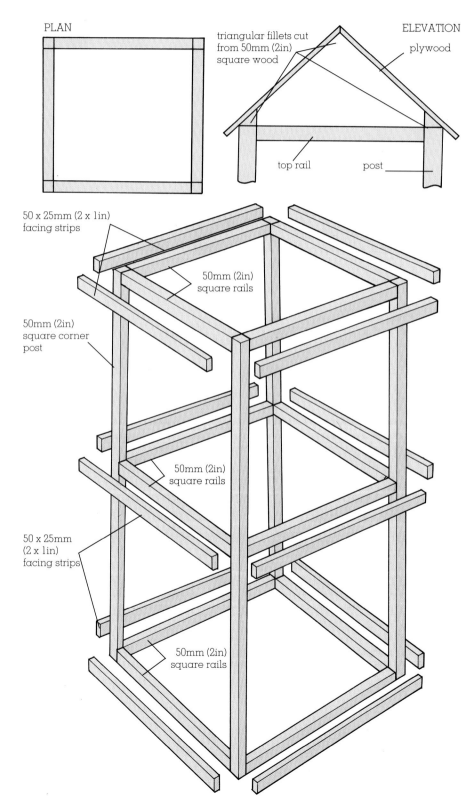

PLAN

ELEVATION

triangular fillets cut from 50mm (2in) square wood

plywood

top rail

post

50 x 25mm (2 x 1in) facing strips

50mm (2in) square rails

50mm (2in) square corner post

50mm (2in) square rails

50 x 25mm (2 x 1in) facing strips

50mm (2in) square rails

Right: *This summer aviary for your budgies can be moved around easily. Be careful not to leave it in full sun.*

Small Weekend Projects

Making a cold frame

If you want to give seeds a head start or protect delicate cuttings, a cold frame is the ideal structure for preventing a touch of frost from nipping them in the bud. This one is made from tongued-and-grooved softwood cladding, fixed to sturdy corner posts, and has two opening top frames. Apart from the usual woodworking tools, you will find a router or a set of shaping cutters for your electric drill invaluable for making the opening frames. Start by cutting the 19mm (3/4in) thick cladding to length – 1169mm (46in) long for the front and back, and 578mm (22 3/4in) long for the ends. Glue and cramp the boards together to make up panels which you can then cut down to exactly the required height – 406mm (16in) for the back and 353mm (13 7/8in) for the front. Mark the ends to be 353mm (13 7/8in) high at the front and 406mm (16in) high at the back, link the marks with a cutting line and saw along it. Use a plane to bevel the top edge of the front and back panels off to an angle of about 20°.

Make up the centre strut next from one 578mm (22 7/8in) length and one 588mm (23 1/8in) length of 75 x 19mm (3 x 3/4in) wood, plus one 537mm (21 1/8in) length of 25 x 15mm (1 x 5/8in) wood. Glue and screw the two wider pieces together to form a beam with a cross-section in the shape of a T, aligning them at one end so that the other end of the on-edge piece of wood projects by 10mm (3/8in). This stub on the upper end of the strut locates in a vertical blind mortise cut in the middle of the back panel, with the top of the cut-out 44mm (1 3/4in) below the top edge of the back panel. Then glue and screw the 25 x 15mm length of wood on edge on top of the assembled T-section so it projects 44mm (1 3/4in) beyond the lower end of the T-section strut.

Now you can cut the corner posts to length from 45mm (1 3/4in) square wood. You need two 406mm (16in) long and two 353mm (13 7/8in) long. Glue and screw them to the corresponding side edges of both the end panels, and then screw the back and front panels to the posts so the ends of these two panels overlap the exposed endgrain of the two end panels. Slot one end of the centre strut into its mortise in the back panel, then screw through the front panel into its other end to secure it in position. Finally, add the top back rail to which the opening frames will be hinged; this is a 1199mm (47in) length of 85 x 25mm (3 3/8 x 1in) wood which is screwed to the tops of the corner posts and also to the centre strut.

The components of the glazed frames are cut from 25mm (1in) thick wood. The

two sides are 572mm (22 1/2in) long and 50mm (2in) wide, and each has a 9mm (3/8in) wide groove cut 12mm (1/2in) deep along its inner edge to hold the glass. The back rail, which is hinged to the top back rail of the cold frame, is a 538mm (21 1/4in) length of 75mm (3in) wide wood, also grooved and with 25mm (1in) long tenons cut on each end so the width between the tenon shoulders is 488mm (19 1/4in). The front rail is 588mm (23 1/8in) long and 80mm (3 1/8in) wide, and has a 50 x 12mm (2 x 1/2in) rebate machined along its length.

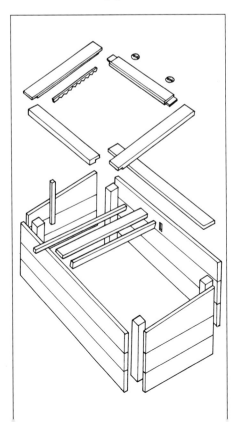

Above: *Attractively painted, the cold frame becomes a practical and attractive addition to any garden.*

The top corner joint of each frame is an open mortise joint, while the bottom corner joints are halving joints; this allows the glass to oversail the front rail, which itself overlaps the front wall of the cold frame. This is to allow water to run off and drip away from the front.

Assemble the frames, slide in the glass – a pane measuring 506 x 490mm (19⁷⁄₈ x 19¹⁄₄in) – and secure the bottom edge of the pane to the bottom rail of the frame with glazing sprigs to keep it in place. Finally hinge the frames to the top back rail of the cold frame.

IN AN AGE WHERE THE POWER TOOL IS KING, IT IS EASY TO FORGET THE ARRAY OF HAND TOOLS AVAILABLE TO THE DO-IT-YOURSELFER. HERE IS A GUIDE TO SOME OF THE HAND TOOLS YOU MIGHT NEED FOR YOUR OUTDOOR ACTIVITIES.

HAND TOOLS

Perhaps the simplest of all woodworking jobs is fixing things together. In each case you have to make a fixing of some sort – either driving a nail or a screw. Nails are easier to use than screws; all you need to drive them is a hammer (see below). However, it is not always easy to drive nails exactly where you want them, and it is difficult to get them out again once they are in. Screws are better: they provide a more secure grip, and can be undone easily if you want to move or change whatever it is that you have fixed. However, you need separate tools to make the hole and to drive the screw.

DRILLS

Requirement number one is a drill. For this job there is little point in buying a hand drill; invest in an electric drill, ideally one with a 13mm (1/2in) chuck,

variable speed control and hammer action, so you can tackle a wide range of drilling jobs in all sorts of materials with just one tool. See page 178 for more details.

For actually making the holes, you need some drill bits. Buy high speed steel twist drills for making holes in wood, plus two or three masonry drills for making holes in walls. Twist drills are sized in millimetres or in fractions of an inch, and are sold in sets as well as singly. Masonry drills are sized by numbers that match screw gauges, or in millimetres.

SCREWDRIVERS

For driving the screws, you need a screwdriver. To be precise, you need several screwdrivers, because screws come in several sizes and have heads of different types. For the driver to work efficiently, its blade must match the slot or recess in the screw head. If it slips out, it will damage whatever you are fixing.

You can probably get by with just two flat-bladed screwdrivers of different sizes for driving slotted screws, plus one cross-point driver for cross-head screws (Pozidriv and Supadriv are the commonest types; a No 2 size screwdriver will drive the most widely-used screw sizes). Most screwdrivers nowadays have plastic handles; choose ones that feel comfortable in your hand.

MEASURING AND MARKING TOOLS

There are several other tools you will find invaluable. The first is a retractable steel measuring tape, to help you get things the right size or the right distance apart and at the right height. Choose one with a tape at least 3.5m (12ft) long, marked with both metric and imperial measurements; it is a good idea to have one with a lock so you can take long measurements without the tape coiling up unexpectedly.

The second tool is a spirit level, invaluable for ensuring that you fix things like posts truly vertical and get rails and other components at a true horizontal. Choose one about 900mm (3ft) long with a metal body and both horizontal and vertical indicators; then you can use it for getting things plumb too. Add a pencil, so you can mark the positions of screw holes, draw guide lines and so on.

The third tool you will need is a try square, used for marking cutting lines at right angles to the edge of the wood you are cutting to length.

HAMMERS

Despite the superiority of screws for making secure fixings, a hammer is a tool you cannot do without. Choose a claw hammer, which can pull nails out as well as drive them. One with a metal shaft and a moulded rubber handgrip will stand up to more abuse than one with a traditional wooden shaft.

A TENON SAW

Even if you plan to do no more carpentry than cutting a few battens to length, you must have a saw. A tenon saw will cope with most small sawing jobs on thin boards and on timber up to about 50mm (2in) thick. Choose one with a 300 or 350mm (12 to 14in) blade and a plastic handle which will not split or crack like a wooden one.

For heavier-duty sawing, either buy a power saw (see page 178) or a hand saw. The cross-cut saw has a blade 600–650mm (23–26in) long with between six and eight points (teeth) per inch, and as its name implies is ideal for heavy-duty cutting across the grain. For ripping

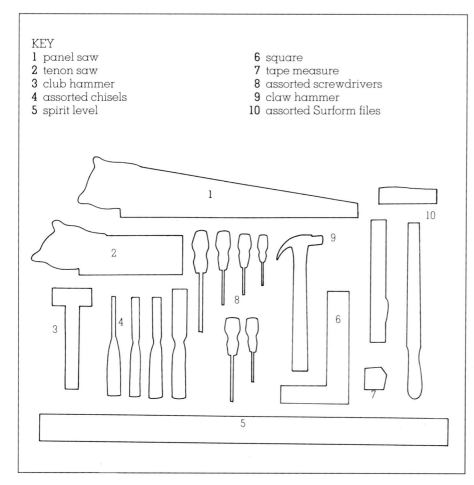

KEY
1 panel saw
2 tenon saw
3 club hammer
4 assorted chisels
5 spirit level
6 square
7 tape measure
8 assorted screwdrivers
9 claw hammer
10 assorted Surform files

wood along the grain direction, use a rip saw instead; this has fewer teeth per inch, and the teeth are chisel-shaped rather than knife-shaped as on a cross-cut saw.

A Surform

There are likely to be a variety of wood-shaping jobs you will have to tackle. A Surform, which is a general purpose plane/rasp, is ideal for this. Surforms come in a range of styles, including flat rasps, planer-files, round files and block planes. All have replaceable blades.

Tools for cutting joints

When it comes to cutting joints, recesses for hinges and so on, a set of wood

chisels is essential. Bevel-edge chisels are more versatile than firmer chisels because you can undercut with them; you need at least four, in 6, 12, 18 and 25mm ($^1/_4$, $^1/_2$, $^3/_4$ and 1in) widths. Choose plastic handles rather than wooden ones, so you can drive them with your claw hammer instead of a mallet. You will need an oilstone to keep them sharp. See pages 182–183 for more details of how to make three essential woodworking joints.

Adjustable spanners (wrenches)

You are likely to be using nuts and bolts to assemble some of the larger outdoor woodwork structures featured in this

book. Obviously, in an ideal world you would have a different spanner for every nut, but a couple of adjustable spanners will do just as well; you need two because often you will have to grip a nut as well as a bolt. Choose one small and one medium spanner, to enable you to cope with a wide range of different nut and bolt sizes.

A pair of pliers

Pliers are a real jack-of-all-trades tool – they will grip all sorts of things you may be trying to undo or tighten up, and will also bend things like stiff wire. Choose a pair of combination pliers with fine and coarse serrated jaws and a wire cutter near the pivot point; plastic hand grips make them more comfortable to use.

wood and 12mm (¹/₂in) or so in masonry. Most two-speed drills now have hammer action as well.

You get even more versatility with variable-speed drills, since you can choose precisely the right speed for the job you are doing and also vary it if necessary while you are working. Variable-speed drills have either one or two speed ranges, the latter being selected by a mechanical gearbox. Others also have reverse gear with variable speed control which is useful for repetitive jobs like undoing screws. Hammer action is a feature of most variable-speed drills. Most have 13mm (¹/₂in) chucks, although some heavy duty models with 16mm (⁵/₈in) chucks are available in 'professional' ranges.

Cordless drills running on internal rechargeable batteries are now very popular, especially as a second drill, because of the convenience of not having to use an extension lead. They are especially useful for work on cars, boats and caravans as well as for jobs in the garden away from a convenient power source. They run much more slowly than a mains-operated drill, but they are still capable of drilling holes up to around 19mm (³/₄in) in wood, 10 or 12mm (¹/₂in) in masonry. Some have two speeds or even variable speed control, and one or two models even feature hammer action. All cordless drills come complete with a charger unit, so the drill can be kept fully charged and ready for immediate use. Most also have reverse gear, making them ideal for removing screws too.

SANDERS

Power assistance is particularly useful for jobs like sanding, especially if you have large areas to tackle. You can choose between two types of power sander: the orbital sander and the belt sander.

An orbital sander has a flat rectangular baseplate covered with a soft cushion over which a sheet of abrasive paper is clipped or stuck. The sander's motor drives the baseplate via an eccentric pin mechanism; this makes it rotate in a sort of high-speed scrubbing action. Most orbital sanders are designed to accept either one-third or one-half of a standard-sized sheet of abrasive paper, which measures 280 x 230mm (11 x 9in). You can also get smaller models called palm-grip sanders; these accept a quarter-sheet of abrasive and are ideal for small areas where a larger tool cannot reach.

Most orbital sanders have motors rated at up to 250 watts and have a high orbit speed and small orbit diameter. This makes them ideal for finishing work, but they are not very good at removing large amounts of material. To

POWER TOOLS

Compare the average do-it-yourselfer's tool kit today with his grandfather's, and you would notice one huge difference: the power tools. Whereas grandfather did everything by hand, we now have the benefit of a wide range of power tools that take the hard work out of many of DIY jobs and in many cases mean we can achieve a more professional finish too. Here, briefly, is what each category of power tool has to offer.

DRILLS

The electric drill is without a doubt the most useful and versatile power tool. It will not only drill holes; it will also drive a wide range of attachments as well.

The simplest and least expensive type is the single-speed drill, which has a motor rated at about 400 watts and a chuck capacity of 10mm (³/₈in), giving it a drilling capacity of about 19mm (³/₄in) in wood. This makes it a good choice for light-duty drilling work. You can also get larger, more powerful models able to put up with heavy sustained use without burning out. Most have a larger 13mm (¹/₂in) chuck.

With two-speed drills you can choose a high speed for drilling wood and a lower one for metal and masonry, which makes this type generally more versatile than single-speed types. Two speed drills have either 10mm (³/₈in) or 13mm (¹/₂in) chucks, with the larger drills having motors rated at up to 600 watts. Drilling capacities for drills with 13mm (¹/₂in) chucks are around 25mm (1in) in

do this you need either a more powerful motor, or else one with a lower orbit speed and larger orbit diameter. Some orbital sanders have variable speed control, and also have dust bags or a dust extraction facility.

Belt sanders have a continuous belt of abrasive that is guided round two rollers, and they can be used freehand or as a bench-mounted tool. They are altogether a heavier-duty machine than the orbital sander, and are capable of removing larger amounts of material much more quickly. However, a dust bag or dust extraction facility is essential to contain the resulting dust if you are working indoors, and belt sanders usually offer one or both options. Most models accept belts 65 or 75mm (2½ or 3in) wide, although larger professional models take belts 100mm (4in) wide. A few machines offer variable speed control.

JIG SAWS

The power jig saw is one of the most versatile of all power tools, since it can carry out all sorts of general-purpose cutting jobs. It can also double up as a coping saw or padsaw when you want to make cut-outs away from the edge of the wood, or to cut curves. You can fit a fence or use a guide batten to keep the saw on line when making long, straight cuts, and you can tilt the baseplate to make angled ones.

Most single-speed saws typically have motors rated at around 350 watts, giving cutting capacities of about 50mm (2in) in softwood. With variable-speed saws you have the option of using a slower speed setting which is essential if you are cutting curves or awkward shapes. They generally have more powerful motors than single-speed models – up to 550 watts or so – and their cutting capacity is generally greater too. You can expect to manage up to 70mm (2¾in).

A variation on the jig saw has the blade projecting from the front end of the saw, enabling it to be used in the same manner as a handsaw and giving greater cutting capacity than a jig saw. It is variously known as the sabre saw or reciprocating saw, and can be fitted with different types of blades for fast or fine cutting. One step on from the sabre saw is a new type of saw with two reciprocating blades, rather like a hedge-trimmer, and which is virtually vibration-free.

CIRCULAR SAWS

Circular saws are mainly favoured by serious woodworkers who prefer to prepare their own timber instead of using off-the-peg sizes from the local timber merchant. They can be used free-

hand or can be mounted in a saw table for use as a bench saw. They have a tiltable soleplate, so you can make bevelled cuts, and can be fitted with an adjustable rip fence so accurate cuts can be made parallel to and a fixed distance away from the edge of the workpiece. Some models feature a dust extraction facility, like the jig saws mentioned earlier.

The smallest type of circular saw takes a 125mm (5in) diameter blade which gives a maximum cutting depth of around 30mm (1¼in), reducing to around 22mm (⅞in) for cuts made at an angle of 45°. Models taking 150mm (6in) blades have cutting depths of up to about 45mm (1¾).

For heavier-duty work, you will need to turn to larger models rated at up to around 1000 watts. These accept blades about 180mm (7in) in diameter and are capable of cutting to depths of about 60mm (2⅜in). Most powerful of all are models taking 235mm (9¼in) diameter blades, giving a cutting depth in wood of up to 85mm (3⅜); their motors may be rated at up to 1500 watts, to provide the cutting power and speed required without risking burning out the motor.

Chop-saws are circular saws mounted on a baseplate and fitted with guides for cutting mitres and bevels accurately – useful for repetitive work. The workpiece is simply placed in the guides and the blade is lowered to make the cut.

ROUTERS

Routers are a favourite amongst specialist woodworkers, because the wide range of cutters available means you can cut a huge range of slots, grooves, chamfers, rebates and decorative profiles. The cutter rotates at extremely high speed – around 24,000rpm – and produces a clean fast cut so long as the cutters are sharp.

The majority of do-it-yourself routers are the plunge-action type, which means that the cutter is plunged down through the soleplate into the workpiece to start the cut – rather like using a drill stand.

POWER PLANERS

Power planers look rather like an ordinary bench plane, but there the similarity ends. The cutting action is provided by a rotating drum with two cutting blades which is mounted in the centre of the sole plate. The cutting depth is adjustable, and may range from about 0.5mm per pass on smaller models up to around 3mm (⅛in) on more powerful machines. Most power planers have a cutting width of around 82mm (3¼in) – wider than a bench plane – and can cut chamfers and rebates as well.

PORTABLE WORKBENCH

If you are working out of doors and away from your workbench, you will find a portable foldaway workbench such as the world-famous Workmate invaluble. It is basically a huge vice on legs, with the flat timber jaws of the vice providing a work surface when closed. The jaws have holes designed to accept push-in plastic bench stops for planing and sawing jobs. A step platform lets you use your own weight to improve the bench's stability, and some models have fold-down legs which allow the work-surface height to be raised from sawhorse height to a more comfortable working level for other tasks. The long vice jaws are opened and closed by two independent screw mechanisms, so you can taper the gap to hold irregularly-shaped objects.

POST-HOLE BORERS

If you have a lot of posts set in the ground, a tool called a post-hole borer is well worth hiring from your local plant hire firm. It is basically a giant auger bit which literally drills out the hole as you turn the T-bar handle, and the resulting hole is both straight-sided and narrower than you can excavate with a spade. You can also get powered versions.

FIXING POSTS

Many of the projects featured in this book involve fixing posts securely in the ground, whether to support a run of fencing or to anchor a building or other structure. It is essential not to skimp on this job; if you do, the next spell of windy weather will simply flatten what you have built, often causing considerable damage to your garden and its contents in the process. Remember too that garden structures are unlikely to be covered by household insurance policies, so you will have to bear the expense of repair and reconstruction work yourself if the worst happens. Do the job properly in the first place and the problem will not arise.

There are two common ways of securing posts: to sink them in the ground and surround them with concrete, or to use metal fence spikes. In some countries, notably the US, galvanized post anchors are also widely used.

DIGGING HOLES

If you plan to sink your posts in the ground, the first thing you have to do is to make a hole for it. The golden rule is to sink approximately one-quarter of the overall post length in the ground; for example, a post that will project above ground by 1.8m (6ft) needs an additional 600mm (2ft) of post underground, so you must buy 2.4m (8ft) posts.

The hole needs to be a little deeper than a quarter of the post length so you can place some drainage material beneath it; add another 100mm (4in) to the overall hole depth to allow for it. This helps to prevent the foot of the post from being constantly waterlogged and therefore prone to rot, even if it has been treated with preservative first. As far as width is concerned, the ideal for a 100mm (4in) square post is a hole about 300mm (12in) across.

In firm, undisturbed ground it is relatively easy to dig a neat, square-sided hole with a garden spade, but in crumbly or recently-dug soil you may find that the sides tend to crumble as you dig. If this is the case, renting a tool called a post-hole borer (see page 179) is well worth considering. Its rotating auger will drill out a cylindrical hole to whatever depth you require, and if the hand-operated types cannot cope with heavily-compacted or stony soil you can get gas-powered borers that provide extra digging power. However, neither can cope with a really rocky subsoil; here you will probably have to turn to a pickaxe or even a pneumatic breaker to make any progress. It's worthwhile digging a few test holes with a spade to see what will be necessary.

GETTING THE POST VERTICAL

Once you have dug your hole to the depth you require, shovel in some gravel and bed half a brick or a piece of paving stone in the center of it on which to stand the post. To set the post to the correct height, nail on a piece of scrap wood so this rests on the ground at each side of the hole when the post is stood in position. Adjust the level of the bedding brick in the gravel as necessary.

Next, cut two braces for each post from scrap wood, and fix them to adjacent sides of the post with a single nail through each brace, about two thirds of the way up the post. Adjust the brace positions until the post is standing vertically, then drive wooden pegs into the ground next to the foot of each brace and nail the brace to the peg (1). Double check that the post is still vertical. If you are setting posts to accept panel fencing, check the post spacing carefully at this stage too to ensure that the panels will fit once the posts are set in position (2). This checking may also apply for other garden structures where the correct post spacing is critical. It is not so important if you are putting up fencing with horizontal rails, since you can cut these to length to suit the actual post separation.

BEDDING THE POST IN PLACE

The next step is to concrete the post in place. The best method is to fill the hole completely with concrete, finishing the surface just below ground level so it slopes away from the post. This allows you to conceal the concrete with a thin layer of soil. However, you can reduce the amount of concrete this method requires by half-filling the hole with carefully-placed pieces of brick or stone, wedged against the faces of the post and well rammed down with a tamper or an offcut of fence post (3). Then top this off with concrete as before (4).

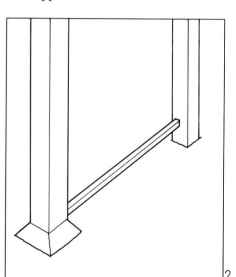

1

Use a 1:2½:3½ cement:sand:aggregate concrete mix, made with coarse 20mm (¾in) aggregate. If you are using combined aggregates, use a 1:5 mix. Add just enough water to moisten the mix, then shovel it into the hole and tamp it well down layer by layer. Give the surface a smooth finish with a trowel (4), then cover it with some soil to help retain moisture while the concrete sets. Leave this to harden for seven days before removing the braces and completing whatever structure the posts will support.

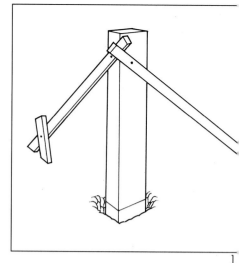

2

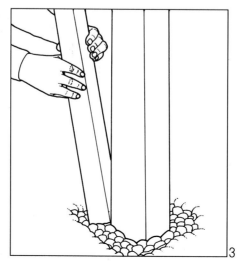

3

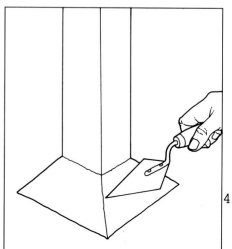

4

Using fence spikes

Fence spikes are a comparatively recent addition to fencing technology. They consist of a square metal socket welded to the top of a long spike, and are designed to be driven into the ground with a sledge hammer. To protect the socket from being damaged by the hammer blows, you either fit an accessory called a dolly – simply a steel block, sold along with the spikes – into the socket, or use a short offcut of fence post instead (1). You need a spike 600mm (24in) long for posts up to 1.2m (4ft) high, and a 760mm (30in) spike for 1.5 and 1.8m (5 and 6ft) posts. Sockets come in three sizes to accept 50, 75 and 100mm (2, 3 and 4in) square posts.

Once you have driven the spike into the ground, you simply set the post in the socket and secure it there by driving in screws or nails, or by tightening the mouth of the socket around the post with a spanner, according to the type of spike you are using (2).

Fence spikes offer a quick and relatively easy way of fixing posts. The main drawback is that it can be difficult getting the spike truly vertical; you need to keep checking that it is with a spirit level and a post offcut as you drive it into the ground, and to make adjustments if it is drifting off line. Spikes work best in dense, undisturbed soil that is comparatively free from buried stones and rocks, and should not be used for anchoring tall posts in exposed locations – anything over about 1.2m (4ft) high is best set in concrete.

Using post anchors

The post anchor is similar in principle to the fence spike. It is a galvanized steel socket into which the foot of the post fits, and is designed to be bolted to the top of a cylindrical concrete footing.

Dig the hole to the depth required by local building codes, than shovel some loose gravel into the bottom and set a concrete tube form in the hole after cutting it to the required length (3). Check that its top is level and about 50mm (2in) above ground level, then pack soil in round it to hold it upright.

Fill the tube form with concrete, tamping it down well and levelling it with the top of the form (4). Then set a J-bolt in the concrete at the centre of the footing so about 25mm (1in) of the threaded end is exposed (5), check that it is vertical with a spirit level and leave the concrete to set. When it has, cut away the exposed part of the tube form with a sharp utility knife.

Next, place the post anchor on the footing, slip the anchor plate over the J-bolt and tighten the nut down with a ratchet wrench (6). Then stand the post in the anchor and drive nails in through the pre-drilled fixing holes all round to lock it in position.

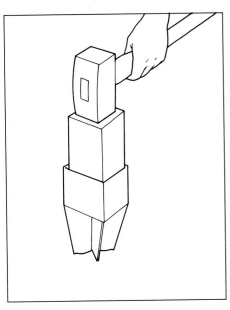

1

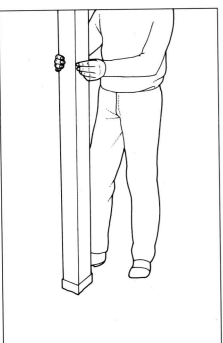

2

3

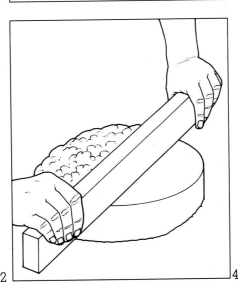

4

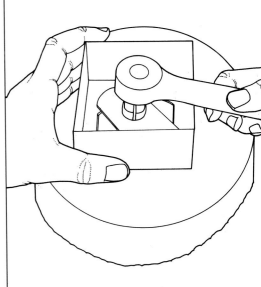

5

6

Woodworking joints and fixings

Many of the garden structures featured in this book can be assembled using nothing more complicated than nails and butt joints. However, some will benefit from the additional strength and neatness of proper woodworking joints, in particular the halving joint and the mortise-and-tenon joint.

Butt joints

A butt joint, as its name implies, is formed by butting one component of the joint against the other, and then fixing the two together mechanically – usually with nails or screws. At corners and in T-joints, the end of the first component butts against the face of the second, through which the fixing nails or screws are driven (1).

As a general rule, butt joints should always be made by nailing through the thinner component into the thicker one, using a nail or screw about three times longer than the thickness of the thinner component. However, since the fixings pass into end-grain, the butt joint is not particularly strong and is prone to pulling apart under load if nails alone are used. For this reason, joints of this type are usually strengthened in some way. Gluing, using a waterproof adhesive, is one option. Skew-nailing (toe-nailing) involves driving the fixing nails at various opposing angles (2). In clench-nailing, over-long nails are driven right through the two components and their protruding points are then hammered flat to lock the components together. Butt joints can also be reinforced by fixing blocks inside the joint angle or adding reinforcing plates to the edges of the two components.

Halving joints

The halving or half-lap joint is a simple joint to cut and assemble, and involves removing half the thickness of each component at the joint position to form a neat-looking joint with the two components fitting flush with each other. Compared with the butt joint, it greatly strengthens corner, T and X joints in frameworks of all sorts since the interlocking shoulders of the joints help to resist twisting and also provide a greater contact area for gluing.

To make a corner halving joint (3), first ensure that the two ends to be joined are cut square. Then lay one component in position over the other and use a marking knife to mark the width of each piece across the face of the other component. Square this line all round each piece, then use a marking gauge to scribe a line to half the wood's thickness on each edge of both components.

Now clamp each component in turn in a vice and saw into the end-grain with a tenon saw, down to the marked line. Then lay each one flat on a bench hook and saw across the grain down to the first cut to remove the waste piece. Check that the two components fit well together, then apply waterproof woodworking adhesive to one component and assemble the joint, clamping it for maximum bond strength until the adhesive has set. Reinforce the joint with nails or screws.

For T and X (cross-halving) joints you need to cut a notch in one (T) or both (X) components. As before, use one piece to mark the position and width of the notch on the other component, then use the marking gauge again to scribe a line to half the wood's thickness. Saw down to this line on both sides of the notch to the scribed line, then use a sharp chisel to pare away the waste wood between the two saw cuts. Check that the notch has a flat base and cleanly-trimmed sides, then assemble the joint. The other component will have a halving-jointed end for a T-joint (4), or a matching notch for a cross-halving joint.

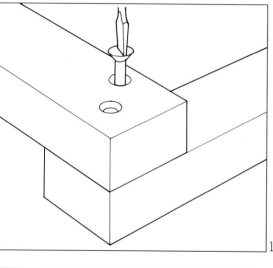
1

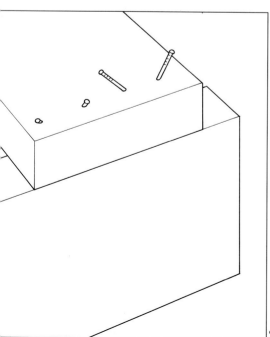
2

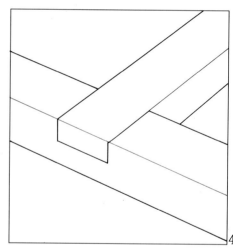
4

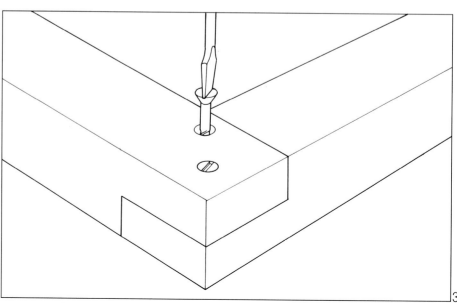
3

Mortise-and-tenon joint

This joint provides the strongest and neatest joint you are ever likely to require for your garden construction projects. It consists of a slot (the mortise) cut in one component into which a tongue (the tenon) cut on the other component fits. There are several variations, but the simplest is the through tenon, where a long tongue passes right through an open slot cut in the mortised component. The stopped version has a blind slot and a shorter tongue, giving a joint where no vulnerable end-grain is exposed to the elements.

To cut a mortise-and-tenon joint, start by preparing the piece with the tenon – component A (5). Lay the piece to be mortised – component B – across the end of A, to leave the tenon slightly over-long for later trimming. Square this shoulder line all round A, then select a chisel with a blade width as close as possible to one-third of the wood's thickness and set the two pins of a mortise gauge to match the blade width. Use the gauge to scribe the tenon width lines onto the edges and end of component A. Cramp it in a vice and saw down the scribed lines to the shoulder line, then set it on a bench hook so you can remove the two pieces of waste wood by sawing down the shoulder lines.

Next, lay A across B at the point where the mortise is to be cut, and mark the width of A on B. Square the lines all round B, then use the marking gauge with the pins set to the same separation as for marking the tenon to scribe the mortise width lines on the edges of B. Hold it edge up in a vice and drill out most of the waste from the mortise using either a spade bit in a power drill or an auger in a brace. Finally, use a chisel to remove the rest of the waste wood, working from both sides of the mortise to leave a neat, square-sided slot. Test the tenon for fit, and pare a little more wood from the sides of the mortise if it is too tight.

To assemble the joint, apply wood-working adhesive to the faces and shoulders of the tenon and insert it in the mortise (6). Check that the joint is square and cramp the two parts together if the structure allows and you have sash cramps long enough to span it. When the adhesive has set, plane off the end of the tenon so it is flush with the surrounding wood.

Using nails and screws

Most of the fixings you use for your garden projects will be nails or screws. Make sure that they are galvanized or otherwise rustproofed for outdoor use. As mentioned earlier, you should always fix the thinner component to the thicker one, using a fixing about three times longer than the thinner component. As far as diameter is concerned, the nail size selected will determine its thickness. For screws, the shank diameter should be no more than one-tenth the thickness of the wood it is being driven into.

When driving nails, ensure that the hammer head strikes the nail head squarely so you do not bend it; pull out and replace any that do bend. Use a nail punch to drive the nail head fractionally below the wood surface.

When driving screws, remember that for all but the smallest screws you must drill two screw holes before you drive the screw in. You need a clearance hole in the thinner component to prevent the shank of the screw from jamming or splitting the wood, and a pilot hole in the thicker component to accept the threaded tip of the screw. If you want the screw head to lie flush with the wood surface, you also need a countersink – a conical recess formed in the wood with a countersinking bit. As a guide, the clearance hole should be the same diameter as the screw shank, while the pilot hole should be about two-thirds of the thread diameter and about 6mm (1/4in) less than the thread length.

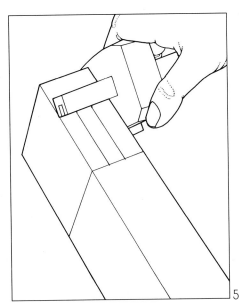

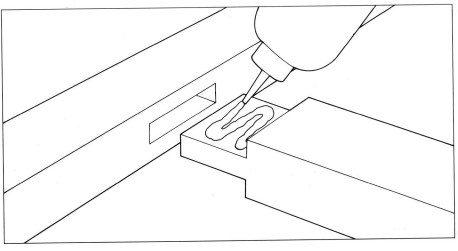

5

6

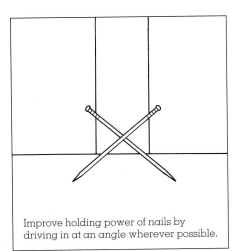

Improve holding power of nails by driving in at an angle wherever possible.

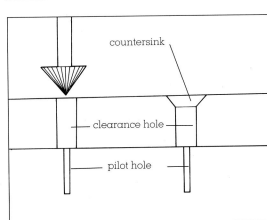

countersink

clearance hole

pilot hole

Using coach bolts

You may prefer to use coach bolts and nuts to assemble heavy-duty structures. Simply drill a clearance hole through both components to match the bolt diameter, insert the bolt, add a washer and tighten the nut with a spanner. The action of tightening the nut will draw the squared-off section beneath the bolt head into the wood, preventing it turning and helping to lock the structure securely together.

Techniques

Wood preservatives and finishes

The trouble with wood is that it is a natural material, and Mother Nature is always trying to reclaim her own – by attacking it relentlessly with sun, wind, rain, wood-boring insects and wood-eating fungi. Preservatives help to stem the attack.

The biggest enemy of wood is moisture, because it provides the perfect conditions for natural forces to thrive and eventually to destroy it. Outside the house, any exposed woodwork will be damp for long periods, and these are precisely the conditions which encourage rot and insect attack. Most at risk is any timber in direct contact with the ground.

Types of preservative

Perhaps the best known and, until recently, the most widely used wood preservative for outdoor use is creosote. This is formed from the distillation of coal tar, and is a dark or golden brown liquid easily applied to surfaces such as fences and sheds by brush or spray. Creosote's main drawbacks are that it soon weathers, so repeated applications are needed; it is unpleasant to handle – many people suffer skin irritation when using it – and is toxic to plants coming into contact with treated surfaces; it is also difficult to overpaint once applied. However, it is cheap.

Organic solvent preservatives were developed precisely to get round these drawbacks. They consist of fungicidal and insecticidal agents dissolved in an organic solvent – usually white spirit – which helps to ensure deep penetration of the wood. They can be applied by brush or spray, or for the best penetration, by immersing the wood in the liquid for a period of up to 24 hours. Once the solvent has evaporated, the wood can be painted or varnished if desired. Some types incorporate wood stains, which help to colour and enhance the look of the wood grain and make other finishes unnecessary. Others incorporate water-repellent additives to further improve the wood's resistance to moisture. They are generally less messy to apply than creosote, and any after-smell soon disappears as the solvent evaporates. However, they are highly inflammable, so must be used with care. Special horticultural grades are available which are non-toxic to plants.

Water-based preservatives have been around for many years, but are mainly used for the pre-treatment of structural timbers and the like by pressure impregnation. Recently-introduced water-based preservatives for DIY application are easier to apply than solvent-based ones, have little smell, are easy to wash from hands, clothes and brushes and are harmless to plants. Some types also incorporate stains and water-repellent additives. However, they do not penetrate wood to the same degree as the organic solvent types, and are therefore recommended for use on timbers not in direct contact with the ground.

Microporous finishes

One of the problems of keeping rot and woodworm at bay lies in the use of traditional paint or varnish systems on much exterior woodwork. These trap moisture beneath the film surface, encouraging rot to spread especially if the wood itself was not preservative-treated.

One solution to this problem is to use so-called microporous or 'breathing' products instead. These form a waterproof coating to the wood, but allow moisture vapour to evaporate through them without causing the tell-tale blisters and cracks that plague traditional finishes. The end result is a finish that stays effective and good-looking for longer, and is also easier to maintain in the future than gloss paint or varnish coatings.

Microporous finishes are available in opaque or translucent form – in other words as 'paint' or 'varnish'; which you choose will depend on whether you want a coloured finish or one that enhances the natural look of the wood grain. Microporous paints are available in a wide range of colours, and have a gloss or semi-gloss finish. Microporous stains come chiefly in natural wood shades – teak, oak, mahogany, cedar and so on – and come in matt and semi-gloss finishes.

To perform as they are intended to, microporous products have to be applied to bare wood – usually as a two coat system. This means that existing paint or varnish films have to be stripped off completely first. They do not themselves have any preservative action (although the translucent stains incorporate ultra-violet filters to help reduce degradation of the wood fibres by sunlight). It is therefore still important that wood being treated with these products has adequate preservative protection. This means either applying one of the wood preservatives mentioned earlier, or ensuring that all bought wood has been pre-treated by the supplier.

Repairing fences

The fences round your property deserve to be as well looked after as any other part of the house and garden. If they are, they will look good, help keep intruders (human and animal) out and define your property boundaries clearly in case of territorial disputes with your neighbours. If they are not, they are just an inefficient eyesore that will be a constant source of irritation to all parties.

Checking ownership

Before you even contemplate any work on your fences, make sure you know which ones are your responsibility and which are your neighbours' preserve. There are no hard and fast rules about this: your deeds may state who owns which fence, and there is a common assumption that the fence is yours if the supporting posts are on your side. Also, with board-and-rail fences it is sensible to assume that the boards were fixed to the rails from the owner's side. Some fences are legally designated as 'party fences', which means both owners must share maintenance costs. If ownership is unclear, try to reach a sensible agree-

Above: *This attractive summer house will soon need attention. Check wooden structures annually for damage.*

ment with your neighbours; ideally this should be in writing so that disputes are avoided in future years.

MAKING AN INSPECTION

Checking your fences is a perfect weekend job. Walk round your boundaries and inspect the condition of posts, intermediate boards, rails and panels, and check that fixings are sound and posts are secure. If everything is in good condition, some simple cosmetic and preservative treatment may be all that is needed, but if you have neglected your fences you may be in for some more substantial repair work.

USING PRESERVATIVES

If you have wooden fences that are in good condition, it will pay you to keep them that way by treating the wood with preservative to keep rot and insect attack at bay. See Types of preservative for more details. It is a simple matter to apply any of these treatments to your fences, although if you have plants growing up the fence or nearby you should either use a type harmless to plants or pull them away from the fence carefully and protect them with polythene. Use an old brush or a garden spray gun, and pay particular attention to end grain and to sections close to ground level.

STRUCTURAL REPAIRS

If you find that your fence is not in particularly good health, it is better to repair it now than to have to replace it completely in another few years.

If you have a close-boarded fence, remove rotten boards by punching their fixing nails through into the rails behind, then slide in a new length of feather-edged board which has been liberally treated with preservative. Use a spacer to gauge the correct overlap between boards, and nail the new board in place to the rails.

Repair breaks or splits in the rails by nailing on proprietary galvanised metal repair brackets – the straight type for breaks in the centre of the rail, the flared-end type for repairs to the ends of the rails where the tenon may have rotted away or pulled out of its mortise.

Remove rotten gravel boards and their fixing blocks, treat the bottom ends of the fence boards with preservative and nail a new gravel board to new blocks (again well treated with preservative).

If you have a panel fence, check that the fixing nails have not caused splits in the sides of the panel, and drive in fresh galvanised nails if the panel is loose. Replace panels that are badly split or warped; you can cut panels down to size by removing the vertical battens, sawing down the panel and replacing the battens.

REPAIRS TO FENCE POSTS

If you find that a fence post has worked loose, dig out the soil round the base of the post to see if it has rotted away. If it seems sound, brush on a liberal dose of preservative; then ram some bricks in firmly round the bottom of the post and anchor it with a collar of concrete about 150mm (6in) thick.

If the underground section of the post has rotted away completely, you can either fit a completely new fence post or else save the sound part and use a concrete fence spur or fence spike to secure it.

With a concrete spur, you avoid having to dismantle part of the fence run. First, saw through the post just above ground level and remove the rotten part. Then dig a hole beneath the post, and set the spur in the hole. Check that it is vertical, then mark the post through the bolt holes in the spur, drill the fixing holes through the post, and brush preservative into the holes. Finally, bolt the post to the spur using galvanised nuts, bolts and washers, ram in hardcore round the base of the spur,

and top it off with a collar of concrete, sloped at the top so rainwater runs away from the post.

With a fence spike, you have to remove the old post first. Cut through the arris rails next to the posts, or prise out any panel fixing nails, ease the adjoining fence sections away from the post, and provide temporary support for them. Lever out the post using stout timber roped to the post as a lever and some bricks to act as a fulcrum, and saw off the rotten part. Compact the ground thoroughly where the old post was removed, then hammer in the fence spike and check that it is vertical. Set the post in the top of the spike, and screw or bolt it in place. Finally, replace panels, either with nails or using small C-shaped metal brackets; with close-boarded types, re-attach the arris rails with metal repair brackets.

Lastly, make sure that the vulnerable tops of the fence posts are protected from moisture penetration by nailing on a shaped wooden capping piece.

OTHER STRUCTURES

Other wooden garden structures also need looking after if they are to remain in good condition, yet many are sadly neglected. Replacements are not cheap any more. so it pays to put right defects before they get serious, and to include such structures in your annual property maintenance round.

If rot has begun to attack but has not yet seriously affected the timber, treat it as a matter of urgency with two or three generous coats of preservative (see above). Before applying this, scrub down the timber surfaces thoroughly to remove surface dirt and growths of lichen or algae. Then brush on the first coat, working from the bottom up to avoid drip marks, and apply a second when the first has dried. Most preservatives are rather splashy to use, so lay polythene sheeting round the structure to protect paving, lawn or plants.

If rot damage has already occurred on a small scale, you may be able to patch it using a wood repair kit. This consists of a hardener to consolidate and strengthen damaged wood, plus a filler to make good missing parts. However, these kits are designed for making repairs that will be overpainted, and the patches will be rather noticeable on a typical timber outbuilding with a natural finish. A better solution is to cut out the rotten timber carefully and to replace it with new, preservative treated wood. You will have to take this course anyway if the damage is widespread.

Left: *Wear gloves when applying creosote as it can irritate the skin.*

BRICKWORK

INTRODUCTION

THIS SECTION IS ABOUT USING MASONRY IN THE GARDEN OR BACK-YARD. BY MASONRY, WE MEAN BRICKS AND BLOCKS, CONCRETE AND STONE, GRAVEL AND SAND AND THE VARIOUS PRODUCTS MADE WITH THEM. THE GARDEN OR BACKYARD IS IDEALLY AN EXTENSION OF THE HOUSE AND AS SUCH SHOULD REFLECT YOUR LIFESTYLE AND CATER TO YOUR OUTDOOR NEEDS. THE FEATURES YOU INCORPORATE AND THE WAY IN WHICH THEY ARE BUILT WILL GIVE YOUR SITE ITS PARTICULAR CHARACTER AND STYLE. WHETHER YOU ARE INTRO-DUCING A TRICKLING WATER FEATURE. LAYING A PATIO OR BUILDING A WALL, THE MATERIALS USED, NATURAL OR MAN-MADE, SHOULD WHEREVER POSSIBLE REFLECT THE MATERIALS OF THE HOUSE OR THE MATERIALS USED IN OTHER OUTDOOR FEATURES.

In this section we look at a comprehensive range of masonry features for your garden area, including pools and ponds (including accessories for creating fountains and waterfalls and for lighting); brick-built planters; outdoor furniture and barbecues; pillars and arches; patios; steps, paths and drives; walls (including retaining walls and concrete screen block walling); and, finally, the construction of a concrete panel garage.

Each section has step-by-step drawings or photographs showing how the project is completed and details of materials and masonry techniques are given in the reference section on page 262.

SOME BASIC RULES

Good planning is essential when it comes to outside masonry work. Consider carefully the existing character of the site and your house before you start to plan any additional structures. For certain projects you may also need to consult the local planning authority.

Decide what you want, where you want it and then choose the materials which will provide the best appearance and function.

Scale drawings will help enormously when planning the work – it's better to make your mistakes on paper rather than on the ground when undoing them later can be difficult, if not impossible.

Think about levels, existing fixed structures, services (especially underground pipes and cables), slopes, and finally soil type (all masonry work is more difficult on soft or clay soils).

Good workmanship and the use of quality materials are important if your structures are to be a sound investment. Remember that well-planned garden masonry work will add to the value of your house when it is time to sell.

Above right: *Bricks and concrete used in a planter, patio and steps.*

Far right: *Reconstituted stone edging used as both a border and a coping.*

Right: *An effective, sinuous brick path.*

Below: *A seat built between planters.*

PLANTERS

RAISED FLOWER BEDS AND PLANTERS BUILT IN OR ONTO WALLS CAN ADD TO THE VISUAL IMPACT OF MOST OUTDOOR AREAS, PROVIDING COLOUR AND FORM. THEY ARE EASIER TO MAINTAIN AND REQUIRE LESS WATERING THAN POTS AND FREE-STANDING CONTAINERS. PLANTERS ARE PARTICULARLY USEFUL FOR SITES WITH POOR SOIL, AS YOU CAN FILL THEM WITH ANY GOOD QUALITY SOIL MIX YOU WANT. WHATEVER KIND OF PLANT CONTAINER YOU DECIDE TO BUILD, THE BASIC PRINCIPLES REMAIN THE SAME.

FUNCTION

Raised planters are usually built against walls, as part of retaining walls or as features arising from existing paving – most typically to frame the entrance to a home. Being raised off the ground, their leafy contents can effectively soften the hard lines of an adjoining wall, or add interest to a dull area.

A practical reason for building a raised planter would be to make a low-lying, swampy area suitable for planting. Vegetables are often grown in this way when drainage is a problem. A raised planter is also a boon to gardeners who are elderly or disabled, since, built to a suitable height, it eliminates the need for bending. Whole gardens can be created with raised flower beds especially for wheelchair users.

Building a raised planter on a patio or as part of a pool surround can successfully enclose and define the area. Planted with pretty flowers, it will add colour; with foliage plants or shrubs, it creates a feeling of privacy.

In a level setting lacking interesting features, the addition of raised beds can create varying levels, improving the landscape and providing character. Use them to frame colourful plants, to break up a large expanse of lawn, or in the place of a dividing wall within the confines of your property.

A free-standing planter constructed alongside built-in seating may become the dominant feature on a patio, adding a decorative touch. If planted with a colourful and striking species, it can have a dramatic effect, as in the planter built in our step-by-step project.

DRAINAGE

A big advantage of raised planters is that they can simply be left open at the base, thus enclosing the plants but allowing for good drainage. However, weepholes should also be included in the design to ensure that the roots do not become waterlogged. See retaining walls, page 250 for details of how to create weepholes and ensure proper drainage.

Additional drainage is especially important when constructing a planter next to the walls of a house. In this case, the inclusion of damp proofing is also essential to prevent moisture from entering the house. This may be in the form of black plastic secured against the back wall of the planter; otherwise a suitable bitumen (asphalt tar) sealant may be painted on the area.

MATERIALS

Planters are commonly built with bricks which are durable and easy to maintain. Facing brick will look especially good if it has been used elsewhere in the garden while clay bricks or inexpensive cement bricks may be used and then rendered (pargeted) and painted. Concrete block walling can be used in place of brick, especially if it blends with other wall or paving features.

Successful raised planters may be constructed from hardwood – the most suitable being railway sleepers (railroad ties) or wooden poles. However, the wood must be treated with preservative and thoroughly sealed, otherwise it will rot over time. A raised bed of unmortared bricks could also be built and can easily be shifted or removed should you decide to alter the layout of your garden or backyard at a later stage.

A mixture of materials is sometimes very effective – for instance, a brick planter with a tiled or wooden coping adds texture and variety to the site. Whatever material you choose, though, make sure it blends harmoniously with the house and the other outdoor features.

Step-by-step planter
To build a planter 800 x 700 mm (2 ft 7 in x 2 ft 3 in) and with a height of 490 mm (19 in) from the foundation and 380 mm (15 in) from the paving, and with a foundation 1,000 × 900 mm (3 ft 3 in × 3 ft) and 100 mm (4 in) deep, you will need:

Foundation
25 kg (or just over ½ x 100 lb bag) cement
65 kg or 1¾ cu ft (143 lb) sand
100 kg or 2 cu ft (220 lb) aggregate

Brickwork
70–75 bricks
10 kg (22 lb) cement
40 kg or 1 cu ft (88 lb) sand
5 kg (11 lb) lime
OR 10 ml (⅓ fl oz) plasticizer

1 Although a strip foundation is sufficient for a small planter, it is easier to lay a concrete slab (in this case 100 mm [4 in] deep). To allow for drainage, place two bricks in the centre and remove before the concrete sets.
2 Peg and set up lines along the outside of two adjoining walls of the planter before you start laying the bricks. Make certain that the bricks are level and that

1

2

Above: The planter has been finished off with paving bricks and any excess mortar removed with a metal scraper.

the corners are at 90°, checking each one with a spirit level and a square.
3 An easy way to create weepholes for drainage is to exclude mortar at several of the vertical joints. This completed planter measures only 800 x 700 mm (2 ft 7 in x 2 ft 3 in), for which three weepholes are adequate. Piping can be inserted for more substantial drainage.

Continue laying bricks for six courses, checking to ensure your surfaces are level and plumb.

3

Pools and Ponds

Pools and ponds can transform the most ordinary setting, giving it a magical, tranquil quality. Even a very beautiful site can benefit from the addition of a sparkling water feature. Water brings life, light, movement and reflection, offering a wonderful contrast to paved surfaces and other fixed structures. Whether it is created in a formal or natural, or ornamental or simple way, a well-planned water feature is always aesthetically appealing and guaranteed to draw visitors to its edges.

Location

The most important factor when planning a pond is its location. Eminently suitable are 'dead' corners, shady nooks which look as if they already fringe a pool, or areas with natural rocks and boulders.

Sometimes a slope where plants will not grow can be used successfully to make a tiered or flowing water feature, following the natural contours of the site. Exploit the fact that water flows downhill

Left: *A half-raised pond built from random stone walling.*

192

and collects in a low area and your pond will look natural and will blend in perfectly.

Trees provide welcome shade over a pond, but roots could damage the base and fallen leaves can look unsightly and cause problems. It is therefore preferable to site a pond in the open or under an evergreen tree.

STYLE

There are numerous ways of designing and creating ponds and water features, but the style you choose should be influenced by other existing features. Also take into consideration the full

extent of the area in which it will be located, since this will affect the type as well as size of your pond or pool.

While water features may, broadly speaking, be formal or informal, several other characteristics are as important. Decide whether you want to hear or only see the water; a still, mirror-like pond reflecting light can be as soothing as the sound of rushing or trickling water. If you simply want a visual feature, consider incorporating it in your patio design. It is true that moving water never fails to attract interest, enlivening any setting. It may be introduced as a fountain, which is usually quite formal and ornamental, or it could flow into a natural-looking

Above: *This formal raised pool incorporates a 'shell boy' fountain.*

waterfall (see picture on page 199).

If you decide on a fish pond, the kind of fish you choose will also affect your choice of construction. A Nishikigoi pond should be filtered so that you can see the brilliant colours of the fish. It should also be at least 600 mm (2 ft) deep and big enough to allow the fish to develop and grow. Try to create a variety of depths so that the koi can move between the cool depths and the warmer, shallow water. Goldfish, however, can survive happily in a small, shallow pool with no special equipment. They require little maintenance and so are often the best choice.

Introducing aquatic plants to oxygenate the water will prevent it from turning stagnant. Note that even if the water does become quite greenish, you do not have to replace it, as long as there are sufficient plants in the pond. In fish ponds, plants perform the additional functions of providing food and a spawning ground for the fish.

The water lily is the queen of all aquatic plants. It flowers throughout the summer and the large floating leaves keep the sunshine from the water, helping to control algae growth. Water lilies are best planted on the bottom of a pond – start by supporting them on bricks and they can be lowered gently as they grow.

There are four other types of plant you can have in a pond:

* *marginal plants* sit on a ledge at the edge of a pond to provide decoration. There is a wide and fascinating variety to choose from with both colourful flowers and leafy foliage.

* *deep marginals* are planted at the bottom of a pool to provide interest in the centre.

* *floating plants* are simply placed on the surface of the water and, like water lilies, help to control algae growth.

* *oxygenating plants* are essential to control algae. They are planted on the bottom of the pond and five bunches are needed for every square metre (10 sq ft) of water area.

Surprisingly, a water feature with plants requires only a few messy hours of cleaning in spring, when water plants that have grown too profusely should be taken out of the water, cut back and replanted.

CONSTRUCTION

Once you have decided on the type and style of pond you would like, you will have to choose your method of construction. The simplest way is to buy a ready-made shell, most commonly available in glassfibre-reinforced plastic (GRP or glassfibre), fibre-cement or high-density polyethylene. Some of these ready-made ponds can stand above ground, while others are designed to be sunken.

On the other hand, you can simply use heavy-duty plastic or synthetic rubber sheeting to line a hollow in the ground or you can build a more permanent structure in concrete or in brick, above or below the ground. This should be lined with plastic or sealed with a non-toxic bitumen (asphalt tar) sealant.

Our first step-by-step section features a simple, formal pond which is built of brick and sealed with non-toxic bitumen (asphalt tar), with its base below ground level and its sides extending above the paving surround.

Our second project shows a pond made using a heavy-duty liner with a crazy paving surround.

SEALING

The biggest and most common problem relating to pools and ponds is, appropriately enough, their ability to hold water. (How many leaking pools have been adapted to make sandpits for the children or filled in with earth and planted?) As always, meticulous preparation should avoid this problem.

Thick plastic or rubber sheeting will undoubtedly provide a waterproof lining, but it is fairly vulnerable to puncturing. In any case, its life-span is limited, and it will therefore have to be replaced periodically.

The interior surface of a masonry pond can be painted with a proprietary bitumen (asphalt tar) sealant, following the manufacturer's instructions. If brick is used, rendering (pargeting) it first will reduce the number of coats of bitumen (asphalt tar) required. Because of their dark colour, both black plastic and bitumen (asphalt tar) will give the pond a feeling of depth and mystery.

Left: *The effect of this circular brick pond has been cleverly enhanced by the leafy planter behind.*

DRAINAGE

While there are obvious advantages in constructing a pond with built-in drainage, deciding on a suitable water outlet may be a problem. Any plughole must be attached to a PVC pipe which should, in turn, feed into a drainage channel. This sometimes increases the likelihood of leaking, but thorough sealing around the hole with a good quality, flexible sealer can eliminate the problem. Most pumps will enable you to drain the pond from the top, thus avoiding the need for a plughole.

Alternatively, provided the base of your pond is higher than the surrounding ground, you can simply siphon all the water out with a piece of garden hose.

Step-by-step raised pond

The height from the foundation is 400 mm (16 in) and from the paving, which incorporates a slope for drainage, 200 to 230 mm (8 to 9 in). The foundation is 1,960 × 1,150 mm (6 ft 5 in × 3 ft 9 in) and varies from 150 mm (6 in) to 200 mm (8 in) deep at the edges. You will need:

Foundation

Concrete: 1:2½:3½ cement:sand: aggregate
50 kg (1 x 100 lb bag) cement
125 kg or 3 cu ft (276 lb) sand
200 kg or 4 cu ft (440 lb) aggregate

Above: *The pond filled with water.*

Brickwork

120–130 bricks
20–30 paving bricks
18 kg (40 lb) cement
108 kg or 2¾ cu ft (240 lb) builder's sand
9 kg (20 lb) lime
OR 8 ml (¾ fl oz) plasticizer

1 Mark the area of the proposed pond (see the section on square in Brickwork Principles, page 268), and excavate to the rquired depth. As this pond will extend above ground, incorporating a low brick wall, the excavated depth is about 300 mm (1 ft).
2 Mix the concrete (see page 269) and roughly line the bottom and sides of the hole.
3 Lay a foundation and build up a five-course wall topped with paving bricks, continually checking levels and corners.
4 If using plastic sheeting, spread this inside the pond when the first three courses are complete, finishing off with a further two courses and paving bricks. Otherwise, seal the pond with several coats of non-toxic bitumen (asphalt tar). When the bitumen (asphalt tar) sealant is dry, create areas of interest within the pond by placing rocks on the bottom and potted plants in groups on rocks near the surface.

POOLS AND PONDS

Step-by-step liner pond

The size and shape of pond you create is a matter of taste, but experience has shown that the minimum size to produce an attractive and clear pool and harmony between volume of water, plants and fish is around 4 sq m (40 sq ft).

The depth of the pond should be between 380 and 450 mm (15 to 18 in) for small to medium-sized ponds; 600 to 750 mm (24 to 30 in) for larger ponds (over 10 sq m or 100 sq ft). Build in shelves 230 mm (9 in) wide and 230 mm deep around the edge for marginal plants.

The pond shown here is constructed using a heavy-duty liner: for this, the sides of the pond should slope by approximately 20° – 75 mm (3 in) inwards for every 230 mm (9 in) of depth. To calculate the size of liner you need, take twice the maximum depth and add this to both the overall length and overall width of the pond, irrespective of the actual shape.

To build a 4 sq m (40 sq ft) pond, you will need:

Base
100 kg or 2½ cu ft (220 lb) builder's sand
Black plastic liner

Surround (600 mm [2 ft] wide)
5 sq m (50 sq ft) paving materials
40 kg or almost one bag (88 lb) cement
80 kg or 2 cu ft (176 lb) sand

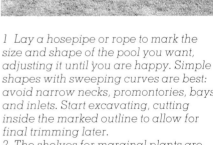

1 Lay a hosepipe or rope to mark the size and shape of the pool you want, adjusting it until you are happy. Simple shapes with sweeping curves are best: avoid narrow necks, promontories, bays and inlets. Start excavating, cutting inside the marked outline to allow for final trimming later.

2 The shelves for marginal plants are cut out around the edges and the edges themselves trimmed back around 50 mm (2 in) to allow for the overlap of the edging stones.

3 Short wooden pegs are inserted about 1 m (3 ft 3 in) apart around the edge of pond and levelled with a spirit level – it is vital that the top of the pond is

6

7

Above: In fine weather the pond edge makes a pleasant place to sit and relax.

horizontal as the water will soon show any discrepancies.

4 After final trimming and excavation, the depth and width of the marginal shelves (here two sets at different levels) should be checked and the inside of the pond inspected for any sharp stones or roots which could damage the liner.

5 A cushion of sand 12 mm (1/2 in) thick should be placed all over the excavated area, making sure it fills any holes. Smooth the sand down – at the top, make sure it is level with the marking pegs and then remove the pegs and fill the holes with more sand.

6 The pond liner is then draped loosely into the hole with an even overlap all the way round with stones or blocks placed at the corners and, if necessary, on the sides. Start filling with water.

7 As the pond fills, the stones should be eased off at intervals to allow the liner to fit snugly into the hole. Some creasing is inevitable, but some creases can be removed by stretching and fitting as the pond fills.

8 When the pool is full, cut off the excess liner, leaving a flap around 100 to 125 mm (4 to 5 in) wide. This can be temporarily secured to prevent slipping by driving some 100 mm (4 in) nails

8

9

10

through it into the ground.

9 Rectangular pools can be edged with pre-cast regular paving: curved ponds are better finished with broken stone flags or concrete paving stones as used in crazy paving. Lay the edging stones on a mortar of one part cement to three parts sand, removing the temporary nails from the liner as you go.

10 Ideally, the pond should be emptied and refilled before planting and stocking with fish – especially if any mortar has been dropped in during the construction. Add fountains, lights and other ornaments – here, a small geyser jet has been used which will not disturb the water lilies or other marginal plants.

Pools and Ponds

Pumps for Ponds

A variety of pumps is available for use with fish ponds and ornamental pools. Choose one which will cope with the water capacity of your pond and which will also power a waterfall or fountain. You should also make certain that the unit will enable you to pump water from the pond, thus draining it when necessary. Relatively small in size, pumps suitable for ponds must be specially designed for the purpose with a completely sealed motor housing so that they can be submerged in the water.

Pumps are available in both mains voltage and extra low-voltage (typically 24V versions). Mains-voltage pumps need an outside electricity supply, the installation of which is a job best left to a professional electrician. ('Mains-voltage' means 240 V in the UK and 110 V in the US.) Low-voltage pumps are supplied from a transformer. For ponds close to the house, this can be plugged in to a convenient power point inside the house and low-voltage cable led to the position of the pond. For more distant ponds, a mains-voltage supply can be taken overhead or underground to the position of the pond where the transformer will need to be placed in a waterproof shed next to the pond.

Most pond pumps will provide a variety of fountain patterns (the fountain can be mounted on top of the pump or can be a separate feature) and can be used, separately or simultaneously, to power a waterfall.

Lights

Once you have installed electricity at the site of the pond, you can add lighting to enhance its appearance at night.

Low-voltage lights can be placed around the pond or special types can be floated on the surface (or, if weighted, under the surface) for a more dramatic effect.

The clever combination of lighting and fountains can create particularly spectacular night-time effects.

Fountain jets

Pond fountain jets fall into four basic types. These are shown above (reading clockwise from top left).

The simple spray jet varies in size and can have as many as three fountains.

The bell jet produces a clear dome of flowing water.

The foam jet is a powerful geyser, which seems to be in constant motion.

The tulip jet creates an endlessly elegant spout of water.

198

Above: An attractive waterfall feature produced using a pond pump. The colourful and exotic plants add to the tropical effect.

Right: This miniature pond, which blends cleverly with the wall behind, has been enhanced by a lion's mask fountain.

Left: The dramatic, crimson water lilies and 'rock baby' fountain have given this raised pond a touch of grandeur and made it more interesting.

Far left: Creative lighting, especially with coloured lights, can give your pond a magical quality at night.

Seat and Table

Built-in outdoor furniture simplifies seating for outdoor entertaining, takes up little room, and adds to the value of your home. Instead of having to move chairs and tables outside whenever you want a meal or a quiet drink in the fresh air, the basic equipment is already there. All you need do is add cushions for comfort.

Location

The design of furniture and its location will depend on your requirements. If you want a place to sit and relax or read, away from the hustle and bustle of normal household activities, you will probably want a simple yet comfortable bench tucked away in a quiet corner. But if you plan to use the furniture for entertaining or for family meals, it will have to meet entirely different needs.

Built-in seats and tables may be combined with other built-in features. The most common location for this type of furniture is on patios, especially when barbecues and other outdoor cooking facilities are included. Other spots where people congregate regularly, for example paved areas around ponds or pools, are obvious sites for both benches and tables.

The furniture itself may blend in naturally or, if attractive and unusual, may become a striking feature. A tiled or mosaic seat, for instance, adds interest as well as providing a place to rest.

Materials

Any furniture left outdoors permanently should be made from weather-proof materials. Brick and stone are certainly very durable, but do not provide particularly comfortable surfaces for seating, and therefore need to be finished off with a more agreeable material.

Wood is a good option for table tops and seats, and it can look very attractive combined with brick. Alternatively, a practical table can be made by topping a stocky pillar with a smooth, pre-cast concrete slab. Keep bricklaying to a minimum by building a bench alongside a

Above: *The perfect setting for a relaxed meal outside.*

retaining or screen wall, with the wall forming the backrest, and timber slats forming the seat.

Step-by-step seat and table
For this project a raft or slab foundation was used, covering the base of the whole area of the structure. This type of foundation is not as deep as a strip foundation, which is used to build walls. For this project the foundation was 2,100 × 1,700 mm (6 ft 11 in × 5 ft 7 in) and 100 mm (4 in) deep. You will need:

Foundation
75 kg (165 lb) cement
200 kg or 5 cu ft (440 lb) sand
300 kg or 6 cu ft (662 lb) aggregate

Brickwork
410–450 bricks
66 kg (1½ x 100 lb bags) cement
396 kg or 10 cu ft (873 lb) sand
33 kg (73 lb) lime
OR 66 ml (2 fl oz) plasticizer
11 pieces of wood, 150 x 38 mm (6 x 1½ in) (length for table 4 x 1,800 mm [5 ft 11 in], 2 x 570 mm [22 in]; for seat 3 x 1,550 mm [5 ft 1 in], 2 x 420 mm [16½ in])
22 x No. 8 x 75 mm (3 in) coach screws (screwspikes) (12 for table, 10 for seat)

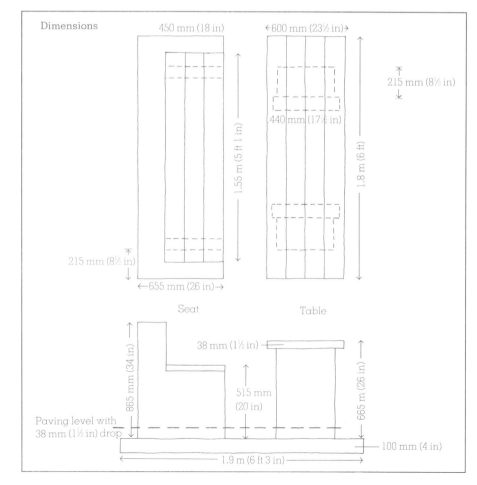

Dimensions

450 mm (18 in)
←600 mm (23½ in)→
215 mm (8½ in)
440 mm (17½ in)
1.55 m (5 ft 1 in)
1.8 m (6 ft)
215 mm (8½ in)
←655 mm (26 in)→

Seat
Table

38 mm (1½ in)
865 mm (34 in)
515 mm (20 in)
665 m (26 in)
Paving level with 38 mm (1½ in) drop
100 mm (4 in)
←1.9 m (6 ft 3 in)→

1 Peg out the area required for your seat and table, allowing an extra 100 to 200 mm (4 to 8 in) on all four sides to accommodate the slab foundation. Excavate to a depth of 100 mm (4 in) – about the depth of a brick on edge. Make sure your surface is level before you mix the concrete and lay the foundation. Check the levels by placing a brick at each corner and using a spirit level placed on a long straight-edge.

2 Mix cement, sand and aggregate in a ratio of 1:2½:3½. Spread the concrete over the entire area, levelling with the back of a spade. You can leave the bricks in the corners to help keep the concrete surface level.

3 Once the concrete is dry, lay a one-brick wall for the seat. Use the straight-edge and the spirit level to keep the back wall level. Check with the builder's square that all corners are at 90°.

4 Now build up two courses at the corners, using the spirit level to check both horizontal and vertical surfaces. Use a gauge rod to make certain that the brick courses are regular.

5 Start building up the two pillars which will support the wooden table top. It is easiest and most practicable to work on the bench and table simultaneously, gradually building up all the walls. Stretcher bond (see page 244) is used for these two features which both have wooden strip surfaces. From the

foundation level, the seat back is built up to 11 courses, the seat itself to seven courses and the table up to nine courses. When planning your final levels, take into account that nearly two of these courses may be below the final paving.

Strips of wood are screwed together and fitted across the walls which form the built-in seat. Thinner brick pavers are used to finish off the top and ends of the seating section, as the wood does not extend to the edges. The table is built in a similar way, but with an extra piece of wood. The cross pieces are cut to slot in on the inside of the two piers, to prevent the table top from sliding from side to side and to reinforce the seat.

Barbecues

When the weather is fine, nothing beats cooking and eating outside. A permanent and well-constructed barbecue provides an effective way for a family or group of friends to socialize while cooking an informal meal. A simple built-in barbecue, maintenance-free and weather-proof, is easy to construct and the enjoyment it will afford you is certainly worth the effort.

Location

The location of any barbecue is a vital factor. Careful thought and planning will provide a pleasant entertainment area which you can exploit to the full. Lack of forethought and inadequate attention to factors such as sun, wind, accessibility to the house and the nearness of neighbours are more likely to result in wasted time, effort and money.

Spend time sitting in various parts of the site and take note of climate-related factors. Take note of the areas that receive hardly any sun or are particularly wind-swept. You are unlikely to want to end up cooking at the barbecue on your own, while guests sit elsewhere. The ideal spot should offer both sunshine and some shade, as well as shelter from the prevailing wind, so that guests can relax around the barbecue.

It is often preferable to site a barbecue near the house to avoid tedious trips to the kitchen for food, water and utensils. However, if it is too near, you may end up with discoloured walls and a smoke-filled house whenever you cook outside. It could also be a fire hazard.

Patios often make good barbecue sites, but if you opt for an established area which is enclosed or covered, construct a properly designed chimney to channel smoke away.

Design

Before considering the design options of a barbecue, determine your needs and those of family and friends who will make regular use of the area. Evaluate your life-style and choose your design to suit it.

Even the simplest barbecue arrangement should have both adequate working surfaces and convenient storage space for those cooking utensils you will use most frequently, as well as for wood and charcoal.

If you cannot afford everything you would like to incorporate at the time of building, plan your barbecue for future improvement or expansion, allowing for additional features at a later date. These could include built-in seating and tables, fitted doors for the storage space, or planters to add colour.

The style of the structure – including seating and other additional features – should blend with your home and complement existing building materials. Match brick, render (parget) and paint and take care that the barbecue does not dominate existing features.

Barbecues may be built with brick, concrete walling blocks or stone; they may be mass-produced or portable; regarding fuel, they may use wood, charcoal or gas.

The advantages of built-in barbecues include convenience, durability and, provided they are imaginatively designed and well-built, an increase in the value of your property.

Design options are endless, and range from simple, functional units, such as the unit for which we have given building instructions, to elaborate designs incorporating grills; simple spits or even rotisseries; pizza and baking ovens, as well as seating and storage facilities.

Foundation

A sturdy foundation is an important factor when building a barbecue. Its depth will, of course, depend on the size and weight of the structure it will support. A smallish unit can be built on a raft or slab foundation 75 to 100 mm (3 to 4 in) deep (see *Seat and Table*, page 200). For this reason, an existing patio will often present a suitable base, provided it is level and firm.

For easy cleaning and drainage, the foundation should be sloped slightly towards the front of the barbecue.

Construction

Mark out the area for your barbecue and excavate an extra 100 to 200 mm (4 to 8 in) on each side. If you are working alongside an existing patio, mark the paving as an additional guide.

Right: *The simple style of this barbecue makes it an excellent project for any do-it-yourself enthusiast who wants to build a basic yet practical structure. The slatted wooden doors and wooden seat were later additions.*

BARBECUES

During bricklaying, check levels and surfaces constantly, using a straight-edge and spirit level, adding or removing mortar from under the bricks if necessary. Place the spirit level diagonally against the bricks as well as in a horizontal and a vertical position. Use a square to check corners, and use corner blocks with a builder's line to help maintain a straight edge. If you find that any bricks are lying skew, tap them gently into place. Scrape off any excess mortar as you work.

Step-by-step barbecue

The base measurements for this barbecue are: 1,800 × 525 mm (5 ft 11 × 20½ in) with a foundation 2,000 × 800 mm (6 ft 7 × 2 ft 7 in) and 100 mm (4 in) deep. The materials you will need to build the barbecue are:

Foundation

Concrete mixture: 1:2½:3½ cement:sand: aggregate
50 kg (1 × 100 lb bag) cement
125 kg or 3 cu ft (276 lb) builder's sand
200 kg or 4 cu ft (440 lb) aggregate

Barbecue unit

240 bricks (30 halved)
53 paving bricks (1 halved)
75 kg (165 lb) cement
300 kg or 7½ cu ft (662 lb) builder's sand
38 kg (84 lb) builder's lime
OR 75 ml (2½ fl oz) plasticizer

4 standard concrete lintels, 1,500 mm (4 ft 11 in) long
8 round iron pegs OR 100 mm (4 in) bolts
450 x 450 mm (18 in square) grid, for cooking

1 Having marked out the area, excavate to the depth of one brick on edge and lay a foundation using concrete mixed to a ratio of 1:2½:3½ (cement:sand:aggregate).
2 When the concrete has set, lay the first course of bricks without mortar and mark pencil lines on the concrete. Remove the bricks. Mix mortar in the ratio of 1:1:6 (cement:lime:sand).
3 Using the pencil markings as a guide, lay a sausage-like bed of mortar, 10 to 12 mm (½ in) thick and about 100 mm (4 in) wide, along the lines where each wall of the barbecue will be built. Use lines and furrows (see page 271) to lay the bricks.
4 Using the line and furrow in the mortar as a guide, follow the pattern shown when the bricks were laid without mortar and lay the first course of bricks which form the two side walls of the structure (10 bricks in all). Use corner blocks and check levels frequently with a spirit level.
5 Now lay the long outer wall and then lay the bricks which will form the two short inner walls. Once again, use the spirit level and square frequently. All

gaps between bricks should be filled in with mortar before you begin to lay the second course of bricks.
6 The stretcher bond used for this barbecue requires six half bricks for every second course. Begin laying at the outside corners of the back wall, but before you set the first brick of the second course in place, lay a strip of mortar on top of the first course of bricks. Build up both outer corners to three courses before starting on the second course of the straight walls. To complete the inside corner of the second course, put a half brick in place. Fill in any gaps with mortar before placing a full brick in position to complete the inside corner of the third course.
7 Continue laying the bricks for a total of 10 courses. Lay a single course of bricks around the outside edges of the structure and four pre-cast concrete lintels across the top of the inside bricks. Spread mortar over the lintels and then build up walls to shield the cooking area.
8 Set bolts into the wall to support a grid. Rake out any excess mortar on the external walls. Thinner brick pavers are used for the final course of bricks on all surfaces, including the floor surface below the barbecue. An alternative option is to build up a last course of bricks over the lintels and then to tile the working surfaces on each side of the cooking area.

5

6

8

7

STEPS AND STAIRWAYS

STEPS – WHETHER BUILT OF BRICK, STONE, CONCRETE BLOCK, SOLID CONCRETE OR A COMBINATION OF MATERIALS – HAVE A CERTAIN WAY OF ADDING CHARM AND INTEREST TO AN OUTDOOR AREA. A FLIGHT OF STEPS IS HIGHLY PRACTICAL ON A SLOPING PROPERTY – PROVIDING SAFE AND EASY ACCESS TO INACCESSIBLE OR INFREQUENTLY VISITED AREAS. STEPS ARE ESSENTIAL ON STEEPLY SLOPING SITES, IF ONLY TO ALLOW ACCESS BETWEEN THE BOUNDARY AND FRONT ENTRANCE OF THE HOUSE.

AS WELL AS HAVING A PRACTICAL PURPOSE, STEPS CAN SERVE A DECORATIVE FUNCTION, BECOMING A FEATURE IN THEMSELVES. ALTHOUGH IT MIGHT SEEM AN AMBITIOUS TASK, BUILDING STEPS IS NOT AS DIFFICULT AS YOU MIGHT EXPECT, PROVIDED YOU OBSERVE A FEW BASIC RULES.

LOCATION AND DESIGN

The style and design of steps depends largely on their location and their intended use. It is always very important to plan your steps carefully. Make certain they will be located practically and to the best visual advantage before you start building. Whether their use is practical or decorative, steps should have some sense of purpose.

You may find that the slope in your plot does not make steps a necessity, but consider the decorative aspect. A gradually stepped pathway could, for instance, become a feature on its own. If possible, avoid making a long flight of stairs follow a straight line.

Plants on either side will enhance any flight of steps. Use trailing greenery or flowering, ground-covering plants to soften stark lines or build planters for dramatic, bold specimens (see our step-by-step project). For a charmingly whimsical effect, you could plant sweet-smelling herbs between the spaced treads of informal steps.

MATERIALS

Whatever style of steps you decide on – be it formal brick or rustic stone – it is important that they enhance your property rather than conflict with existing features. For instance, if your house has a very distinctive style, it might be best to treat steps leading to the front door as an extension of the building, and use materials which blend with or reflect its style of architecture. On the other hand, continuing the colour and texture of existing pathways or paving could be equally effective.

A popular choice for outdoor steps is concrete paving slabs for the treads laid on brick or block walls as the risers. A typical method of construction is shown in the drawing – the bottom riser is built on a concrete base, the space behind filled

Below: *A standard method of constructing steps with pavers and brick risers.*

Below right and detail: *Formwork needs to be constructed for solid concrete steps.*

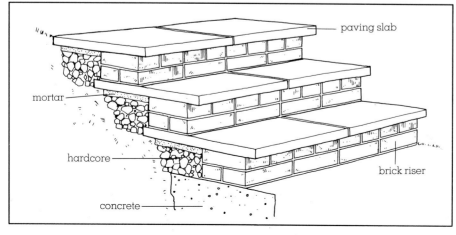

paving slab

mortar

hardcore

concrete

brick riser

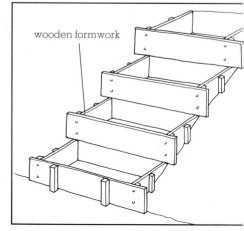

wooden formwork

with hardcore and earth and the paving slab then laid on a bed of mortar across the riser and the hardcore. The second riser is then built on top of the paving slab and so on to the top of the flight.

Steps can be made entirely from brick, as in our first step-by-step example, or can be built from concrete blocks bedded in sand, as in our second example.

To build solid concrete steps, formwork needs to be constructed for each of the steps. Concrete is poured in for the bottom step, levelled off and allowed to set until firm enough to take the weight of the second step.

A popular and particularly practical material for constructing steps is paving bricks. Consider, however, combining brick with other materials to add textural interest – treads of concrete paving blocks or tiles; or perhaps incorporating railway sleeper (railroad tie) ends.

The instructions given for building steps with brick are a general guide, and the same method may be applied when using bricks in combination with concrete paving blocks, regular-cut slate or crazy paving.

EXCAVATION

Once you have decided where to site the steps and what materials to use, mark out the area with a profile (see diagram) and excavate. You should try to avoid cutting bricks and should therefore take the size of the bricks, pavers and slabs you are using (plus mortar where necessary) into account when choosing the size of the steps, especially the risers (see table).

If you build on a steep bank, you will probably have to construct side retaining walls first (see page 250). Failure to do this could result in erosion and eventual collapse of the steps. Be sure to measure the width of your stairway first.

Left: *Bricks seem the obvious choice for the steps leading up to this house.*

Below: *Here a dramatic effect has been created by building steps over an arch.*

tamping beam

HEIGHT

The rise of a step should not exceed 200 mm (8 in), while the length of a tread should be at least 250 mm (10 in). Outdoor steps are, however, often much more gradual than this.

As a rule, the higher each step, the brisker your pace will be as you walk up and down them. Long, shallow steps invite a leisurely stroll. Steps planned for the garden or backyard will therefore be less steep than, say, a stairway providing access to the entrance of your home. If your plot is very spacious, the gradient of your steps can be as gradual as 1 in 15. A long gradual slope may look better with a series of steps, rather than with a single stairway. Alternatively, break the steps with planters or seating.

TREADS AND RISERS

The relationship between the length of the tread and the height of the riser between treads is important since they must be in proportion to each other. The more gradual the slope and the longer the tread, the shallower the riser should be.

Some successful combinations may be used as a guide; for instance, a tread which is 300 mm (12 in) long works well with a 175 mm (7 in) riser, while a 500 mm (20 in) tread should be combined with a shallower 100 mm (4 in) riser.

Above: Green vegetation in the planters sets off the red of the brickwork.

WIDTH

Ideally, garden steps should be 1.2 to 1.5 m (4 to 5 ft) wide, which is wide enough for two people to walk comfortably abreast. Functional steps built purely for access should be at least 600 mm (2 ft)

Recommended tread/riser combinations

Tread length	Riser height	Possible riser materials
500 mm (20 in)	100 mm (4 in)	one course of bricks plus 25 mm (1 in) paving slab
450 mm (18 in)	115 mm (4½ in)	one course of bricks on edge or one course of bricks + 38 mm (1½ in) slab
400 mm (16 in)	140 mm (5½ in)	one course of concrete-based walling blocks + 38 mm (1½ in) slab
350 mm (14 in)	150 mm (6 in)	two courses of brick laid flat
300 mm (12 in)	175 mm (7 in)	two courses of brick + 25 mm (1 in) slab

wide. To prevent puddles forming, steps should be given a gentle slope of, say, 1 in 100 (5 mm/500 mm or ¼ in/4 ft).

PROFILES

To measure the depth of your slope and to establish exactly how many steps will fit, it is advisable to make a simple profile device with two straight-edged pieces of wood joined at right angles. The vertical must be placed at the point where the steps should end, and the horizontal at the top of the steps. Place a spirit level on the horizontal plank to ensure your profile levels are straight. The depth of the slope is the distance along the horizontal section of the profile, A-C, while the vertical section indicates the total change in level, A-B.

Use these figures to decide the best number of steps. For example, if (as shown) the total length is 1.2 m (4 ft) and the total height is 420 mm (1 ft 4½ in), you might think of having two, three or four steps. Two would give too great a riser (210 mm or 8¼ in); four would give steps with 105 mm (4 in) risers but a tread length of only 300 mm (1 ft), which is too short for this combination. So the best choice is three steps, 140 mm (5½ in) high and 400 mm (16 in) long.

It may sometimes be necessary to change the extent of the depth of the slope to enable you to fit in steps which

Brickwork
72 bricks
56 brick pavers
15 kg (33 lb) cement
60 kg or 1½ cu ft (132 lb) sand
8 kg (18 lb) lime
OR 15 ml (½ fl oz) plasticizer

1 Establish the level of both the top and bottom step by using your profile and set up a building line as a guide. It is not necessary to dig away all the earth. Simply cut out the general shape.
2 Lay a concrete foundation 50 mm (2 in) thick and to the length and width of your tread. When this is dry, lay your first course using bricklaying mortar. In this case, the first step will be an extension of the path, so only paving bricks are laid.
3 Fill in the gap behind the tread with concrete, to the level of your paving bricks. This new concrete base will form the foundation for your second step. Once it is dry, you can start laying the riser.
4 Now build up the riser (here with two courses of brick) behind the first tread, using corner blocks and a builder's line to ensure that the bricks are laid straight. Use your spirit level to ensure that the bricks are level and vertical.
5 Fill in the gap behind the bricks with concrete, extending into a level 'platform' for the tread pavers. When this is dry lay the pavers on a bed of mortar, using the spirit level frequently.

conform satisfactorily to the tread/riser proportions required and to suit the size of your bricks (plus mortar) or other materials.

Step-by-step steps
For three steps 900 mm (3 ft) wide with 200 mm (8 in) risers and 290 mm (11½ in) treads, you will need:

Foundation
10 kg or ⅛ bag (22 lb) cement
30 kg or 1 cu ft (66 lb) sand
45 kg or 1 cu ft (100 lb) aggregate

Below: *A simple profile for building steps.*

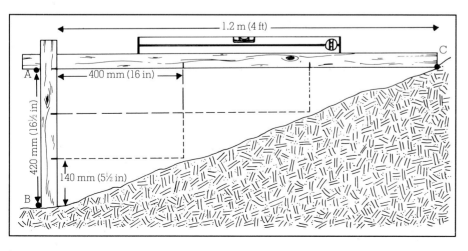

Step-by-step concrete block steps

For three steps 1,800 mm (6 ft) wide with 200 mm (8 in) risers and 500 mm (20 in) treads, you will need:

55 curbstones
110 concrete paving blocks

Foundation/sub-base

35 kg or ⅔ bag (77 lb) cement
90 kg or 2¼ cu ft (200 lb) sand
140 kg or 3 cu ft (308 lb) aggregate
100 kg or 2½ cu ft (220 lb) concreting sand
200 kg or 4 cu ft (440 lb) hardcore

1 Start with two side brick walls and the site roughly excavated.
2 Wooden formwork is used to form the concrete for the riser curbstones. This must be correctly positioned, levelled and secured.
3 Concrete is shovelled into the formwork and roughly levelled off.
4 Once the concrete has set (allow three days or more), remove the formwork.
5 Use a string line to position the curbstones and place them on a mortar bed.
6 Lay all the curbstones.
7 Now shovel in a mixture of small stones and finer granular material.
8 Compact the sub-base thoroughly until it is at the required depth (add more material if necessary).
9 Shovel fine concreting sand in and compact this with the hand compactor. Lay two screeding rails 60 mm (2½ in) below the finished step height.
10 Screed off the sand and remove the screeding rails.
11 Use a block splitter (masonry saw) to cut blocks for filling in small gaps.
12 Lay the paving blocks in the required pattern – here basketweave.
13 Compact the sand by tamping down with the hand compactor, using wood to protect the block surface.
14 Brush fine sand across the blocks, making sure it gets into all the joints.
15 Compact again to force sand in between the joints and to level the blocks.
16 A fine set of steps.

8

11

14

9

12

15

10

13

16

Arches

While solid walls provide privacy and protection, the inclusion of arches at entrances or other points of access can add visual interest and a pleasing new dimension to the design of your garden or backyard.

Location

Arches may be introduced into the design in several ways – to frame an entrance, add interest to a plain wall or to provide a framework for fragrant flowering climbers. It is not usually advisable to construct a single arch – unless it has a definite sense of purpose it will simply look out of place. So, in the planning stages, decide whether your arch will bridge a functional opening, separate sections of the plot or offer support for plants to trail over.

An arch can be introduced to frame an opening in a wall, as an extension, rising above a wall, or as a free-standing structure. Whichever type is used, it should mirror any other arches within view. These may recur within the wall itself, perhaps as a second utility entrance, or be incorporated in the shape of nearby structures such as garage doors, a patio wall, window frames or the entrance to the house itself.

Small-scale arches may also be included in your design. They can be used to frame a postbox, a refuse bin (garbage can) or a nook.

Construction

Building an archway is a project that needs to be tackled very carefully, particularly if it is to span a wide opening. The most widely accepted method is to work with a supporting formwork (also called former or a turning-piece), which is cut in the shape of a semicircle or arc or, where a less pronounced effect is desired, as a smaller segment of a circle (a segmental arch).

A semicircular arch is generally simpler to set out and to build – a segmental arch means some geometrical drawing

Below: *An arch built into a wall is an unusual way to frame features such as this gargoyle fountain.*

and the wall bricks on either side have to be shaped to take the first arch bricks (which will not be horizontal). The formwork may be made up of two pieces of chipboard or plywood nailed together, but separated with blocks of wood around the edges. This is positioned where the arch is to be constructed, and bricks are then laid over it.

Formwork for

Semicircular arches

The formula for setting out an arch in a semicircle is simple: half the span of the opening is equal to the rise of the arch.

Above: A striking arch which adds visual interest to the gate while providing a framework for the plants to grow over.

Right: This diagram shows how to set out a segmental arch geometrically.

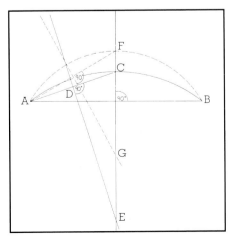

The base of the completed formwork must be equal in width to the span and must line up with (and therefore mark) the baseline of the rise.

To draw the shape, lay your board flat on the ground and mark out a semicircle with a pencil attached to a piece of string, measuring the rise as half the width of the span. Cut out the shape with a jigsaw

and then use it as a template to cut a second piece.

Now lay one cut-out piece of board flat and line the inside edges with blocks of wood, approximately the same thickness (less the thickness of the boards) as the wall. Cover with the second piece of board and nail this to each block; then turn over the board and attached blocks, and nail on the remaining board. Cover the edge with a strip of hardboard, nailing to secure.

FORMWORK FOR
SEGMENTAL ARCHES

While designed along the same principles as a semicircular arch, a segmental arch will give a less pronounced curve. When making the formwork for such an arch, it is sensible to include a little extra below the baseline of the rise, for ease of handling.

The first step is to decide on the height of the riser, which should never be less than a sixth of the span (for the purpose of this explanation, 900 mm [3 ft]). Lay out the board and draw a straight 900 mm (3 ft) baseline from A to B (see diagram). Mark the centre point and draw a second line at right angles through it. Measure the height of your rise (150 mm [6 in]) from the same centre point and mark C. Draw a line from A to C, bisect and draw another perpendicular line through the new centre point. The point at which it intersects your original perpendicular line, E, is the base point for drawing a segment of your circle, using the method described for semicircular arches.

Note that if your rise had been 250 mm (10 in) to F, G would then mark the base point for drawing the circle.

BUILDING THE ARCH

While the construction of an archway may seem like a formidable task, it is possible for a novice bricklayer to master the skills required by systematically following a few basic rules.

Once the formwork has been made it is placed in position in the wall opening and is supported by a timber framework constructed from pieces of wood at least 100 x 50 mm (4 x 2 in). Pairs of wedges are placed under the framework to ensure that the formwork is absolutely level at the correct height (these will also help when it comes to getting the formwork out once the arch has been built).

If the former has not been marked with the brick positions before putting it in place, these can be marked by laying the bricks 'dry' with wedges in between to represent the mortar courses. If you are continuing upwards with the wall over the arch, check with a gauge rod that the top of the keystone will line up with the first full course of bricks.

1

2

3

4

5

6

It is best to build up the arch evenly from both sides to prevent it being pushed out of position – as you lay the bricks, check that they are in the correct place (i.e. lined up with the marks on the former) and use a spirit level (or straight-edge) to ensure that each face of the arch is level with the faces of the former.

The last block to go into place is the 'keystone' at the very top of the arch. Make sure this is firmly in place and leave the mortar to dry for at least three days before removing the former.

Step-by-step arch
To make the formwork, you will need:

1,200 mm (3 ft 11 in) chipboard
50 mm (2 in) square wood, cut into a 1.2 m (4 ft) length
Strip of hardboard, whose width equals the thickness of the arch and whose length is 1:6 times the arch width
75 mm (3 in) wire nails to nail chipboard and blocks together
40 mm (1½ in) wire nails to nail hardboard onto formwork

Bricks/blocks
Apart from a separate keystone, you can use the same bricks or blocks that you are using for building the wall to make the arch.

1 Using one of the two methods described, draw the shape of your formwork onto the board and cut out two with a jigsaw.
2 Cut the square length of wood into six blocks, each 190 mm (7½ in) long, and nail these in place between the two pieces of board.
3 Cut a strip of hardboard to fit the perimeter of the arc and nail it on to the wooden blocks lining the edge of the formwork. This will give you a smooth and continuous surface over which the bricks can be laid.
4 Using the gauge rod, work out the position of the blocks to be laid over the top of the formwork. Avoid having to cut blocks by making mortar joints slightly thicker than usual, if necessary. Mark the formwork as a guide.
5 Before the arch former is made, the wall needs to be built up to the level of the bottom of the arch – here with concrete blocks.
6 Wedges can be used to position the blocks around the former so that the lines can be drawn back to the centre of the circle showing the position of each of the blocks.
7 Blocks are laid in mortar from either side, checking all the time that they have the correct alignment and are level with the face of the former.
8 The last block to go into place is the keystone – here one three courses deep and standing slightly proud of the surrounding blockwork for effect.

7

8

215

PILLARS AND PIERS

FREE-STANDING BLOCK AND CONCRETE BLOCK PILLARS AND PIERS HAVE VARIOUS USES, INCLUDING ACTING AS SUPPORTS FOR BASIC PERGOLAS OR ARBORS, AS POSTS FOR GATES AND DRIVEWAY ENTRANCES, AS BASES FOR SUNDIALS OR BIRD BATHS AND AS ESSENTIAL UPRIGHTS WHICH FORM THE SUPPORTING STRUCTURES FOR CARPORTS. INTERMEDIATE OR END PIERS ARE PUT IN FREE-STANDING BRICK WALLS FOR ESSENTIAL ADDITIONAL SUPPORT. BUILDING A PILLAR OR PIER IS RELATIVELY EASY ONCE YOU HAVE ACQUIRED THE BASIC SKILLS OF BRICKLAYING AND UNDERSTOOD THE BASIC METHODS OF CONSTRUCTION.

FOUNDATION

The minimum foundation depth for a brick pillar is 200 mm (8 in) although it may be advisable to make it as deep as 600 mm (2 ft), depending on its height and the weight (if any) it will carry.

The concrete mix used for a small pad foundation of this kind should be the standard 1:2½:3½ mix. This mixture was used for the pillar in our step-by-step project since it was less than a metre (3 ft 3in) high and its purpose was to be decorative rather than supportive.

REINFORCING

Some pillars must be built to take a considerable load, like those which are part of a carport and support the weight of a roof. They should also be able to withstand the force of wind gusting underneath the roof. For this reason both reinforcing rods and a strong mortar mix should be used in their construction.

Of course, any roof structure must also be securely fixed to a pillar and metal reinforcement should be built into the final five courses.

When building brick piers and pillars, it is usually advisable to incorporate vertical metal reinforcing rods. One or two rods are set in the centre of the foundation and propped up with timber while the concrete dries. The bricks are then laid around the rods, and additional mortar is used to fill in the central cavity as you work. It is advisable to let the mortar set for seven days if the pillar is to support a roof or covering of some sort.

For tall pillars or piers, embed a 'starter rod' into the foundation concrete and then tie further reinforcing rods to this with galvanized wire.

BUILDING PILLARS AND PIERS

It is best to make free-standing pillars out of an even number of bricks, whether they are solid or hollow, and to make them square. Intermediate or end piers in walls can be an odd number of brick sizes – a hollow square pier, with sides the width of three bricks, is a popular choice in half-brick walls, for example.

With piers in or on walls, there is a choice between bonding the brickwork of the pier to the bonding system of the wall

Left: *Brick pillars have been used here to support a wooden pergola over a patio area. The same technique could also be employed to build a carport.*

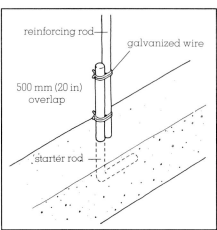

reinforcing rod

galvanized wire

500 mm (20 in) overlap

starter rod

Above: *In long high walls like this one movement joints and supporting piers need to be placed at regular intervals.*

Right: *The brickwork of the pier has been bonded to the half-brick wall.*

Below: *Expanded metal used to reinforce the joint between piers and wall.*

Bottom left: *Movement or control joint. Half of the metal strip has been greased to prevent a bond.*

Left: *'Starter rod' reinforcement is required for tall pillars and piers. The starter rod is concreted in place.*

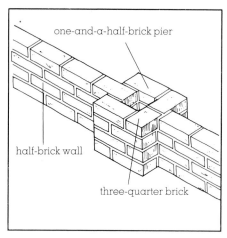

one-and-a-half-brick pier

half-brick wall

three-quarter brick

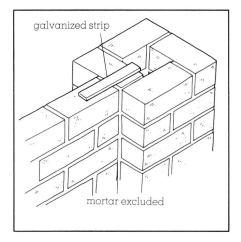

galvanized strip

mortar excluded

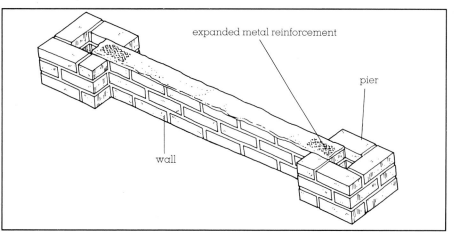

expanded metal reinforcement

pier

wall

PILLARS AND PIERS

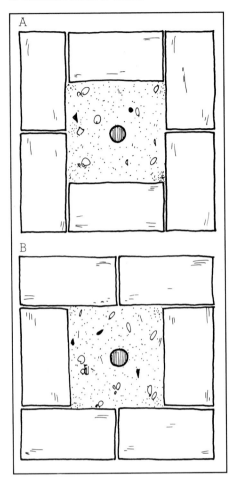

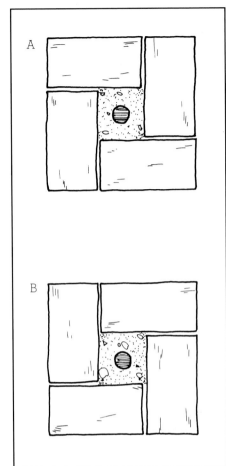

Left: *The diagram shows the brick courses for pillars and piers. Lay one course as in A, one as in B, one as in A and so on until the full height is achieved. This ensures proper bonding.*

or cutting bricks in half in alternate courses and leaving a vertical joint at the sides of the pier and reinforcing the horizontal courses with expanded metal or wall ties.

Leaving a vertical joint has the advantage that it can be used to create a movement (or 'control') joint in longer walls. Here, mortar is left out of the vertical joint and a flat strip of galvanized metal laid in the horizontal joints with one half of it lightly greased. This allows the wall to expand and contract along its length but supports the wall in a sideways direction. The sides of the otherwise open vertical joint are filled with non-setting mastic.

Step-by-step pillar
To build a hollow four-brick pillar, 900 mm (3 ft) high (excluding brick pavers), with a foundation 600 × 400 mm (2 ft × 16 in) and 110 mm (4½ in) deep, the materials you will need are:

Foundation
10 kg or ⅕ bag (22 lb) cement
25 kg or ½ cu ft (55 lb) sand
40 kg or 1 cu ft (66 lb) aggregate

Brickwork
50 bricks
5 brick pavers
10 kg (22 lb) cement
40 kg or 1 cu ft (88 lb) builder's sand
5 kg (11 lb) lime
OR 10 ml (⅓ fl oz) plasticizer
Metal reinforcing rod, about 1 m (3 ft 3 in) long

Render
8 kg (18 lb) cement
48 kg or 1¼ cu ft (106 lb) builder's sand
4 kg (9 lb) lime
OR 8 ml (¼ fl oz) plasticizer

1 An area of 600 x 600 mm (2 ft sq) must be excavated for a free-standing four-brick course pillar such as this, but this pier is attached to the wall and was built at the same time. The foundation must be laid first and allowed to dry thoroughly. Set out the first course of bricks without mortar.
2 It is essential to ensure that the four corners of the pillar are at exactly 90° to each other. Once you have laid the first course, check the corners with a builder's square. As you work, remember to check the height with a gauge rod and to use a spirit level to

Left: *The completed piers blend well with both the brick wall and the path.*

ensure each course is level and plumb.
3 A reinforcing rod is inserted into the still-wet mortar which has been poured into the central cavity of the pier. The top of the rod extends to the finished level of the wall and the pier. To keep it from falling over, prop up the rod with pieces of timber and continue to work around it.
4 The completed pillar, one of a pair, is bonded to the wall and could be used as a support for a gate. For uniformity and a harmonious design, both the pillar and the wall have been rendered (pargeted) and then washed with diluted paint. While the wall was finished off with bricks laid on edge, brick pavers were used to top the pillars.

PATIOS

A PATIO CAN EXTEND YOUR OUTDOOR LIVING SPACE AND PROVIDE YOU WITH A COMFORTABLE PLACE TO RELAX AND ENTERTAIN DURING SUMMER MONTHS. A PATIO IS NOT ONLY DURABLE AND PRACTICAL BUT IT WILL ALSO BE RELATIVELY EASY TO BUILD YOURSELF. LAYING A PATIO LIES WELL WITHIN THE CAPABILITIES OF ANY ENTHUSIASTIC HANDYMAN AND NEED NOT TAKE LONG TO COMPLETE.

PLANNING

Before planning your patio, try to get everyone who will use it to agree on what needs it should fulfil. Then you can decide on where, ideally, it should be sited, the features it should possess, its size, as well as other details.

SITE

There are usually several possibilities when it comes to siting a patio on any one property. It may lead off a living area of the house or may even be sited away from any buildings, perhaps alongside a pool or barbecue area. The decision will depend largely on the function your patio will fulfil although certain additional, yet basic, factors must be taken into account.

Will it, for instance, receive any sun; be sheltered from the midday sun and pro-tected from the full force of the wind? If you are looking for a place where you can sit and read, try to make use of the shade from any existing trees when siting your patio, especially if they are growing in an unappealing, 'dead' area in your garden or backyard that is not being util-ized. A paved area could transform such a spot into a pleasing and easily main-tained retreat.

A patio to be used for frequent sun-bathing should be exposed to the sun for most of the day, but if you intend to use the patio for dining or entertaining, it should offer both sun and some shade, as well as being accessible from the kitchen.

Right: *Mellow brick in a 'basketweave' pattern creates a traditional effect.*

Below: *A well-lit paving slab patio.*

SIZE

The patio should be built to a size that will serve your purpose for it. It is usually best to make it slightly larger than you think you would like it to be. If yours is a grow-ing family, try and assess what your needs will be in years to come so that you are not forced to extend the patio later on.

For a patio which will be used for din-ing, there must be enough space to ac-commodate a table and sufficient chairs. When planning your patio area, leave enough room for a table and chairs, as well as any other furniture you may want to use. If space is at a premium, built-in furniture takes up much less space than

MATERIALS

You can use many different paving materials for a patio, including bricks, concrete paving blocks, stone 'flags' and concrete paving slabs. The range gives a choice of colours and of finishes, ranging from smooth (easy to clean, but potentially slippery) to a rough-hewn or 'riven' finish (safer to walk on, but more difficult to keep clean). You do not have to use only one material: interest can be created by mixing materials and colours.

PRINCIPLES

When it comes to building a sound and attractive patio, several important principles must be considered.
* The area to be paved must have a firm, well-compacted sub-base to avoid sagging and possibly even the eventual collapse of the paving.
* Proper drainage is essential to direct the flow of rainwater away from buildings and prevent unsightly puddles forming during rainy periods.
* All brick and block paving (but not slabs) should be contained within a sound framework to prevent it from breaking up at the edges over time.
* The paving should be laid flat with a slight slope for drainage. Protruding bricks, blocks or slabs not only look ugly; they can also be hazardous.

With an appreciation of these priorities, you will be ready to consider the principles of patio-building in detail.

DRAINAGE

The very nature of outdoor patios and other paved areas makes drainage essential. Proper planning and thorough preparation will prevent puddles from forming whenever it rains.

A patio should be built on a well-drained site that will dry out quickly after rain. The finished surface of a patio adjoining any building should be at least 150 mm (6 in) below the existing damp-proof course (vapor barrier). This is formed by inserting a strip of plastic sheeting or other impervious material into the brickwork of external walls just above ground level and below your final floor level to prevent damp from rising.

The patio must slope away from the building at a gradient of 1-in-50 or a drop of 20 mm in every 1 m (1 in/4 ft), to prevent water from collecting at the base of the walls or in puddles on the patio itself.

The paved area can be sloped towards its outer edge, to drain away naturally into a lawn or a large flower bed. In high rainfall areas, however, your lawn could become swampy, in which case rainwater must be channelled away, either to the road, a stormwater drain or simply into well-drained soil. It must not be

free-standing pieces. Seating can be built in to accommodate a movable table in a corner.

If the patio adjoins the house, French or sliding doors often make access and movement between the two areas easier. In this way your patio could become a natural extension of your home.

SHAPE

Your patio's shape should complement existing features and buildings. If your flower beds follow gentle curves, try to design a patio that mirrors their flow, even if it does mean putting a little extra work into the paving.

STYLE AND FINISH

The way you design and furnish your patio will largely depend on the style of your house, but try to keep it simple. Too much colour and too many plant containers or pieces of movable furniture dotted about can sometimes create visual confusion and a cluttered effect. The key is to link together all aspects of the house and patio so that they blend harmoniously.

If you are not a keen gardener, opt for a low-maintenance patio with hardy plants. There is no reason for the area to look dull: many shrubs, climbers, ground-covering plants and even trees that need little attention are available.

channelled to any drain leading to a sewer, septic tank or cesspool, but can be taken to a rainwater soakaway. A patio that is completely enclosed will certainly need a drainage channel or underground piping to lead off water.

Edging

Brick or concrete paving blocks must be held in place by some sort of edging. However, where it is laid alongside existing structures – such as boundary walls or the sides of your house – edging may not be necessary as the structure will help contain the paving.

Where there are no abutting struc-tures, an edging can be formed with a pre-cast concrete curbstone or by pour-ing concrete *in situ* around the perim-eters of the paving. Alternatively, and more commonly, a brick or block edging may be laid. Bricks or blocks can be set end to end, against the paving, or length-ways at right angles to the paving, depending on the area to be contained. Either way, they should be set in mortar on a concrete strip foundation.

A freestanding brick or concrete block patio will have to be held in place by such an edging on all four sides in much the same way as a brick or concrete block drive (see page 237). Do not lay the edg-ings first, however, as you could end up with an odd-shaped space which forces you to cut a number of bricks or blocks to make them fit. Instead, begin by laying your edging on one side only.

To lay the edging, use a builder's line to mark out the area, and dig an even, shal-low trench around the outside. Lay a strip of concrete for a foundation and let it dry. Butter the bricks and lay them in the usual way (see page 271). Finish by forming a flaunching of mortar along the outside.

Patios made from stone flags or con-crete paving slabs do not need a separ-ate edging, though one could be added for visual effect if required. Bricks on edge make an interesting contrast.

Types of paving bond

Left (reading clockwise from top left):

Herringbone creates visual interest.

Basketweave (parquet) looks neat.

Staggered or half basketweave.

Stack bond is acceptable for paving but not for walls.

Bordered grid for a traditional effect.

Stretcher bond provides strength.

P<small>REPARATION</small>

Common sense indicates the importance of a solid foundation, especially if your patio is planned for a high traffic area or is to form the base for a carport. A solid, level and well-compacted sub-base is imperative. If necessary, get an expert's opinion on the type of soil you are planning to build on.

Soil with a high clay or peat content, making it unstable and highly water retentive, will often need a layer of hardcore, which consists of broken bricks, stones or other hard material. The depth of the hardcore will depend on the instability of the soil and on the use to which the patio is put, but it is usually 50 to 100 mm (2 to 4 in) deep for garden patios and 100 to 250 mm (4 to 10 in) for patios used regularly by vehicles.

The surface of the patio should end up at least 150 mm (6 in) below the damp-proof course (vapor barrier), and should have a slight slope for drainage. To work out the exact depth to which the soil needs to be excavated, add together the depths of the layer of hardcore (if used), the paving material, and the layer of sand on which they will sit.

The soil from a patio site must first be excavated to the right depth and the site levelled. Lighter-coloured subsoil should not be used for levelling – use hardcore instead. Well-compacted hardcore forms

Right: *Different and interesting effects can be created if paving slabs of varying sizes are used. Reconstituted concrete paving slabs, arranged in a neat pattern, have been used here.*

Edging patterns

Left (reading from left to right):

Bricks laid at an angle in concrete.

Curbstones positioned where the public road adjoins a brick driveway.

Curved soldier course edging.

the first layer, followed by a 25 to 50 mm (1 to 2 in) layer of fine concreting sand which can be compacted with a garden roller. Bricks and blocks can be laid directly onto the sand (see *Driveways*, page 235 for details); paving slabs are put down on dabs of mortar.

TOOLS AND MATERIALS

Once you have planned the area to be paved, you can estimate the quantity of bricks required. A useful rule of thumb is to allow 45 clay bricks or blocks for every square metre (38 per sq yd). Concrete and clay bricks are both suitable and available in various colours. For 450 mm (18 in) square paving slabs, allow five per sq m (four per sq yd).

You will need hardcore for the base and cement, sand and aggregate for the foundations, for the edging and for holding slabs in place (see *Quantifying Materials* on page 269) and clean concreting sand for the paving base.

Your base surface must be firm and well-compacted before you start paving. You will need either a tamping or ramming tool, or a compacting machine

Left: *How to break a slab neatly.*

Below: *A brick patio provides a mellow setting for a colourful flower bed.*

(which may be hired in most large centres). For the various other tools required for paving, see page 262.

Step-by-step paving slab patio
To cover an area of 6 x 5 m (19 ft 8 in x 16 ft 5 in), you will need:

150 paving slabs 450 mm sq (18 in sq)
2,650 kg or 53 cu ft (5,830 lb) hardcore
2,100 kg or 53 cu ft (4,620 lb) fine concreting sand, for bedding

Mortar
Cement and sand mixed in the ratio 1:5
45 kg or 1 bag (110 lb) cement
225 kg or 5½ cu ft (495 lb) builder's sand

1 Clear the site of all existing material (soil, vegetation etc) and excavate to an even depth of 150 to 350 mm (6 to 14 in) below the final level of the paving (depending on the thickness of the slabs and the depth of foundation required), ensuring the patio is at least 150 mm (6 in) below the house wall damp proof course (vapor barrier) and that it has a slope away from the building of 20 mm in each metre (1 in/4 ft).
2 Spread a layer of hardcore appropriate to the use (50 mm [2 in] for most patios; more for unstable soils or heavy use) and compact with a hand compactor – a heavy weight on the end of a pole. Spread 50 mm (2 in) of fine concreting sand on top of the hardcore and rake and roll this level.
3 To ensure accurate alignment of the paving slabs, mark out the area carefully with string and line pegs. To lay the first slab, put five fist-sized lumps of mortar on the sand and lower the slab into place. Use the handle of a club hammer to tap the slab into place, checking its position with a spirit level – in the direction of drainage, use a wooden off-cut under one end of the level to ensure the correct fall.
4 Subsequent slabs are laid, using the first as a guide, with thin (6 to 8 mm, ¼ in) plywood spacers between the slabs. As well as the five lumps of mortar, place a thin strip of mortar along the edge of the slabs already laid, which will form most of the finished mortar joint.
5 Check the level of each slab as it is laid and if too low or too high at any point, lift it and add or remove mortar.
6 Lay all the full-size slabs first. At the edges, you will need to cut or shape slabs to fit. Score a groove all around the slab with a wide-bladed cold chisel and club hammer and then tap the back of the slab with the club hammer until it breaks.
7 To finish off, remove all spacers after 24 hours and 'point' the joints with fresh mortar, making sure with a wooden or thin sheet material 'mask' that mortar does not get on to the face of the slab and is well pushed down into the joint.

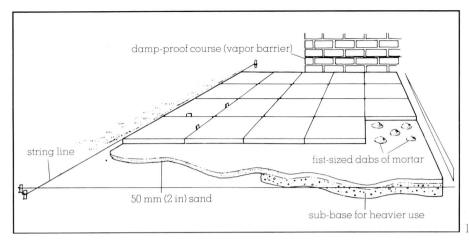

damp-proof course (vapor barrier)
string line
fist-sized dabs of mortar
50 mm (2 in) sand
sub-base for heavier use
1

hand compactor
hardcore
2

plywood spacer
5

3

groove
6

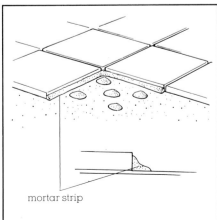

mortar strip
4

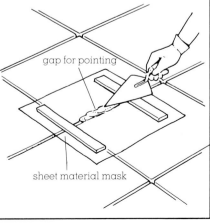

gap for pointing
sheet material mask
7

Paths

Strategically positioned, paths can provide convenient access and a firm surface between the house and other parts of the property or its boundary. They can follow a defined route from the garage or carport to the front door, from a swimming pool, clothes drying area or barbecue to the house, or simply lead to special features such as a pond, a herb garden or perhaps a bench. The pathway itself should be visually attractive but unobtrusive.

Location

Including a path in your outdoor design will usually be motivated by the simple need to link two or more areas, but sensitive planning is essential.

While the shortest route between points may frequently be indicated by a worn stretch of lawn, it may not be the best line to follow. Unless your setting is formal and symmetrically planted, try to avoid pathways which run straight down the middle of the lawn from entrance gate to front door, ruthlessly bisecting the space. Instead, consider curving the path to echo a line of flower beds. If necessary, move the gate to create a less rigid design. But beware of making paths *too*

curved – the result could be that everyone takes a short cut across the grass!

A large site can often accommodate winding paths which lead to alluringly concealed corners and shielded features. If yours is a small site, however, a maze of little paths will simply make the area seem smaller.

Materials

Paths should generally be made of hardwearing materials which are easy to maintain. For safety, the surfaces should be level and non-slip. Taking this into consideration, the most sensible materials to choose are brick, stone or concrete, either solid concrete or

concrete blocks or slabs. Other possible materials include gravel (or pea shingle) and cobblestones. Materials can be used on their own or in combination. Railway sleepers (railroad ties) become slippery when wet, but strips of paving between the sleepers (ties) would solve this problem, and look attractive too. Laying paving bricks in between concrete paving blocks cuts down on material costs and creates interest at the same time. Otherwise, a sweet-smelling ground-covering plant like thyme or minty pennyroyal could be planted between bricks at intervals, to lend colour and aroma.

For best effect, a path must blend with the overall environment. Ideally, materials used should correspond with those used elsewhere in the garden – around a pool, on an existing patio or for any walls. Steps should also be constructed from the same material as any paths that extend from them.

Safety

As well as having a non-slip surface, it is important that paths are safe in other ways. Steps can be a particular hazard and should not be positioned where they might come as a surprise – just around a

Left: *Stone chippings add visual appeal to these concrete paving slabs.*

corner, for example. Both steps and the main path surface should be kept clean (especially if moss or slime start to form) and kept clear of slippery leaves in the autumn. To make paths and steps safer at night, good lighting is essential – either overhead or at low level or built into a wall alongside the path.

Width

Common sense will tell you how wide a pathway should be, as this will largely be dictated by its function. Its width should, though, be in proportion to the size of the surrounding site. To accommodate two people walking abreast, a path should theoretically be about 1.5 m (5 ft) wide. Few modern houses, however, have paths of such generous proportions. The brick pathway in our step-by-step project, which links a pool area with the patio, is 900 mm (3 ft) wide, which fits in well in a site of this size.

The height of the top of a path should be level with or slightly below the surrounding grassed areas so that a lawnmower can be used without damaging the paving (or the lawnmower blade!).

Foundations

Paths do not normally need quite the same depth of foundations as either patios or drives. For most materials, a 50 mm (2 in) layer of sand is all that is required: on clay and peat soils, a hardcore sub-base may be needed.

Edging

Solid concrete paths and paths made from concrete paving slabs do not need any edging, though a contrasting edging could be added for visual effect. All the other main materials (brick, concrete block, cobbles and gravel or pea shingle), however, do need some kind of edging to hold the material in place and prevent it from spreading.

This edging could be pre-cast concrete strips (or, for curved paths, plywood or flexible plastic). For a concrete block path, the blocks themselves can be used as an edging, mortared onto a concrete foundation.

When building a brick path, the most common method of laying an edging is to set the bricks in concrete – lengthways or end to end. Alternatively, a single row of bricks could be laid in an upright soldier course, or they may be set in a zig-zag course like a row of falling dominoes.

Left: *This curved brick path echoes the shape of the wall beside it.*

Paths

Preparation

The first step is to mark the outline of the path. Pegs and string lines can be used for a straight path; for a curved path, a hose or string can be adjusted to give different curves and will help you to visualize the end result at the planning stage.

It is quite feasible to lay a path on slightly sloping ground, but steps (see page 206) should be incorporated if the incline is too steep to use comfortably.

To make a path, the first task is to excavate the site to the required depth (50 mm [2 in] plus the depth of the paving material, allowing for any mortar needed) with a drainage crossfall of 1 in 40 (25 mm/m or 1½ in/5 ft). If required, the centre of the path could be the highest point with a gentle slope equally in either direction. With an otherwise flat path, there should ideally be a fall along the length (away from the house) of 1 in 100 (10 mm/m or 1 in/8 ft).

The sand sub-base (plus any hardcore if required) must be well compacted (hand compaction with a hand compactor or roller is enough for a garden path) before the paving material is laid.

Paths in different materials

You can choose any material you like for a garden path (and you may want to have more than one path, each in a different material), but the guideline should normally be that the material matches another material elsewhere in the site – either a patio area, a drive or the walls of the house itself.

Each material has its advantages and disadvantages and sometimes you may be able to compensate for these by combining one or more different materials in the same design.

Paving slabs
Pre-cast concrete paving slabs come in various sizes, shapes, colours and textures – for a path (especially a sloping path), the smoothest surfaces should obviously be avoided.

Least expensive are the plain square and rectangular designs, but these can be made to look more interesting and attractive by combining different sizes, colours and shapes.

Paving slabs can be laid directly on to sand or, preferably, on dabs of mortar on a hardcore sub-base (see *Patios*, page 225). Edging is unnecessary.

Gaps are left between paving slabs which can be filled with mortar at the end. This is done by brushing on a mixture of 1 part cement to 4 parts sand, making sure it goes down all the gaps and then hosing the surface off with water.

Paving slabs are not suitable for curved paths because of the amount of cutting and shaping involved.

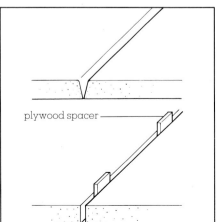

plywood spacer

Crazy paving
This uses broken slabs and looks less monotonous than regular designs. With crazy paving, time is needed to find a satisfactory pattern with minimum gaps and also to adjust the thickness of the sand below the paving since the slabs will often be of an unequal thickness.

No edging is needed. You may need to go over the gaps two or three times with dry mortar to fill them. Crazy paving can usually accommodate gentle curves.

Left: *Plywood spacers are used to hold the gaps between paving slabs until they are filled in with mortar.*

Left: A concrete path is often best in a functional part of the garden.

Stone

Flagstones are laid in a similar way to concrete paving slabs and crazy paving, but because stone is a natural material, it can look more attractive.

Granite sets (paving blocks)

Granite sets are commonly found on older city streets as a paving material, but can look effective in the home as well. You will need to excavate more deeply than with other materials as the sets are themselves thicker; sets are best laid on a mortar bed and the gaps filled with a dry mortar mix as for paving slabs.

No special edging is required, provided the outer rows of sets are put firmly in place first.

Bricks

Bricks can be used for paths, but may need to be frost-resistant. Special, thinner brick pavers can also be used.

The advantage of brick is that it has an attractive finish and can often match well with a brick house. On the other hand, it is a fairly expensive material and is time-consuming to lay. Bricks can either be laid on a bed of sand (see the step-by-step instructions in the next section) or on a 50 mm (2 in) layer of mortar. In either case, firm edging is required to retain the bricks in place.

Concrete blocks

Concrete blocks are generally thicker than concrete paving slabs and come in a range of different shapes, colours and textures. They are laid on a compacted bed of sand (see *Driveways*, page 235) and require a firm edging.

Gravel

Gravel is the name given to sharp edged chippings of crushed stone and the size

Below: Using a mallet to level crazy paving slabs on a bed of sand.

compacted sand base

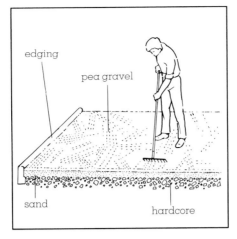

Above: Raking pea gravel evenly across a hardcore base.

and colour depends on where it comes from. It can either be laid loose or bonded to an emulsion base which will stop it moving around.

Gravel is laid to a thickness of around 25 mm (1 in) over a hardcore sub-base blinded with sand (to fill in the gaps). It needs a stone, concrete, brick or timber edging to keep it in place, but even so will need frequent raking to keep an even spread plus occasional weedkilling. It is very suitable for use on curved paths, but not suitable for sloping ones.

Pea shingle is treated in the same way as gravel – it consists of small rounded stones sold in graded sizes.

Solid concrete

A solid concrete path can be inexpensive, but may look dull (and be slippery) unless it is textured by pressing stone chippings into the surface or by brushing as it sets to roughen the surface or to expose some of the aggregate. An unusual and attractive path can be created by adding coloured pigments to the concrete.

Although concrete does not need an edging, it does need formwork in order to lay it. For a garden path, a thickness of around 75 mm (3 in) is sufficient: it can be laid directly onto firm soil, though soft soil will need a hardcore base.

Solid concrete is particularly suitable for making a curved path; here, it will be best to hire flexible metal 'roadforms' to give the correct shape. For details of how to lay concrete, see *Working with Concrete*, page 273. For paths, you should use paving mix – 1 part cement, 1½ parts sand and 2½ parts aggregate – and put a joint in the path every 2 m (6 ft 6 in) or so.

Below: Here a raised pond forms the focal point while brick paths lead off to other areas of interest and elegantly divide up the space.

Cobbles

Cobbles are egg-shaped stones which can be used to create paved areas by laying them in a bed of mortar.

There are two ways to lay cobbles – on edge, where you want to *discourage* people from walking on a particular area or flat, where they are to be used as part of a path or other paved area.

Cobbles are commonly used to break up the monotony of other paving materials rather than on their own.

Paving in a lawn

To create a different effect, individual concrete slabs or stone flags can be laid as 'stepping stones' across a lawn surface. They do not need to be regular shapes – in fact, odd-shaped pieces are often best if the 'path' is to be curved.

To lay this type of paving, holes have to be made in the lawn to put in hardcore and the slabs or flags can then be laid on dabs of mortar so that the surface is flush with or just below the lawn surface. Use the slab itself as a guide for cutting through the turf and then dig carefully to keep the sides of the hole vertical.

Above right: *Using a tamping beam to tamp cobbles into a dry mortar mix.*

Right: *Laying individual paving slab 'stepping stones' in a lawn.*

dry mortar mix

tamping beam

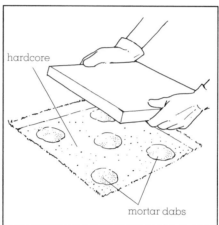

hardcore

mortar dabs

Step-by-step curved brick path

You will need normal bricklaying tools for constructing the edging and a rubber mallet for firming the bricks into place (or a club hammer used on top of a piece of timber). For a path 6 m (22 ft 2 in) long and 0.9 m (3 ft) wide, following our method, you will also need:

Edging foundation

Concrete mix 1:2½:3½ (cement:sand: aggregate) and 1:2:6 (cement:lime:sand) for mortar
50 kg (110 lb) bag of cement
70 kg or 2 cu ft (154 lb) sand
110 kg or 2¼ cu ft (242 lb) aggregate
60 kg or 1½ cu ft (132 lb) builder's sand
8 kg (18 lb) lime
OR 16 ml (½ fl oz) plasticizer
Black polythene sheet (optional)

Brickwork

240 paving bricks
235 kg or 6 cu ft (517 lb) concreting sand

1 First peg out your path and lay string or a hose along the perimeters of the area to be paved. Demarcate the width with loosely laid paving bricks. Excavate to accommodate one brick depth and a 50 mm (2 in) layer of sand, removing all grass and vegetation. To accommodate a stretcher bond pattern, which is the pattern used here, two bricks in each alternate course will have to be cut prior to laying the paving bricks.

1

2 Level and compact the excavated site and lay plastic sheeting over the whole area to be paved. Lay a concrete foundation – about 200 mm wide and 40 mm deep (8 x 1½ in) – along the outer perimeters. Leave it to dry. Using the mortar mix, lay bricks along the edge, taking care to maintain an equal distance at all points, exactly the width of four bricks and to give a fall of around 20 mm (¾ in) across the path.

3 Fill in the area between the edgings with sand to just above the base of the paving bricks already laid. Smooth the sand with a shaped screeding board. Now press the bricks into the sand without mortar joints. Tap them gently with a rubber mallet to level them. If a brick is lower than it should be, pack a little extra sand under it. When all the bricks are snugly in position, sweep a dry cement: sand mixture (1:4) over the path and gently hose down so that all gaps are filled with mortar.

4 An attractive, curved brick path now connects the patio with the barbecue and pool area. The paving design used was stretcher bond, chosen to match both the new patio and other existing brickwork. Notice that all the extraneous black plastic sheeting along the outer edges of the path has been trimmed close to the brickwork with a utility knife. The re-established grass forms a lush green outline for the red brick.

3

2

4

231

PATHS

Step-by-step concrete path

A concrete path is laid very much in the same way as a concrete slab, except that it is longer and thinner and you may well want to make it curved.

Use paving mix concrete (1 part cement: 1½ parts sand: 2½ parts aggregate) laid 75 mm (3 in) thick with joints every 2 m (6½ ft) along the path. A sub-base will not normally be needed except on clay or peaty soil, but one can be used to build up levels if the top soil is thick (excavation should go down to subsoil level). The quantities of concrete and hardcore required for your path will depend on its width and length.

A curved path is likely to be more suitable for most outdoor settings – curves can be made in the formwork either by using metal 'roadforms' or by notching (kerfing) the wood on the inside face forming the curve. For really sharp bends, use hardboard strips secured firmly in place.

The curved concrete path shown here was built in sections with expansion joints between each section. We take up the story as the last section is being laid.

1 A thin layer of hardcore was used as a sub-base 'blinded' with sand between straight and curved formwork.
2 Walking on the sand is sufficient to compact it and the hardcore.
3 Paving mix concrete is shovelled in between the forms making sure it gets right into the bottom corners.
4 A home-made hand compactor is sufficient to compact the first layer of concrete.
5 The space between the forms is slightly overfilled and compacted with a sawing motion of a home-made wooden tamping beam.
6 Extra aggregate is then sprinkled on to the surface and pushed in with a float.
7 A stiff brush and water spray exposes the aggregate to give an attractive and safe finish.

Right: *The completed concrete path is durable and provides a useful walkway.*

5

6

7

DRIVEWAYS

A SOLID CONCRETE, BRICK OR CONCRETE PAVING BLOCK DRIVEWAY NOT ONLY MAKES A GOOD FIRST IMPRESSION BUT ALSO PROVIDES A SURFACE ON WHICH YOU CAN PARK A CAR OR VAN.

OF ALL THE PAVED SURFACES AROUND THE HOME, THE DRIVEWAY IS THE ONE WHICH NEEDS TO BE ESPECIALLY WELL CONSTRUCTED WITH PROPER FOUNDATIONS. IF IT IS NOT, THE NEW SURFACE WILL SOON GET UNEVEN OR CRACKED AND WILL LOOK UNSIGHTLY.

ALTHOUGH IT IS HARD WORK, LAYING A NEW DRIVE IS A JOB WELL WITHIN THE CAPABILITIES OF AN ENTHUSIASTIC HANDYMAN (PREFERABLY WITH AN EQUALLY ENTHUSIASTIC HELPER), THOUGH SOME SPECIALIZED EQUIPMENT WILL NEED TO BE HIRED: A CONCRETE MIXER FOR SOLID CONCRETE DRIVES, AND A PLATE VIBRATOR AND BLOCK SPLITTER (MASONRY SAW) FOR CONCRETE BLOCK DRIVES.

PLANNING

Although the siting of a driveway will usually be fairly obvious (typically between the road and the garage or leading to the front of the house if there is no garage), there are several points to bear in mind when considering the size and the exact location.

For a start, the drive must be wide enough so that the car doors can be opened on either side with enough room for people to get in and out and, if between garage and road, long enough so that the garage doors can be opened and the front gates closed with the car in position. The drive should not slope so much that the car will 'bottom' as it moves from

the garage to the drive or from the drive to the road.

For a drive in front of the house, you will want to ensure that parked cars do not obscure natural daylight and do not obstruct access to the house. The drive should not be so near to the house that the walls can be stained by exhaust fumes and should not be too close to the neighbouring houses.

MATERIALS

There is a wide choice of materials for constructing front drives.

Solid concrete is hard-wearing when properly laid and can be attractive if given a textured finish. Concrete is, however, susceptible to oil stains and although inexpensive is not easy to lay properly, especially on a slope. For information on how to lay a concrete slab, see page 274: a concrete drive needs to be at least 100 mm (4 in) thick or 150 mm (6 in) if on clay or other soft soil.

Concrete paving blocks give the strength of concrete but can be arranged in a much more attractive pattern. They can be laid in rectangular or interlocking 'shaped' patterns (see the diagram on the next page): they are laid on a compacted layer of sand with 100 mm (4 in) of crushed stone as the sub-base. Fine sand is then brushed on to the surface and compacted so that it 'locks' the blocks together by getting into the joints. No cement or mortar is needed, but the blocks must be positioned between firm edgings to keep them in place.

The most common size of concrete block is 200 mm (8 in) long, 100 mm (4 in) wide and 65 mm (2½ in) thick. The four common laying patterns are stretcher bond (similar to that used for a brick wall), parquet (basketweave), 45° herringbone and 90° herringbone.

The two herringbone patterns are good choices for a drive as they give a very strong bond.

Asphalt is often used for drives because it resists oil spills. However, it can be expensive to lay and is a job best left to a specialist contractor.

Concrete paving slabs can be used to construct a drive, but the necessary 'hydraulically-pressed' type and the deep foundations needed make laying a paving slab drive difficult and expensive (see *Patios*, page 225 for details on how to lay concrete slab paving).

Bricks can be used for constructing drives as they are quite strong (especially

235

DRIVEWAYS

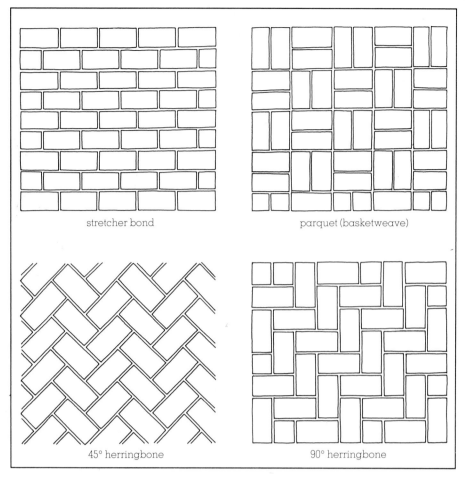

stretcher bond

parquet (basketweave)

45° herringbone

90° herringbone

Right: *The edge blocks of a drive are held in place with mortar.*

if laid on edge) but they may have to be the frost-free type. They can be laid on mortar, but need proper foundations.

Gravel is an attractive and inexpensive material for a drive and easy to maintain as you simply shovel on more gravel. It also copes well with oil spills, but in time can become untidy. Gravel is best used with other materials – perhaps as an oil trap in a paved or concreted area.

PRINCIPLES

Installing a drive means following some important constructional principles.

* The area to be paved must have a firm, well-compacted base to prevent the paving from sagging and/or cracking.

* The drive surface must have a slope to carry rainwater away across and, preferably, along the surface. If the drive slopes towards the house or garage, a drainage channel must be incorporated.

* Drives which are constructed from bricks or blocks must have proper edging restraint to prevent them from breaking up at the edges.

If these principles are not followed, the drive will look unsightly and will be damaged by the weight of vehicles on it.

FOUNDATIONS

Most drives need a foundation of at least 100 mm (4 in) of crushed stone, quarry waste or 'hoggin' (clayey gravel) – do not use normal hardcore. The sub-base must be well-compacted. For concrete block drives, this is covered with a 65 mm (2½ in) layer of fine concreting sand which is compacted down to 50 mm (2 in).

DRAINAGE

The minimum drainage crossfall for a drive is 1 in 40 (25 mm/m or 3 in/10 ft). If you do not ensure a proper slope, water will collect and may damage the house walls. If possible, there should also be a fall of 1 in 100 (10 mm/m or 1 in/8 ft).

The rainwater needs to be disposed of properly. For a large drive draining into the garden or a drive sloping back towards the garage, you will need to incorporate drainage channels to collect it, connected to underground drainage pipes to take it to a soakaway or storm drain – not to a drain leading to a sewer, cesspool or septic tank.

Drainage channels can be pre-cast concrete, fibre-cement sections, *in situ* concrete, bricks or plastic with a metal grid on top.

Left: *A complicated but rewarding pattern known as 'hopsack'.*

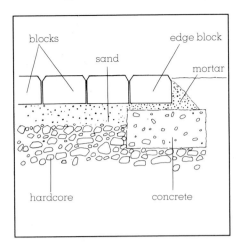

EDGING

When making a brick or concrete block drive, a firm edging, mortared in place, must be provided to prevent the bricks at the sides from cracking or falling out. The edging can be the same material as the drive, or pre-cast concrete edging strip can be used. Either way, it needs to be installed with the correct drainage fall and is put in before the main paving material – which makes calculating the exact size of the drive crucial.

Below: *A brick drive in herringbone.*

SITE PREPARATION

All soil, vegetation (including tree roots) and old drive materials must be removed from the site. For concrete drives, the depth of excavation will need to be 200 to 250 mm (8 to 10 in) below the final finished surface; for concrete block drives around 215 mm (8½ in).

Make sure that the base of the hole has the correct drainage fall from the start so that an even layer of sub-base material can be put down.

TOOLS AND EQUIPMENT

The tools needed for constructing a concrete drive are the same as those needed for laying a concrete slab (see page 274); a compacting machine would be useful for the sub-base.

For a concrete block drive, you will need normal bricklaying tools, but here a plate vibrator and a block splitter (masonry saw) are essential pieces of equipment which you will be able to hire from most major building centres.

Below: *Using a plate vibrator to compact paving slabs.*

Bottom: *It is important to protect the finished paving while using a block splitter.*

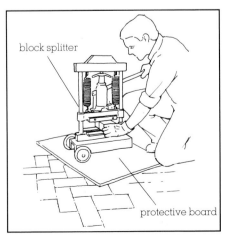

DRIVEWAYS

Step-by-step concrete block drive

For a drive 4 m (13 ft) by 8 m (26 ft), you will need 1600 paving blocks (100 x 200 x 65 mm [4 x 8 x 2½ in]) and:

Sub-base/foundation

5½ tonnes or 110 cu ft (5½ tons) of hoggin, Type 1 base material or similar
3 tonnes or 70 cu ft (3 tons) of sand
67 kg or 1⅓ bags (145 lb) cement
170 kg or 4¼ cu ft (375 lb) concreting sand
280 kg or 5½ cu ft (620 lb) aggregate

Mortar

25 kg or ½ bag (55 lb) cement
110 kg or 3 cu ft (240 lb) builder's sand
13 kg (28 lb) lime
OR 25 ml (1 fl oz) plasticizer

1 Dig out the foundations first, taking care not to disturb any underground pipes or cables. Distribute top soil elsewhere in the garden, but dispose of subsoil and old drive materials. Dig out to the required depth with the correct slope and tamp the soil down firmly with a hand compactor – a large weight on a pole (also known as a punner).
2 Shovel in the hoggin or crushed stone to a depth of at least 100 mm (4 in), raking it out so that it is level.
3 The plate vibrator is then used to compact the sub-base.
4 The next stage is to install the edging blocks which are mortared in place onto concrete 75 to 100 mm (3 to 4 in) deep: careful measurement is necessary to ensure the edging blocks are correctly spaced to take the block pattern between them using an exact number of block widths and also to make sure that they are laid to the correct fall either across or along the drive. A good 'fillet' of mortar should be placed outside the edging blocks so that it will hold them in place. Let the mortar set before moving on to the next stage.
5 The sub-base should be 115 mm (4½ in) below the level of the edging. To estimate the thickness of sand you need, lay a small area 65 mm (2½ in) deep, place some concrete blocks on it and compact them with a piece of timber and a hammer. They should come down to just above the edge restraint. Work out whether you need slightly more or slightly less than this for the whole site and then make up a shaped screeding board which you can use to get the correct thickness. Rake the sand roughly before using the screeding board.
6 The blocks are laid, starting at the bottom of a slope or from one edge. Lay the blocks on the sand base, sliding them down the side of the blocks already

---

Right: *The completed drive has been neatly finished off at the edges and around the central drain.*

in place so that they fit snugly together. Where you are laying a pattern which means that full blocks will not fit at the edges, leave a gap and continue. Always work from the previously laid blocks (kneel on a board) and never from the sand.

The edge blocks can be cut to shape with a hammer and a wide-bladed cold chisel, but it is easier and more accurate to use a block splitter (masonry saw) – mark a chalk line on the block where you want to cut it, put it in the splitter and cut it. Lay all the edging blocks until the whole surface is covered (or for very large areas, until you have done around 10 sq m or 100 sq ft).

Use the plate vibrator to lower the surface of the blocks. It does this by compacting the sand layer and, at the same time, levelling the blocks and forcing some sand up into the joints to hold them secure. If vibrating a partly laid drive, stay at least 1 m (3 ft 3 in) away from the laying face or the blocks will be disturbed. Two or three passes are usually necessary to get the blocks to the correct height; if any blocks crack during this process, replace them with new ones. Finish off the rest of the drive if necessary and vibrate that.

7 The final stage is to brush fine joint-filling sand over the whole drive and make two more passes with the plate vibrator to force this down into the joints.

6

7

WALLS

TRADITIONALLY, WALLS WERE BUILT TO DEFINE BOUNDARIES AS WELL AS TO ACT AS A DEFENCE AGAINST ANIMALS AND OTHER INTRUDERS. WHILE SECURITY IS STILL A MAJOR MOTIVATION FOR MANY PEOPLE, THE BUILDING OF WALLS ON URBAN PROPERTIES IS INCREASINGLY INFLUENCED BY A NEED FOR PRIVACY AND PROTECTION FROM NOISE AND UNSIGHTLY VIEWS. BUT AS WELL AS BEING FUNCTIONAL, WALLS CAN BE AESTHETICALLY PLEASING AND ATTRACTIVE FEATURES IN THEIR OWN RIGHT.

BOUNDARY WALLS

The extent of the average boundary wall may be enough to daunt even an ardent do-it-yourselfer initially. Plan it logically, tackle it at your own pace, and you will find that it is not such an impossible task after all. For novice wall builders, the place to start is with low walls – perhaps retaining walls, dividing walls and screens – and to move on to higher boundary walls and walls on slopes when the basic techniques have been mastered.

When planning a wall around your property, make sure that you identify the exact boundary line and build within it, ensuring that the foundations do not extend beyond the line. If you are having

a new house built, boundary walls should ideally be part of the initial construction. This way it may also be possible to finance the work from your mortgage (bond), thus saving capital outlay later. Suitable materials for boundary and other types of walls are as follows:

Bricks come in a wide range of different colours, textures and shapes. For outside use, you need ordinary-quality *facing* bricks – special-quality bricks are needed only for sites subject to severe frost or extreme weather conditions.

Below: *A low dividing wall incorporating planters and protruding headers.*

Natural stone can be expensive and difficult to obtain as a wall-building material. Although one of the most attractive of materials, it can be difficult to work with if the sizes are very uneven and, for most do-it-yourselfers, reconstituted stone is a more practical choice.

Concrete blocks used for outside walling generally have textured faces with an aggregate of crushed natural stone built into them – hence the term 'reconstituted stone'. The blocks can come in clay brick-sized lumps, as 'multistones' (the size of several bricks with imitation mortar courses already built in) or as random sizes to simulate the effect of building a natural stone wall.

Above: *An ambitious boundary wall in reconstituted stone.*

Screen blocks are also concrete but have a smooth face. They are pierced with an open pattern and can be used on their own to build a wall or with solid bricks or concrete blocks as decoration. Screen blocks are more suitable for decorative, rather than strictly functional, walls.

Right: *Walls do not have to be straight and flat. Here the planters and the gaps between the bricks create interesting and unusual effects.*

Dividing walls

Walls can be used to create interesting visual breaks outside – between patio and lawn, for example, or along the edges of a path or drive. Even low walls can be used to make a site more interesting, especially on a site which otherwise has no distinguishing features.

Higher walls can be built as a windbreak, to screen off certain areas (the compost heap, garbage area or vegetable patch, for example), or to create a private area. To reduce the cost, and to avoid completely hiding the area beyond the walls, screen walls can be made from pierced screen concrete blocks or with 'open bond' brickwork, both of which will let in light and air.

Retaining walls

A retaining wall is used to hold back the soil where a sloping site has been terraced or where there is a difference in level between two parts of the site.

Retaining walls are not difficult to build, but care needs to be taken in choosing the correct materials and in the detailed design.

Left: *A reconstituted stone wall forms the perfect backdrop to this pond.*

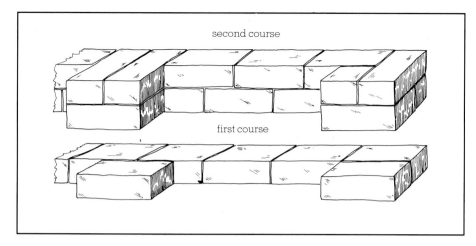

second course

first course

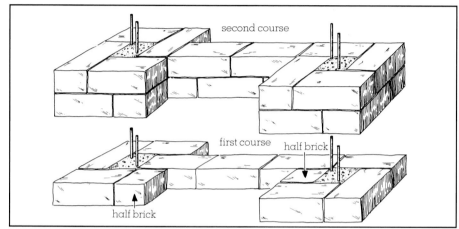

second course

first course

half brick

half brick

675 mm (2 ft 3 in) if piers of at least twice the wall thickness are incorporated no more than 3 m (9 ft 9 in) apart. A one-brick wall 215 mm (8½ in) thick can go up to 1.35 m (4 ft 5 in) high without piers, but with piers of at least twice the wall thickness spaced no more than 3 m (9 ft 9 in) apart, the maximum height goes up to 1.8 m (6 ft).

Piers are built at the ends of the wall, at regular, intermediate points and where additional strength is required – for supporting a gate, for instance. When planning a wall which requires supporting piers, measure out the distance the wall will cover and plot the area where each pier will be built, so that you can lay a slightly wider foundation at these points to accommodate each one.

Building a pier is much the same as building a pillar (see page 216) and reinforcing rods should be provided where necessary. It should also be bonded in a similar manner to a pillar (see diagrams on page 219 for examples of three-brick and four-brick pillars). The opening is then cast full of mortar when the piers are completed (see diagram). When building a very large pillar or pier, or one that would have to bear load, concrete can be

STRUCTURAL WALLS

Building the walls which go to make up a house is not a job for most experienced do-it-yourself enthusiasts. But low walls for a conservatory or garden building are no more difficult than any other type of outside wall, provided a damp-proof course (dpc or vapor barrier) is included in the construction (if necessary tying up with the house dpc) and the design of the wall meets any local planning or building legislation.

HEIGHT AND WIDTH

First evaluate your needs carefully. For boundary walls, 1.8 m (6 ft) is a safe and suitable height from more than one point of view. It would be difficult for the average person to see or climb over such a wall, and it is around the maximum height to which a one- (or full-) brick wall (see our step-by-step project on pages 247 and 248) should be built, according to the local planning/building regulations in many areas. It may be a good idea to consult your local planning authority.

If this height is not adequate for your needs, bear in mind that wider and deeper foundations, expansion joints,

Left: *Concrete block walling can blend in well with concrete block paving.*

supporting pillars and, in some cases, brick reinforcement will be necessary.

Walls below 1.8 m (6 ft) will, however, need supporting piers, depending on their height and their thickness. For instance, a half-brick wall 102.5 mm (4 in) thick (sometimes called a single-brick wall as it is the thickness of one brick) can be built to a height of 450 mm (1 ft 6 in) without piers (except at the ends) or up to

Right: *Free-standing walls need supporting piers at regular intervals.*

Below: *Two half-brick walls built close together to act as a planter.*

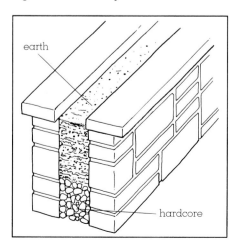

earth

hardcore

used instead of mortar for extra strength.

For added effect, two half-brick walls can be built alongside one another and the space in between filled with hardcore and then earth to act as a planter. Drain holes need to be made as with a retaining wall; for added strength, galvanized wall ties should be used at intervals to hold the two walls together.

Expansion joints

It is essential to provide expansion joints (a vertical joint that extends to the full height of the wall) to allow horizontal movement in walls. They should be provided at least every 6 m (19 ft 8 in) in

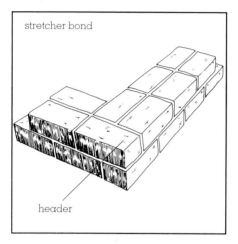

stretcher bond

header

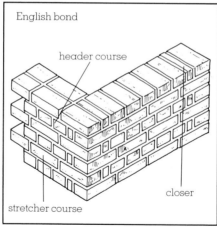

open or honeycomb bond

quarter-brick gap

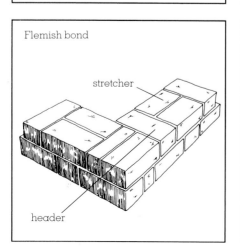

Flemish bond

stretcher

header

walls. The easiest place to incorporate an expansion joint is at a pier.

Bonds

There are a variety of bonds, all of which stagger joints in particular ways, producing different patterns when bricks or blocks are laid. While the visual effect will of course vary according to the bond chosen for construction, the practical reason for bonding the bricks or blocks is to tie them together in a solid mass. An unbonded wall would have vertical joints in straight lines, which would not distribute the load evenly along the length of the wall. It could even result in the eventual collapse of the wall.

Stretcher bond is the most commonly used bond and has bricks overlapping each other by half their length. Bricks are laid lengthways along a double or single line. In a half-brick wall, half bricks must be laid at the beginning and end of every second course to allow for bonding. In a one-brick wall, the end bricks may be laid across the two lines of brick.

Open or honeycomb bond is a decorative form of stretcher bond with quarter- or half-brick spaces between the ends of each brick. It looks attractive and cuts

---

Left and below: *The different types of bond produce various patterns.*

English bond

header course

stretcher course

closer

English garden bond

header course

closer

stretcher course

down on the number of bricks required to build a wall, thus saving money.

Flemish bond is used for one-brick walls and consists of headers and stretchers in the same course. To stagger the joints at the corners, it is necessary to incorporate closers (bricks cut in half lengthways) in alternate courses.

Flemish garden wall bond is similar to ordinary Flemish bond, but has two or three stretchers followed by a header in every course. Once again, closers must be used to aid bonding.

English bond is formed by alternating courses of headers and stretchers so avoiding a vertical joint in the centre of the wall. Some say this is the strongest bond, so it is often used for retaining walls. Closers are used to stagger the joints in the header course.

English garden wall bond is formed by laying three courses of ordinary stretcher bond followed by one header course. Once again closers should be used to stagger the joints.

Joints

When building walls and other features of brick, it is necessary to neaten and shape the joints between bricks. This process, also known as pointing, usually takes place when the mortar is still wet. A variety of pointing tools may be used (see *Tools*, page 266) or you can cut a piece of

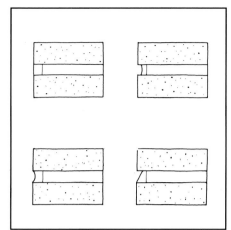

Above: *The diagram shows the four main types of joint. They are (reading clockwise from top left): flush, recessed, weather struck and concave.*

metal and use it to rake out the joints.

Flush joints are quite literally flush with the brickwork. They may be formed by scraping off excess mortar with a small pointing trowel and then wiping clean the brickwork with sacking.

Weather struck joints are made by using a pointing trowel to form an angled recess in the mortar. This angle must slope downwards towards the outer surface of the wall, to allow rain to wash off. Vertical joints can slope to the left or right – but must all be the same!

Concave joints ('bucket-handle') are formed by smoothing the mortar with a pointing tool, a round jointer or a piece of reinforcing metal.

Recessed joints have a section raked out with a piece of wood or metal but, because they do not shed water well, are generally used only inside the house.

FOUNDATIONS

Low (less than 600 mm or 2 ft) half-brick walls can be built on top of paving slabs which have been laid on a full bed of mortar. But for strength and stability (especially on clay or peaty soils), all garden walls should be built on proper strip foundations.

The normal recommendation for half-brick walls up to 1 m (3 ft 3 in) is a concrete strip 100 to 150 mm (4 to 6 in) deep and 300 mm (12 in) wide. For one-brick walls up to 1 m (3 ft 3 in) high, the thickness

Above right: *The first step with foundations above ground is the formwork.*

Right: *Concrete is poured into the formwork and then levelled.*

Left: *To create a strip foundation for a wall, a trench must first be dug out of the ground.*

increases to 225 to 300 mm (9 to 12 in) and the width to 450 mm (18 in). For higher one-brick walls up to 1.8 m (6 ft), the depth should always be 375 to 450 mm (15 to 18 in) and the width 450 to 600 mm (18 in to 2 ft).

To save expense, well-compacted hardcore can be put in the trench first with concrete used to make up the total thickness. The depth of the trench should be 75 or 150 mm (3 or 6 in) more than the depth of the foundations so that the first one or two courses of the wall are below ground level. On very damp ground, you could use engineering bricks for these. The one-brick wall built for our step-by-step project is just over 800 mm (2 ft 8 in) high. A 110 mm deep x 400 mm wide (4¼ x 16 in) strip foundation was therefore quite adequate.

If you are unsure about your site, consult a surveyor or your local building inspector for advice.

Construction

Once you have decided where to site the wall, mark out the area along which it will extend, using pegs and a builder's line or string. The following measurements are based on the foundation built for our wall project; adapt them as required.

Remove all vegetation. Excavate a trench approximately 170 mm (6¾ in)

deep. Knock in the first peg at the lower end so that it protrudes 110 mm (4¼ in) from the trench bottom. Use a straight-edge with a level on top to bring the other pegs to the same level. On sloping ground steps need to be formed in the foundation strip. The height difference in the steps is equal to one or more courses of brick, depending on the steepness of the slope. The length of each step should be equal to the whole number of bricks. Use plywood off-cuts to retain the concrete in the step shapes until it sets. Overlap the steps by about 100 mm (4 in) so that they form continuously bonded structures; otherwise the steps could separate if there is any ground movement. Use a gauge rod to insert the pegs of the next level. Now wet the trench and pour in concrete up to the top of each peg. Leave it for 24 hours to dry.

Tools

Tools required will include most of those in your basic toolkit, the most important items being your spirit level, builder's square and a trowel. in addition, you will need a gauge rod and corner blocks, both of which are simple to make (see page 262); pegs and a builder's line (or string) as well as jointing tools. A tingle (see page 264), which can also be home-made from a scrap of metal or thin plywood, is very handy for keeping your

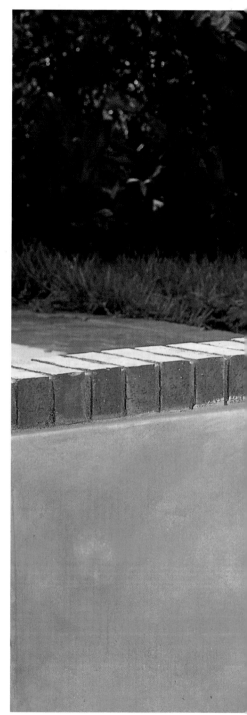

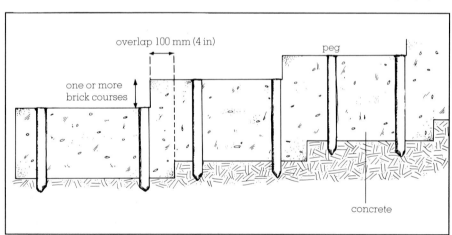

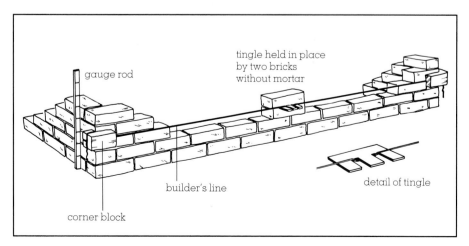

builder's line level over considerable distances.

You will also need a brick hammer (ax) or club hammer and bolster (brick set). If you anticipate cutting a large number of bricks, it would be a good idea to use an angle grinder.

Above left: *This profile shows how, on a sloping site, the trench foundation has been formed into steps, each of which is equal to one or more brick courses.*

Left: *Corner blocks and a tingle ensure that the wall is straight and that the courses are level.*

M<small>ATERIALS</small>

Once you have established the required length, width and height of your wall, it will be an easy exercise to determine how many bricks should be ordered. Remember that 55–60 bricks will be required for one square metre (45–50 a square yard) of half-brick walling, not including piers.

You will need cement, sand and aggregate for the foundation, as well as cement, lime (or plasticizer) and sand to mix mortar for laying the bricks.

Decide on how you wish to finish off the wall – rendering (pargeting) and painting is very effective and attractive.

Above: Although rendered (pargeted) and painted, the wall has a brick coping which maintains the brickwork theme.

Step-by-step one-brick wall

To build a 2 m (6 ft 6 in) long, 820 mm (2 ft 8 in) high, solid one-brick wall, with a foundation 2,200 mm × 400 mm (7 ft 3 in × 16 in) and 110 mm (4¼ in) deep, the materials you will need are:

Foundation

Concrete – 1:2½:3½ cement:sand:aggregate
25 kg or just over ½ x 100 lb bag cement
65 kg or 1¾ cu ft (143 lb) sand
100 kg or 2 cu ft (220 lb) aggregate

Brickwork

Height: 700 mm (2 ft 3 in) excluding 120 mm (4¾ in) facing brick coping
160 bricks
24 facing bricks (for coping)
38 kg (84 lb) cement
228 kg or 5¾ cu ft (503 lb) builder's sand
13 kg (29 lb) lime
OR 25 ml (1 fl oz) plasticizer

Render

16 kg (35 lb) cement
96 kg or 2½ cu ft (212 lb) builder's sand
8 kg (18 lb) lime
OR 16 ml (½ fl oz) plasticizer

Walls

1 Using wooden pegs and a builder's line or string, mark out the planned area for your wall. Excavate a trench as described. Lay the strip foundation and leave to dry.

2 When the foundation has dried hard, set out your first course of bricks, without mortar, to ensure they will fit. Then lay them with mortar, checking carefully to make sure that they are square, level and plumb.

3 As your levels are crucial, continually check vertical and horizontal planes with a spirit level. Lightly tap bricks down with a trowel handle if necessary.

4 When building your end pier, ensure that the corners are at an angle of 90° with the use of a builder's square.

5 For a neat and efficient job, it is important to clean off excess mortar as you work, scraping the trowel upwards against the brick.

6 Although you are buttering the end of each brick as you go, it will be necessary to add mortar between the joints with a trowel.

7 With the gauge rod, continually check that the courses (and mortar joints) are even and regular. Rake out or point the joints with a metal scraper or trowel.

Continue laying brick courses until the full height of the wall is reached. In this project we have also rendered (pargeted) and painted the wall and added a brick coping.

2

1

3

6

5

7

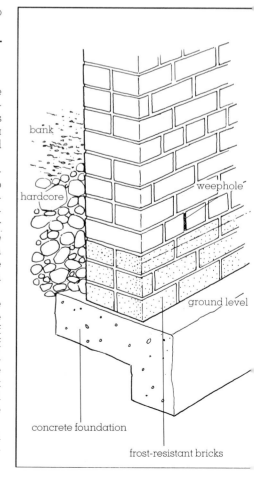

Retaining walls

Retaining walls usually support earth on sloping sites or where one plot is higher than the next. The weight of the soil increases as water collects behind the wall, and earth-retaining walls therefore have to be considerably more solid than free-standing walls. It also follows that the drainage of a retaining wall is of the utmost importance.

Function

On a steeply sloping site, a high retaining wall could be used in the creation of a single terrace offering a good view. Unless you are creating a patio, gradually sloping land is probably more appropriately moulded into several shallow terraces.

A retaining wall can often fulfil a dual purpose, by forming the backdrop to a waterfall or the back wall of a structure, such as a barbecue or a summerhouse. A flat, uninspiring site can be improved by a raised or terraced lawn, or a stylish sunken patio. As a border for a raised flower bed, a low retaining wall (not more than 600 mm [2 ft] high) can be finished or topped with paving bricks or wood and used as seating. A different effect can be created by covering a retaining wall with creepers or climbers, thus turning it into an attractive feature.

Above: A brick retaining wall used to enclose a flourishing flower bed.

Drainage

If the earth behind a retaining wall were to become waterlogged, the whole structure could collapse, with disastrous consequences. Drainage is therefore a critical factor when building a sound retaining wall.

To ensure proper drainage, it is essential to leave adequate weepholes or to install drainage pipes at regular intervals along the base of the wall, thus preventing the accumulation of water behind the wall. Weepholes may be created by leaving quarter-brick gaps in the wall or by inserting a PVC drainage pipe, which is at least 40 mm (1½ in) in diameter.

For major walls or wet areas, it is wise to build a soakaway (see diagram). The space between the wall and the bank of earth is filled with hardcore, consisting of rubble, broken bricks, stones and gravel with the large aggregate towards the bottom. Lengths of PVC drainage pipe, at least 40 mm (1½ in) in diameter, should be inserted at regular intervals in the lowest course above ground level.

If a great deal of water drains through the pipe, it should drain away into a gutter or channel at the base of the wall.

bank

hardcore

weephole

ground level

concrete foundation

frost-resistant bricks

Above: *This retaining wall cleverly matches the elegant flight of steps.*

MATERIALS

It is essential that your retaining wall is strong and solid enough to withstand the lateral pressure of soil and rainwater that it will have to bear. The strength of the wall lies in the foundation bonding and the mortar mix. Tough bonds which work well for retaining walls are the Flemish, English and English garden wall bond (see bonds, page 244).

Facing bricks are suitable for building a retaining wall, as they are strong and durable, though bricks below ground level should be frost-resistant or engineering bricks. For a smallish wall, such as the retaining wall in our step-by-step project, ordinary bricks would be adequate, provided they are rendered (pargeted). A wall which does not have to bear a considerable load may also be built using stretcher bond.

Left: *Here a quarter-brick gap has been left between two bricks to provide a weephole for drainage.*

Right: *A simple soakaway behind a retaining wall will ensure that excess rainwater drains away.*

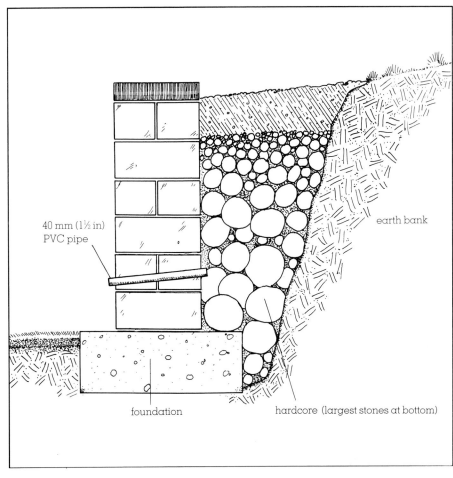

40 mm (1½ in) PVC pipe

earth bank

foundation

hardcore (largest stones at bottom)

Construction

A retaining wall has to be much more solid than the average wall and its load-bearing capacity should be in proportion to the amount of earth it will have to retain.

Try also to keep your retaining wall proportionate to the scale of your garden or backyard – it should not dominate. If the slope is quite steep, it would be better, if possible, to make use of terraces, rather than build one high retaining wall. They will also be stronger, as a result, since each wall will carry less weight.

The higher and steeper the slope you plan to retain, the more critical the construction work will be. Foundations will certainly have to be more substantial than those for ordinary walls. For a one-brick wall up to 1 m (3 ft 3 in) high, for example, use foundations 150 to 300 mm (6 to 12 in) deep and 375 to 450 mm (15 to 18 in) wide.

In some cases, the earth bank will have to be held back during the building process, to prevent it from collapsing onto the new brickwork. Formwork (see diagram) is ideal for this purpose, and can easily be made of timber struts and plywood. The formwork is placed against the face of the soil while you build. A gap of 300 to 600 mm (1 to 2 ft) should be left between the proposed wall and the formwork for easy movement while building.

When the lower courses are completed, mortar the drainage pipes in place so they extend into the hardcore – unless weepholes have been left. On long walls, be sure to add expansion joints at least every 10 m (33 ft) (see page 244). Once the wall is completed, leave the formwork for 24 hours to allow the mortar to dry before removing. Back-fill the trench behind the wall with hardcore and soil and compact well.

Reinforcing

Walls over 1 m (3 ft 3 in) high should be supported by end piers, as well as by intermediate piers, if they are quite long (see *Pillars and Piers*, page 216). Where piers are included in retaining brick walls, it is essential that they project from the face of the wall which is not in contact with the fill. They should also be bonded into the bonding system of the wall and must be the same height as the wall.

Under extreme pressure, bricks tend to buckle outwards. To prevent this, hooked metal rods can be set into the mortar joints of the wall, projecting through the back of the wall into retained earth where they are fixed to blocks of *in situ* concrete, acting as stabilizers.

Below: *Formwork in position.*

Step-by-step retaining wall

For a retaining wall, you need more substantial foundations, so roughly double the amounts of cement/sand/aggregate given for a one-brick wall on page 247.

Otherwise quantities are the same – but note that the bottom three courses of brick should be frost-resistant.

1 Peg out the area to be excavated and mark with string or a builder's line. Digging the soil out may be awkward because of the slope. You may also have to make use of formwork. Make sure the foundation depth is in keeping with the height of the wall as well as the weight which it will retain.

2 Lay your foundation (see Walls, page 245) and start laying bricks as soon as it is thoroughly dry. The number of weepholes required will depend on the size of the retaining wall. To accommodate a pipe you may have to chip off the corner of a brick. We used a PVC pipe, 40 mm (1½ in) in diameter.

3 Finish the wall off with paving bricks. Once all the bricks have been laid and the mortar has set, fill in the area between the earth and the wall with hardcore and soil. Even a low retaining wall will benefit from the extra drainage that hardcore provides.

4 A 50 mm (2 in) gap is wide enough to accommodate a drainage pipe. Hold it in place with mortar.

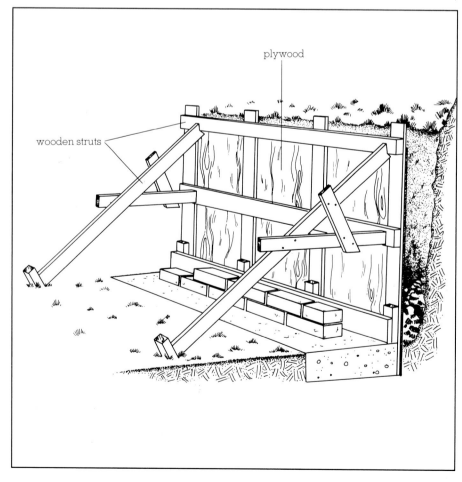

plywood

wooden struts

Walls

Wall finishes

If you can afford a good solid wall – and you can cut costs by building it yourself – make sure the finish will harmonize with the rest of your house and garden. Facing bricks should match other existing brickwork. For instance, a red brick wall should be avoided in a garden with autumn hued paving and it is usually best to give outdoor walls the same finish as the house.

Rendering (pargeting)

Render (parget) may be applied to many surfaces, including bricks and cement blocks. It may be put on smoothly for an even finish; applied in a rough manner to achieve a Spanish-style effect; or it may be stippled manually with a wet plaster mix in a simple stippling machine. Another alternative is to 'bag' the walls, by smearing on a wet plaster mix, so the profile of the bricks still shows.

Render requires the same ingredients as mortar (see page 269) for bricklaying. However, for an exterior wall which will be exposed to the weather, you will need to mix cement, lime and sand in the ratio of 1:1:6. For interior or protected patio walls, a weaker 1:2:9 mix may be used.

Apply the render with a plasterer's trowel, working from bottom to top and left to right (the other way around if you are left-handed). Once you have finished, splash some water onto the wall and trowel over the whole surface. When the render has hardened, continue trowelling it, using water every time, until you achieve a smooth finish.

Coping

Many free-standing walls benefit from a coping to give them an attractive finish and to throw the rainwater off. While tiles, slate, paving slabs or even wood may be used for coping, the usual practice with clay bricks is to use bricks on-edge or on-end, depending on the thickness of the wall. Paving bricks may also be used. Usually a plastered wall does not require a coping, but a combination can sometimes be effective: our step-by-step one-brick wall (see page 247) was rendered (pargeted), painted and then finished with facing bricks on-edge.

Manufacturers of concrete reconstituted stone walling also make single width and double width (overhanging) coping for use with their walling products to enable you to match and tone your colours exactly.

Right: *This brick wall has been finished off very effectively with curved clay coping bricks, which ensure that rainwater does not collect on the top of the wall.*

Above left: *Rendering (pargeting) can make an interesting contrast with the original brickwork. Brick pavers supply the finishing touch.*

Above: *A rendered (pargeted) and painted brick wall here provides an elegant setting for the inset planter.*

Right: *Sloped coping bricks and pier caps look very neat and shed rainwater most efficiently.*

Below: *On this curved wall, contrasting brick-on-edge coping cleverly frames the colourful flowers behind and looks very attractive.*

SCREEN BLOCK WALLS

Pierced screen concrete blocks can be used to provide a screen wall which allows air and light through – either on their own or combined with other walling materials. Each block may have its own pattern or it may take four blocks to make up the design. The block size is generally around 300 mm (12 in) square and the blocks are laid one on top of the other with no bonding pattern.

Proper support is essential for screen block walling. For vertical support, the blocks can be built between masonry block piers or you can use special matching grooved pilasters (into which the blocks fit) every 3 m (10 ft) or less. End pilasters have one groove, corner and intermediate pilasters have two and tee posts have three. For walls more than 1.2 m (4 ft) high, metal reinforcing rods (or lengths of angle iron) should be mortared into the (hollow) centre of the pilasters and reinforcing wire mesh incorporated into every other horizontal mortar joint.

A screen block wall can be built on top of a low masonry wall, or can be built on its own – either on top of paving slabs for a very low wall or with its own foundation similar to that used for a brick wall (see page 247) covered with an *in situ* concrete plinth. No part of the blocks should be below ground.

MATERIALS

To build a screen block wall, you will need normal bricklaying tools and a mortar mix of 1 part cement, 1 part plasticizer and 5 parts sand. Normal cement will tend to give a slightly dirty appearance to white concrete blocks so masonry cement could be used instead – or the mortar joints could be raked out afterwards and repointed with white mortar.

SETTING OUT

Exact measurement is essential when building a screen block wall as the blocks cannot be cut, so the overall wall length will need to be an exact multiple of the block size plus allowance for mortar and the pilasters.

Once the foundations have been laid, lay the bottom row of blocks and pilasters 'dry', allowing 10 mm or ⅜ in for each mortar joint so that you can mark out exactly where the wall will start and end, and where the pilasters will come. Note that the height of three pilasters usually equals two courses of block.

Above left: *A screen block wall can provide a light and airy boundary.*

Left: *Screen blocks positioned on top of a low masonry wall.*

Make up a gauge rod marked with the pilaster heights and the block heights.

Step-by-step screen block wall

For a wall 1.2 m (4 ft) high and 3 m (10 ft) long, you will need:

36 screen blocks
12 pilaster blocks
6 kg (13 lb) cement
30 kg or ¾ cu ft (66 lb) sand
6 kg (13 lb) lime
OR 12 ml (½ fl oz) plasticizer

Foundation

50 kg or 1 bag (110 lb) cement
145 kg or 3½ cu ft (320 lb) sand
235 kg or 5 cu ft (520 lb) aggregate

1 Prepare the foundation with a strip footing 300 mm (1 ft) wide with concrete at least 150 mm (6 in) deep. If reinforcing rods are being used, embed these in the concrete at the correct spacing. Build up from the footing either with a concrete plinth (built in formwork) or with a low masonry wall built between piers.

2 Build the first pier by placing an end pilaster on a mortar bed with the groove facing along the wall. Build up three pilaster blocks, checking that they are vertical and horizontal and using the gauge rod to ensure the correct height. Where reinforcing rods are used, pack the centre of each pier with mortar around the rod.

3 Position an intermediate pilaster block (or another end pilaster block for a short wall) the correct distance away and build this up in the same way. Position a string line across the blocks to mark the edges of the wall blocks.

4 Spread a 15 mm (⅝ in) layer of mortar on the foundations and inside the pilaster groove. Lay the first screen block in place, pressing it into the mortar.

5 Prepare a mortar bed on the foundation for the second block, but first 'butter' the side of the block to form the vertical joint.

6 With a spirit level and your gauge rod, check that the two blocks are level at the right height. If you need to tap a block down with a hammer handle, use a piece of wood to spread the load.

7 Work along the bottom course until you get to the position of the next pilaster pier and slot the last block into place. Build the second course of blocks in the same way and lay wire reinforcing strip along the whole wall from pier to pier. Then build up the piers by another three pilaster blocks and lay two more courses of blocks as before, placing the wire strip in the bottom mortar course. Do not attempt more than 1.2 m (4 ft) in the same day – let the mortar set first.

8 When you get to the required height, finish off the top with coping stones on the blocks and caps on the pilasters and, if necessary, point all the mortar joints.

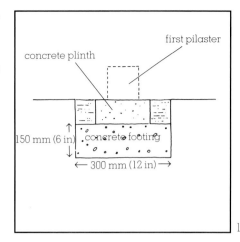
first pilaster / concrete plinth / concrete footing / 150 mm (6 in) / 300 mm (12 in) — 1

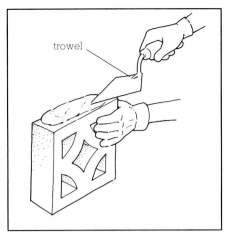
trowel — 5

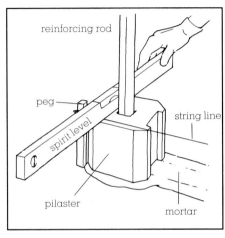
reinforcing rod / peg / spirit level / pilaster / string line / mortar — 2

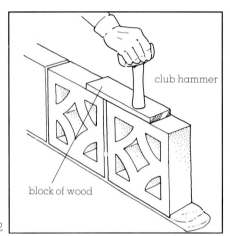
club hammer / block of wood / wire reinforcing strip / mortar — 6

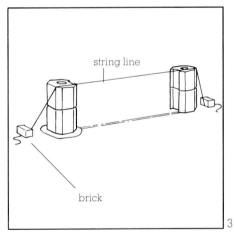
string line / brick — 3

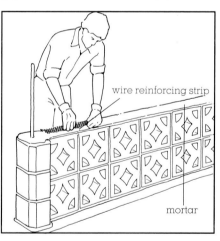
pilaster groove / mortar bed — 4

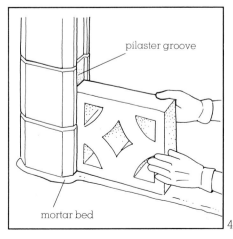
coping stone — 8

GARAGE

A GARAGE IS NOT ONLY SOMEWHERE TO KEEP THE CAR DRY AND
SECURE, BUT IT IS ALSO USEFUL STORAGE SPACE FOR TOOLS AND MA-
TERIALS. ERECTING A PRE-FABRICATED CONCRETE PANEL GARAGE IS
A JOB WELL WITHIN THE CAPABILITIES OF THE AVERAGE HOMEOWNER,
THOUGH IT IS A JOB WHICH IS BEST DONE WITH A HELPER.

Step-by-step garage

The first stage is to excavate the site and
to lay a concrete base 100 mm (4 in) thick
on a sub-base of 100 mm of hoggin
(clayey gravel). This should be at least
100 mm (4 in) longer and 50 mm (2 in)
wider than the garage, but check the
detailed instructions with the garage.
Lay the concrete slab level (i.e. with no
drainage fall) and use a float to smooth a
strip 300 mm (1 ft) wide around the edges.

Use general-purpose mix (1 part
cement: 2 parts sand: 3 parts aggregate);
for a slab of 20 sq m (215 sq ft), you will
need 13 bags of cement, 1,350 kg (2,976 lb)
of sand and 2,350 kg (5,181 lb) of aggregate. You will also need 3½ tonnes or
70 cu ft (3½ tons) of hoggin or a similar
material. Allow the slab a week or so to
cure before building the garage.

*1 Mark out an exact right angle at one of
the rear corners of the garage (using a*
*builder's square or the 3:4:5 method –
see page 266) and start in this corner
bolting panels together. Ensure that
each panel is vertical and that its
external surface lines up with the
previous panel and provide support
until the whole back wall is built.*
*2 To fit a window, use two short panels
beneath the window opening, apply
self-adhesive foam sealer around the
window frame and then slot the window
in place. A lintel is then bolted in place
over the window.*
*3 The frame of a 'personal door' is
secured to the adjacent panels with
coach bolts and a lintel bolted in place
above it. The door can be positioned
either at the back of the garage or in one
of the side walls.*
4 Continue building the walls and then

Right: *The completed garage.*

3

4

5

6

8

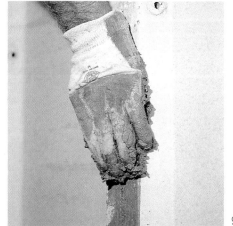

9

start on the roof. A timber wall plate is fitted over the lintel at the front of the garage and timber 'firrings' (wall plates) along the side walls. Steel purlins are secured on top of the firrings to support the roof sheeting.

5 The link arm of the up-and-over (overhead) door is bolted to the front post of the garage.

6 The side tracks for the door are similarly bolted to the garage walls and the door can then be lifted into place and firmly secured in position, following the detailed fixing instructions supplied by the manufacturer with the garage equipment.

7 The final part of fitting the door is to fix the handle and the lock.

8 A general-purpose mastic sealant is used to seal all the joints outside the garage. Additional granules to match the finish of the garage are supplied which can be pushed into the surface of the mastic to camouflage the joints and give a uniform finish.

9 Inside, the joints should be pointed with a cement/sand mortar (1 part cement to 3 parts sand): the mortar should be rubbed into the joints by hand using an old glove and brushed down lightly before it has dried. Apply a cement mortar fillet where the garage walls meet the floor to ensure that there is no leakage and that the garage is watertight.

Small Weekend Projects

There are lots of small projects demanding masonry techniques – many are suitable for beginners who are not yet ready to tackle large areas of paving or a long wall.

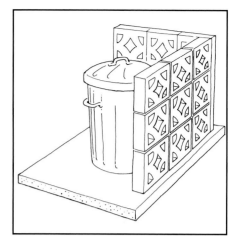

Garbage Bin Surround

Garbage bins can be an eyesore in the garden, but can easily be concealed by building a simple screen block wall three to five blocks high around it. This can also be used for trailing plants but will still allow light through. The walls can be built on their own foundations or on top of concrete paving slabs. You could also add a removable wooden roof, covered in roofing felt, to provide a setting for potted plants.

A more ambitious garbage bin surround could take the form of an L-shaped double wall with a planter in the middle – here constructed from random reconstituted stone.

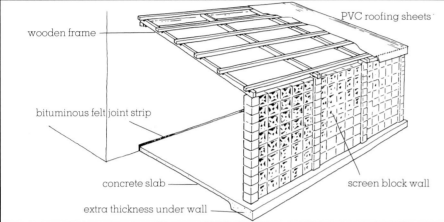

wooden frame

bituminous felt joint strip

concrete slab

extra thickness under wall

PVC roofing sheets

screen block wall

Compost Bin

Masonry can be used to construct a simple compost bin. A 100 mm (4 in) thick concrete slab forms the base; dense concrete blocks or bricks the walls. Leave weepholes to provide drainage and ventilation by excluding the mortar in some vertical joints in the bottom course of bricks. The finish on the concrete should be smooth for easy cleaning.

A compost bin should have at least two compartments and preferably three – one for two-year old compost ready to use, one for last year's compost (to use next year) and one for this year's fresh organic matter.

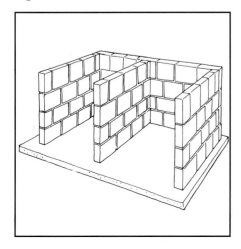

Carport

Screen block walling can be used to provide the support for a carport canopy. The ground slab needs to be 100 mm (4 in) thick concrete on top of 100 mm (4 in) of hoggin (clayey gravel) with the outer edge twice the thickness to act as a foundation for the wall. Use paving mix (1 part cement: 1½ parts sand: 2½ parts aggregate) and follow the instructions given on page 256 for building the screen block wall which must be reinforced with metal rods for added durability.

The roof structure can either be timber framing (as shown) or lightweight metal. Both should be covered with self-extinguishing sheeting (bitumen fibre sheeting). Follow the instructions.

Sundial

A simple pillar, built from brick or concrete blocks, will provide the perfect setting for a sundial. This is an unusual feature which will provide a useful starting point for your building skills.

Detailed instructions on pillar building are given on page 219; if the sundial's own base is square, work out the positioning of the pillar, being careful to make sure that the sundial aligns when it is in the correct position relative to the sun. This is a handy way to tell the time when you are working outside!

Top and above: Two types of garbage bin surround – one built using screen block walling and the other using reconstituted stone blocks.

Above left: Screen blocks with matching piers form this basic carport which has been roofed with corrugated PVC.

Below left: A useful compost area constructed using concrete blocks. Weepholes must be left in the bottom course to allow for drainage.

Below: An attractive plinth and pillar support for a sundial, built with matching bricks and pavers.

REFERENCE INFORMATION

CAREFUL PLANNING IS A VITAL PART OF SUCCESSFUL BRICKLAYING. BE SURE TO STUDY THE PRINCIPLES AND METHODS PROPERLY AND TO EQUIP YOURSELF WITH GOOD QUALITY TOOLS.

TOOLS AND MATERIALS

The basic toolkit required for outdoor brickwork projects (see illustration) is easily obtainable at all major do-it-yourself or hardware stores.

TOOLS

A straight-edge is made from a straight piece of wood, such as pine, and is used to level sand or concrete, or in conjunction with a spirit level.

A gauge rod is simply a flat, straight-edged piece of wood which is marked off at intervals equal to one brick or block plus a mortar joint. It is used to ensure that masonry courses are kept regular. In addition, it can double as a straight-edge and may be used under a spirit level when the level is not long enough or to level sand or concrete.

Trowels are essential items for bricklaying. A large trowel is handy for spreading mortar, while a smaller trowel may be used as a pointing tool. A plasterer's float has a rectangular plate, used for spreading render on walls, and a corner trowel is shaped specifically to shape the mortar or render at corners.

Pointing tools are used to scrape out and shape the mortar joints in brickwork. A small pointing trowel, a special jointing tool or simply a piece of curved metal are all suitable, although each will create a different finish.

Corner blocks are used to string up builder's line as bricklaying progresses. They are not readily available commercially, but are easily and quickly made from wooden off-cuts (see page 268). Metal line pins may also be used.

A builder's square is used to check that corners are at right-angles. If a regular builder's square is not big enough, make one from three pieces of wood, cut in the ratio 3:4:5.

Brickwork Toolkit

1 straight-edge; 2 gauge rod; 3 plasterer's float; 4 corner trowel; 5 bricklaying trowel; 6 small pointing trowel; 7 jointer; 8 corner blocks; 9 builder's square; 10 mortar board; 11 rubber mallet; 12 two brick hammers; 13 bolster; 14 measuring tape; 15 chalk line reel/plumb bob; 16 ordinary plumb bobs; 17 tenon saw (backsaw); 18 scrubbing brush; 19 carpenter's pencil; 20 pegs; 21 builder's line; 22 two spirit levels.

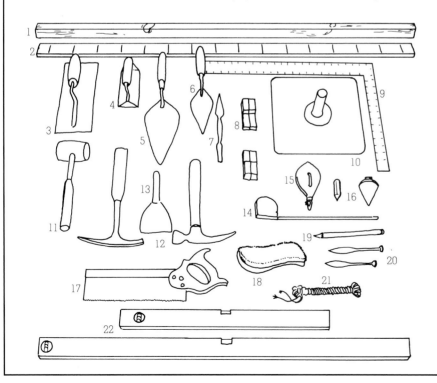

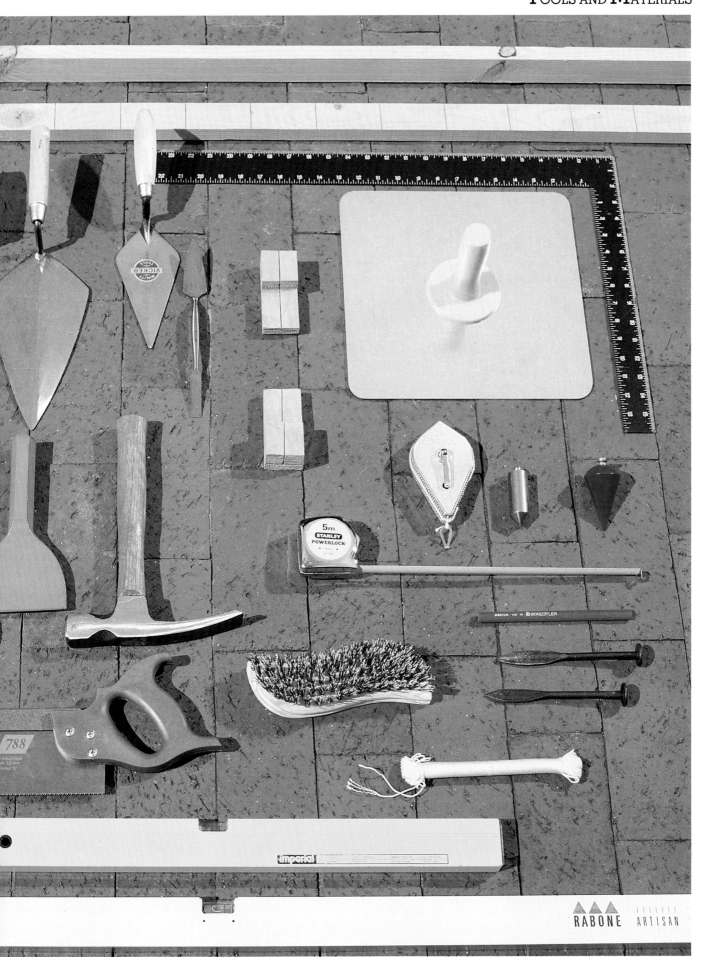

A **mortar board** is rather like a plasterer's hawk and is used to hold the mortar during work. Pieces of flat iron or drum tops make good substitutes for mortar boards.

A **rubber mallet** is used for tapping paving bricks, blocks or slabs into position. A wooden mallet could also be used or the wooden handle of a club hammer.

A **brick hammer** (or **ax**), which has a chisel end, is used for the rough cutting of bricks.

A **brick bolster** (**wide-bladed cold chisel** or **brick set**) has a spade-shaped chisel at one end and is used together with a club hammer (see page 272) to cut bricks.

A **steel measuring tape** is an indispensable item in the toolkit, used for measuring and checking distances, lengths and heights.

Plumb bobs come in various sizes, shapes and forms and are useful for checking that wall surfaces are vertical. The simplest plumb bob is attached to string and may be wound around a piece of wood to ensure it hangs securely. More expensive plumb bobs have a built-in line reel.

A **tenon saw** is useful for cutting the wood used to make a straight-edge, gauge rod or corner blocks.

A **builder's line** or **string** is used with either steel or wooden pegs to mark out an area where building or paving is to take place. It is also used to guide the level of each brick course during bricklaying.

Spirit levels are used to ensure that all surfaces are flat and level. They are available in several lengths with both a horizontal and vertical vial. Individual line levels are also available, working on the same principle as the spirit level, but serving specifically to check that a builder's line is level. The spirit level can double as a gauge rod, by marking off the courses on the underside.

In addition, you will need items such as spades, shovels, perhaps a pick, if excavating hard ground, a wheelbarrow and a scrubbing brush to clean mortar off paving. When long walls are built, a tingle must be used in combination with the corner blocks (see diagram on page 246) or line pins to support your string line. If a number of bricks need to be cut, it might be a good idea to hire an angle grinder or, for concrete paving blocks, a block splitter (masonry saw). Hire shops also supply plate vibrators (for laying concrete paving blocks) and hand compactors (for compacting hardcore or sand prior to laying paving or foundations).

Materials

The basic ingredients of masonry work are bricks or concrete blocks, cement, sand and aggregate, as well as lime or plasticizer.

All of these are available from local suppliers. Pre-mixed quantities of sand, cement and aggregate – useful for small projects – are available from these same outlets in various-sized bags. Alternatively, check your local Yellow Pages for firms which will deliver materials in bulk.

For very large projects, such as laying a foundation slab for a garage or as a base for a drive or patio, *ready-mixed* concrete can be bought and delivered by truck. You must ensure that you have enough people to help unload it and spread it as soon as it arrives.

Bricks may be made from baked clay, cement or concrete and are available in a selection of shapes and sizes, at a variety of prices. The range includes ordinary bricks, facing bricks and thinner paving bricks – as well as highly durable engineering bricks. Your local supplier will be able to give you more information on the types of bricks available.

Although the proportions of ordinary clay bricks do vary a little, it is safe to assume that 60 bricks are required for one square metre (1.2 sq yd) of single walling.

Paving bricks are available in similar sizes to ordinary bricks, but are generally thinner. Remember that if you need accurate dimensions of bricks for planning (or other) purposes, it is wise to ascertain these by contacting the supplying manufacturer.

To achieve an exact match with existing brickwork, the use of second-hand bricks is often a good idea.

Concrete blocks also come in a range of shapes, sizes and finishes and in versions suitable for both paving and walling. Normal structural lightweight concrete blocks are not suitable for use in outdoor masonry (they have no aesthetic appeal and normally will be covered up in house building).

Concrete facing blocks for walling generally have one decorative face which will often include crushed stone aggregate to give a stone-like finish. Sizes can be regular or random – or they are available in large blocks which look like several smaller blocks already with mortar courses.

Cement may be bought in 50 kg or 100 lb bags from local supply stores. Most commonly used is ordinary Portland cement, which is suitable for both mortar and concrete work. White Portland cement is more expensive.

Cement bags should be closely stacked to a height of not more than 12 bags and they must be kept watertight. Ideally, store under cover, on waterproof plastic and covered with plastic, for not longer than two to three months.

If cement becomes lumpy due to damp, it should be used for unimportant work and then only if the lumps can be broken easily in one's hand.

Sand is the fine aggregate used for mixing mortar and concrete. Although it can be purchased in 50 kg or 100 lb bags from some suppliers, building sand is less expensive when ordered by the cubic metre (or cubic yard). It will be off-loaded in a pile outside your house. If you live in

a particularly windy area, make sure you cover it with plastic immediately.

Order 'soft' (bricklaying) sand for making mortar, and 'sharp' (concreting) sand for making concrete. Very fine 'silver' sand is used on concrete block paving after it has been laid, to fill in the gaps.

Aggregate (or ballast) is a mixture of coarser stones used for making concrete. It is available in 50 kg or 100 lb bags, or it may be ordered in bulk.

The important factor is the average size of the stones, which is why commercial suppliers ensure their aggregate is sieved prior to sale. It is available in several sizes. Note that the proportions given below are based on 20 mm (¾ in) aggregate, which is most commonly used for domestic work.

Sand and aggregate bought already mixed is often known as combined or 'all-in' aggregate.

Lime may be added to mortar to increase its binding and water-retentive properties. It is available in 25 kg or 50 lb sacks. Note that agricultural and road limes are not suitable for brickwork.

Plasticizer, available in minimum quantities of five litres (305 cu in), can be used instead of lime. For small projects where it would be wasteful to buy such a large quantity, it is quite acceptable to substitute the liquid soap, that is used for washing dishes.

Water is necessary to mix both mortar and concrete. Only ordinary tap water is suitable, sea water is not.

Reinforcing rods are necessary when building some pillars and piers. Made from metal, they are available from builders' merchants and supply stores.

Below: *A selection of masonry materials, including clay and concrete bricks, paving bricks and various facing bricks.*

BRICKWORK PRINCIPLES

Any experienced bricklayer knows that there are several golden rules when it comes to laying bricks. If your structure is not square, level and plumb, it simply will not have a professional finish and may not stand up properly.

Square

For a structure to be 'square', the sides making up its corners must be at a 90° angle to each other. For this reason, it is essential to check every corner with a builder's square as the wall (or other structure) takes shape. Never rely on guesswork or you will end up with crooked walls and uneven paving.

To set out a paved patio, or walls which meet at right angles, use the simple '3:4:5' method (see diagram). A corner formed in this way should always be exactly 90°. If in doubt, double-check the corner with your builder's square.

Level

It is essential to check your horizontal surfaces continually, including foundations and paving, with a spirit level. If a surface is not level it will slope, and a wall with sloping courses will immediately look peculiar – if, in fact, it stays up at all.

When the bubble is centred, you will know that the surface is level. If the spirit level is too short to use on large surfaces, put it on top of a longer straight-edge or straight length of wood.

Plumb

Applying a similar principle, a vertical surface which is not plumb will appear to lean. All vertical surfaces should therefore be checked continually.

When laying bricks, the simplest way of checking for plumb is to use your spirit level. On the other hand, a plumb bob may be used (see page 264) at corners and when setting up profiles, as well as for building garden walls.

It is not advisable to build when wet weather has been forecast, as heavy rain can wash freshly pointed mortar out of the joints. If this happens, the brickwork should be scrubbed clean as soon as possible to prevent staining. If necessary, use a proprietary masonry cleaning agent. Do not hose down newly pointed walls as the force of the water will have the same effect as heavy rain. If it does rain suddenly, drape plastic sheeting over brickwork to prevent any possible damage, securing the ends away from the brickwork with loose bricks.

Make certain that the brickwork will not receive any knocks before the mortar has hardened. If it is in a vulnerable position, erecting some type of barrier around the structure will help.

Never attempt to lay bricks in very cold weather – less than 3 °C or 37 °F. Remember that even in spring, clear sunny days often result in overnight frost which can damage uncovered work.

Setting out a square corner

Knock a peg into the ground at one corner of the site and measure and mark off 3 m (or 9 ft) to point A on a builder's line stretched along your base line, securing the line with a peg. Now fix a second line at the corner and mark a position 4 m (or 12 ft) at point B on this line and ask a helper to hold this tight at roughly 90° to the first line. With a second helper and a tape measure, adjust the angle of this second line until the distance between points A and B measures exactly 5 m (or 15 ft). The corner is now square and you can secure the line. Repeat for the three remaining corners and finally check that the diagonals are equal.

You can make a permanent builder's square with three pieces of wood nailed together such that the sides of the triangle formed are in the ratio 3:4:5 – say 0.9 m, 1.2 m and 1.5 m (or 3 ft, 4 ft and 5 ft).

Checking level A spirit level is essential for checking that all the horizontal surfaces are level.

Checking plumb A spirit level is also used to check vertical surfaces to ensure that they are plumb. As a final check, a plumb bob may also be used. This can be attached to a piece of wood so that it hangs clear of the brickwork surface.

See page 264 for details of these tools and how to use them.

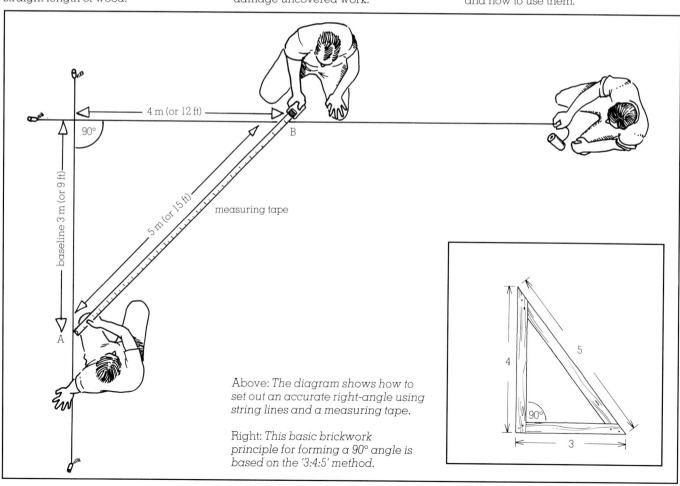

Above: *The diagram shows how to set out an accurate right-angle using string lines and a measuring tape.*

Right: *This basic brickwork principle for forming a 90° angle is based on the '3:4:5' method.*

Checking level.

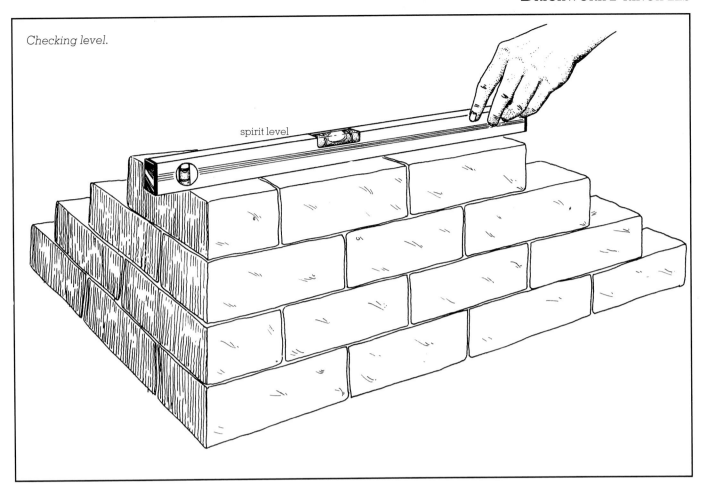

spirit level

Checking plumb.

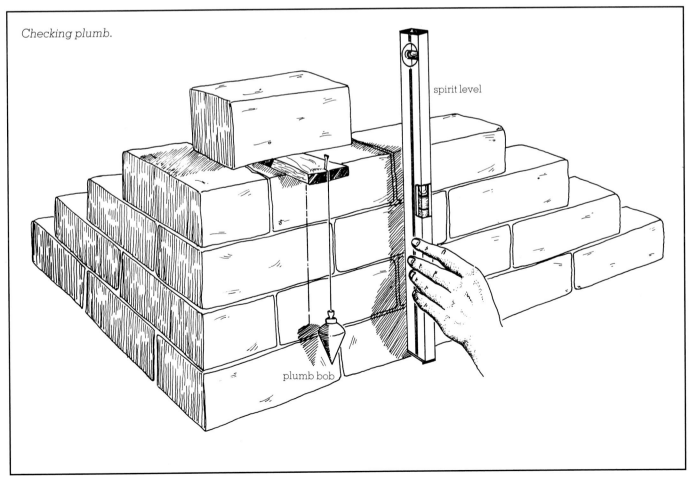

spirit level

plumb bob

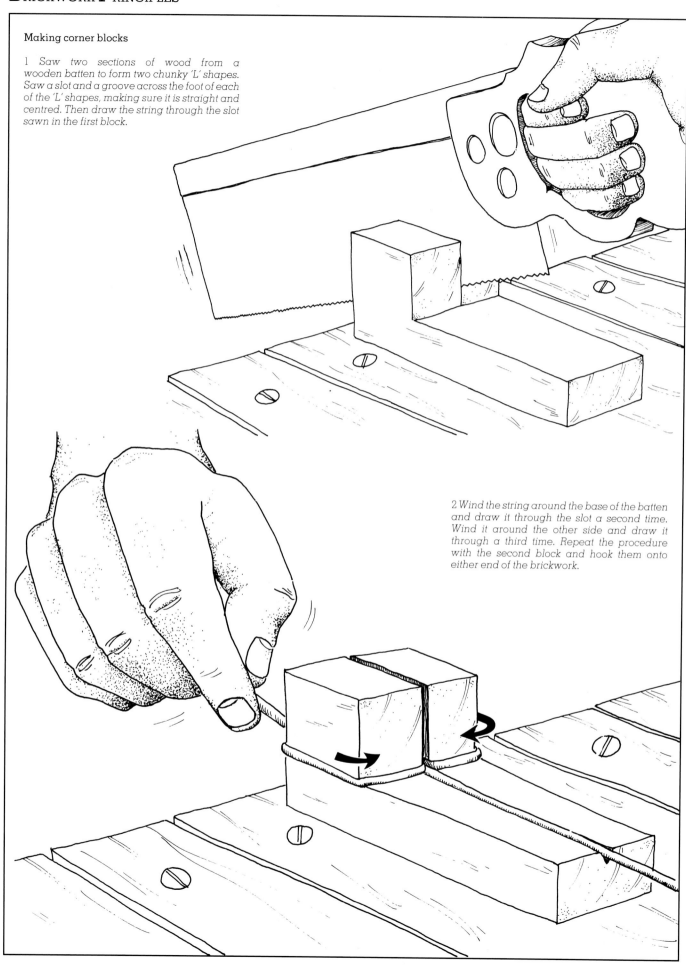

Making corner blocks

1 *Saw two sections of wood from a wooden batten to form two chunky 'L' shapes. Saw a slot and a groove across the foot of each of the 'L' shapes, making sure it is straight and centred. Then draw the string through the slot sawn in the first block.*

2 *Wind the string around the base of the batten and draw it through the slot a second time. Wind it around the other side and draw it through a third time. Repeat the procedure with the second block and hook them onto either end of the brickwork.*

QUANTIFYING MATERIALS

Before ordering materials you will have to assess your requirements. Base these on the following formulae and also use the quantities given with the various projects in this book as a guide.

Bricks are generally ordered in bulk. You will need 55–60 bricks for every square metre (1.2 sq yd) of single (sometimes called half-brick) walling. For every square metre (1.2 sq yd) of paving, you will need about 45 bricks.

Concrete is a mixture of sand, cement, aggregate and water. It is used for foundations, for walls or as a slab for buildings and paved areas in other materials. It can also be used on its own as a paving material. The thickness and proportions required will depend on the kind of brick-work you plan to undertake. The recommended depths of foundations are detailed for the various projects in this book. To ascertain the volume of concrete needed, simply multiply the length x width x depth of the foundation.

Use the following recommendations to ascertain the ratio of materials required. General purpose mix is suitable for most uses, except foundations and exposed paving. Cement, sand and 20 mm (¾ in) aggregate are mixed in the proportions 1:2:3 (1:4 if you are using a combined aggregate). Foundation mix is used for footings, foundations and bases for precast paving. Mix cement, sand and aggregate in the proportions 1:2½:3½ (1:5 for combined aggregate). Paving mix is suitable for all exposed paving, especially drives. Mix cement, sand and aggregate in the proportions 1:1½:2½ (1:3½ for combined aggregate) – or use ready-mixed concrete.

Mortar, the general name for any mixture of cement, sand and water, is used for bedding and jointing brickwork. It is also used in the form of render (parget) to cover walls if required. Mortar mixes vary according to the type of work being done and the strength of mortar required.

A mix of 1 part cement to 1 part builder's lime and 5 to 6 parts sand is suitable for exterior brickwork. One bag (50 kg or 110 lb) of cement mixed as above will lay approximately 600 bricks. For retaining or exposed walls, use a stronger mix: 1 part cement, ½ part lime and 4 parts sand (400–500 bricks/50 kg bag). Plasticizer can be used instead of lime.

Plasticizer Use about 50 ml with every 50 kg of cement (1½ fl oz with 100 lb), in place of lime. For small projects, use the equivalent quantity of liquid soap.

Render requires the same ingredients as mortar used for bricklaying and bedding. For a wall which will be exposed to the weather, you will need to mix cement, lime and sand in the ratio of 1:1:6. For interior or protected patio walls, the proportions of lime and sand may be increased to 1:2:9.

Integral water-proofing solution is available in handy sized packs (2½ litres). Add 1 litre per 50 kg (110 lb) of cement for water-proofing against ground water pressure and ½ litre per 50 kg (110 lb) for general rendering and concrete work.

Mixing materials

The technique used for mixing both concrete and mortar is exactly the same.

First, thoroughly mix the dry materials on a hard, clean, dry and level surface. Then form a crater in the centre and gradually add enough water to make the mixture pliable. When adding the last of the water, be careful, as it tends to become too wet very suddenly.

Carefully mix from the outside inwards, preventing the water from escaping. Too little water will make the mixture stiff, porous and difficult to work with, while too much will weaken it and cause the cement to 'float'. The consistency of concrete should be soft, rather like thin porridge. Mortar must be workable and spread easily.

Consider the weather when mixing materials. Frost may mean that you have to postpone mixing your concrete, and rain could affect your mix dramatically.

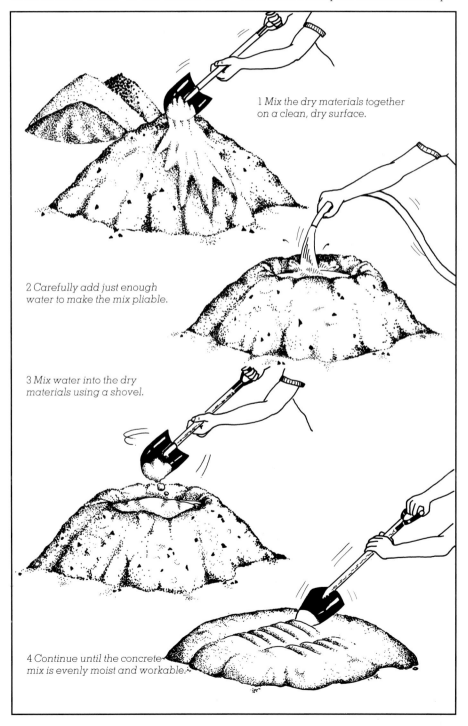

1 Mix the dry materials together on a clean, dry surface.

2 Carefully add just enough water to make the mix pliable.

3 Mix water into the dry materials using a shovel.

4 Continue until the concrete mix is evenly moist and workable.

SETTING OUT SLOPES

Patios, driveways and paths must have a slight slope away from the house or any other building so that water cannot accumulate and undermine the foundations. This gradient may not be evident to the naked eye, since a mere 10 mm for every 1 m (½ in/4 ft) or a gradient of 1-in-100, is adequate along a path or drive, though paths and driveways should incorporate a fall of 1 in 40 in a consistent direction across their width, as well as their length. For patios or paving by the house a slope of 1 in 50 is generally recommended.

There are several ways of measuring a drainage slope, the most usual being to use a spirit level on a straight-edge with a block underneath one end. Read the spirit level in the normal way (with the bubble centred). The size of the wooden block used will depend on the length of your straight-edge and the slope required – for a 1 in 50 slope, for example, a piece of wood 40 mm thick is suitable for a straight-edge 2 m long (or 1 ½ in for a 5 ft straight-edge). This will enable you to establish the correct slope easily and to keep it consistent, so that you can set up your building line along it.

A rubber or plastic hose can also be used to determine a slope (as well as to check levels). This method, which is based on the principle that water finds its own level, is especially useful over a long gradient or around a corner.

To measure a fall of, say, 25 mm in 3 m (1 in/10 ft) take two wooden stakes, each about 750 mm (2 ft 6 in) long. Mark off 500 mm (20 in) from the top of one stake and 525 mm (21 in) on the other. Set them into the ground, 3 m (10 ft) apart, knocking in the first stake to the 500 mm (20 in) mark. Now set two short pieces of transparent plastic tubing (obtainable from some motor spares shops) into either end of the hose.

Attach one end of the hose to the first stake with wire, so that the tubing is opposite the top of the stake. (Note that the hose may be any length for this method to work, which means that you do not have to cut up your hose in order to make it fit.) Fill the hose with water until the water in the tubing is level with the top of the first stake.

Hold the other end of the hose in position next to the second stake, and, with the hose held against the stake, knock the stake into the ground, until the top is at the same level as the water in the transparent tubing. Check back at the first stake and add more water if necessary to reach the required height. Now attach the hose to the stake with wire.

Mark two points 450 mm (18 in) from the top of the first stake and 475 mm (19 in) from the top of the second stake and tie a builder's line between them. This now gives you a guide for excavating to the correct slope until you get down to the two original marks.

Two Methods of Setting out a Slope

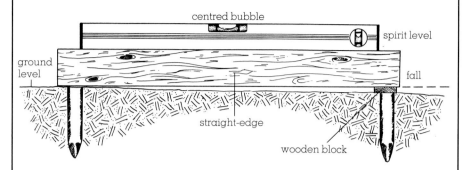

Above: *Place a block of wood under one side of the straight-edge, to allow for the required slope, before taking a regular spirit level reading.*

Below: *Utilizing the principle that water finds its own level, a hose is used to set out a slope of 25 mm/3 m (1 in/10 ft) – see text for details.*

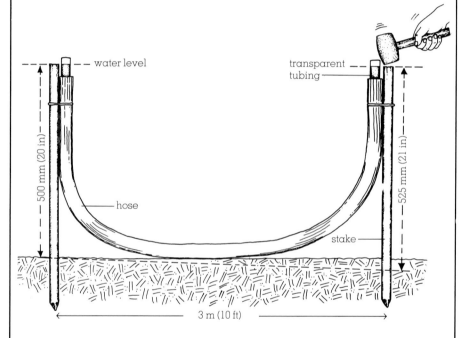

Marking out a Circle

Below: *Knock a peg into the ground at a central point; attach a piece of string with a stick fixed to the other end; pull the string taut across the radius and then mark the circle in the ground with the stick.*

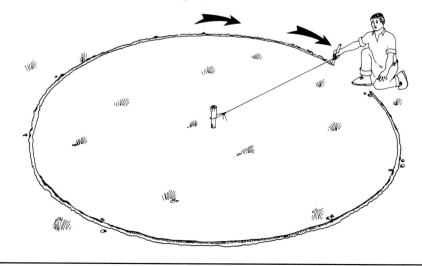

BRICKLAYING TECHNIQUES

Before attempting to lay bricks, it is important to practise using a trowel, as you will need it to form a bed of mortar for your first, most important course and thereafter to spread and butter the bricks with mortar as the wall takes shape.

Bedding bricks in mortar is what bricklaying is all about. Once your concrete foundation is thoroughly dry, set out your first course of bricks without mortar, to ensure they fit. Mix your mortar, in manageable amounts, on a firm, dry surface and pick up a small amount by pushing your trowel sideways into the mixture, then lifting it. Lay a sausage-shaped bed of mortar, 10 to 12 mm (approximately ½ in) thick and 100 mm (4 in) wide, along the line where your first course of bricks will be laid. To ensure that all your walls will be straight, you need to lay a builder's square along the slightly flattened lines of mortar. With the point of a trowel, draw a straight line in the mortar to indicate where the outer edge of the bricks will be. Remove the square and run a furrow down the centre of the mortar to allow better bonding with the first course of bricks.

You can either butter the ends as you work (see below), or fill in the gaps between the bricks once they have been laid. Lay the first brick, using the line and the furrow in the mortar as a guide. Follow the pattern shown when the bricks were laid without mortar and lay the first course of bricks. Continue to spread mortar on each subsequent course, scraping excess mortar off the sides of the brickwork as you press and tap each one into place until it is level.

Set up corner blocks or line pins with a builder's line to help maintain a straight edge. Each corner brick or block must be checked for height with the gauge rod. The vertical and horizontal levels are then checked with the spirit level, adding (or removing) mortar from under the bricks if necessary. Use a builder's square to double check that all corners are at right angles. These safeguards will ensure that you do not end up with lopsided walls. If you find that any bricks are lying skew, tap them gently into place with the handle of your bricklaying trowel. Fill any gaps between bricks with mortar before you lay the second course of bricks.

Using your spirit level and gauge rod, check your levels and planes continually. This is essential because any discrepancies will soon become obvious and may also make your brickwork unstable and thus dangerous.

Check all surfaces throughout to ensure vertical walls. If your corners are skew, the entire structure will be out of alignment. Place the spirit level diagonally against the bricks as well as in a horizontal and vertical position.

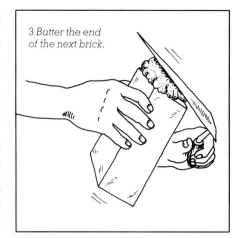

3 Butter the end of the next brick.

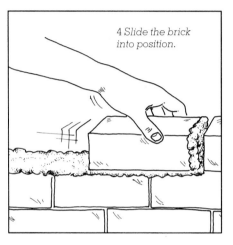

4 Slide the brick into position.

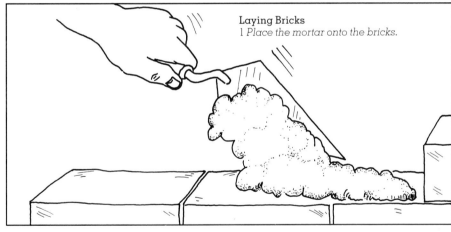

Laying Bricks
1 Place the mortar onto the bricks.

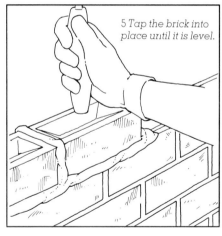

5 Tap the brick into place until it is level.

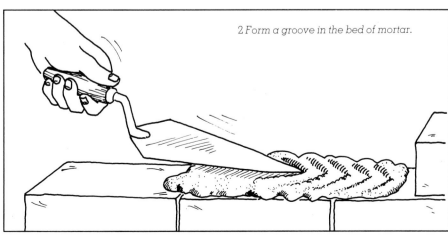

2 Form a groove in the bed of mortar.

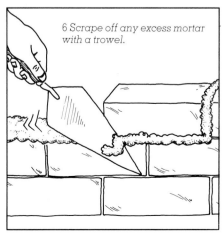

6 Scrape off any excess mortar with a trowel.

BRICKLAYING TECHNIQUES

Buttering bricks is an art which must be mastered before any large-scale bricklaying can be done. To do this, lift a small amount of mortar with the trowel and spread it onto the end of the brick to be laid. Squash the mortar down firmly to ensure it does not drop off and then lay the brick in place.

Cutting bricks manually is relatively simple once you acquire the knack. This can be done with a brick hammer (ax) or with a bolster (wide-bladed cold chisel or brick set) and a club hammer. To cut a brick with a brick hammer (ax), hold the brick in your hand and, using the chisel end, tap a line all around the brick where you want it to break. A final, sharp blow on this cutting line should result in its breaking evenly along the line.

To use a bolster, place the brick on the ground (ideally on a bed of sand) and score the surface on all sides with the chisel end. Then hold the bolster firmly on the cutting line and gently tap the handle several times with the club hammer. Once again, a final, sharp blow should result in its breaking neatly in two.

Right: *Cutting a brick with a bolster (chisel) and a club hammer.*

Below: *Cutting a brick with the chisel end of a brick hammer (ax).*

WORKING WITH CONCRETE

The basic ingredients of concrete are cement, sand and aggregate – see page 269 for details of the different mixes.

When the dry ingredients of concrete are mixed with water, a reaction starts, causing the cement particles to stick to one another, to the sand and aggregate particles and to anything else such as surrounding brick – and even metal (including your concreting tools if you do not clean them!).

Concrete takes some time to set once it has been mixed. Unless retardants have been used, it remains 'workable' for between 1½ and 2 hours but it takes three days before it has any useful strength. After seven days, concrete will have two-thirds of its ultimate strength – it is then important to prevent it from drying out. This can be done by covering it with polythene or damp sacking and, if it is very dry, by spraying it with water – the hardening process is one of curing rather than one of drying out.

Laying concrete

Details of mixing, site preparation and foundations are covered elsewhere in this book. Here, we look at the actual process of laying the concrete once it is mixed and ready to use.

Except where concrete is being poured into a prepared trench, formwork is essential to hold it in place while it cures. Normally, this will be lengths of wood securely held in place and with no gaps at the corners or the edges through which stray concrete could escape. Formwork can either be wood (at least 25 mm or 1 in thick) held in place with pegs firmly driven into the ground, or special steel 'roadforms' – these are particularly useful for making curved areas.

Concrete is placed on the prepared site by upending a wheelbarrow (taking care not to damage the sides of a trench or the formwork) or from the chute leading to a ready-mix delivery truck. Shovels are used to spread it evenly over the site allowing a little for compaction.

Compaction itself can be carried out either with a hand compactor (suitable for stiffer concrete used in trenches) or with a tamping beam – a length of 50 x 150 mm (2 by 6 in) wood held on edge. This is used in a sawing motion across the area – not simply dragged along the tops of the side forms. If the concrete still shows an open texture, it is undercompacted and more concrete should be shovelled on and the process repeated.

Concrete finishes

Concrete can be finished in several different ways.

If left as tamped, it will have a level but rippled finish – depending on how well the tamping was carried out. If the leading edge of the tamping beam is slightly raised during the final tamping, a slightly rippled but otherwise smooth struck-off

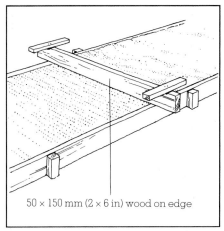

50 × 150 mm (2 × 6 in) wood on edge

Above left and right: *Compaction can either be carried out with a hand compactor or with a tamping beam – a straight length of wood.*

---

finish will be produced on the concrete.

A soft broom can be used to give a fairly smooth finish while a stiff nylon broom will give a pronounced 'corduroy' texture, which is especially suitable for paths and drives.

An exposed aggregate finish can be produced by spreading loose coarse aggregate on the fresh concrete after initial tamping and then tamping this firmly in with a float. When the concrete has

hardened a little, brush and spray the surface with water which leaves the aggregate exposed, highlighting its colour and texture. Finish off with a stiff broom 24 hours later.

A fine sandpaper-like finish can be produced on concrete by using a wooden float on the surface before it has gone off, while a steel float, if kept clean, will give a very smooth finish.

Below: *Various finished surface effects can be produced on concrete. Decide whether you wish to have a smooth or rough look and you can then choose your method accordingly.*

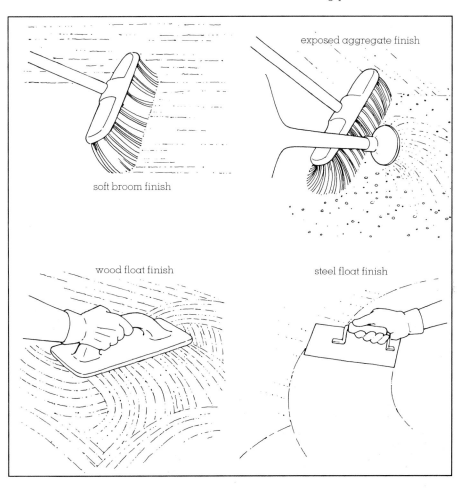

exposed aggregate finish

soft broom finish

wood float finish

steel float finish

3

Step-by-step concrete slab

The concrete slab and surround foundation shown here were the basis for a paving slab patio and concrete brick wall surround. Because the ground was soft, concrete foundations were used and, because a large quantity was needed, we used ready-mixed concrete (Mix C7.5P to BS5238, high workability, 20 mm maximum aggregate).

The patio measured 4.05 m (13 ft 4 in) × 2.25 m (7 ft 5 in) and a 600 mm (2 ft) wide foundation was used for the walls. 50 mm (2 in) of hardcore was used for both the foundation and the patio sub-base and 50 mm (2 in) of fine concreting sand for the patio. The materials you will need to construct this concrete slab are:

1

Patio sub-base
790 kg or 15.8 cu ft (1738 lb) hardcore
632 kg or 15.8 cu ft (1390 lb) fine concreting sand
0.68 cu m (24 cu ft) ready-mixed concrete

Wall foundation
510 kg or 10.2 cu ft (1122 lb) hardcore
0.87 cu m (30.7 cu ft) ready-mixed concrete

1 The prepared site showing turf and topsoil removed and trenches dug for the foundation with depth pegs in place around the edge of the patio area.
2 Formwork erected around the slab, hardcore put in place and well-compacted and the patio surface 'blinded' with sand which is then rolled out level.
3 Help is at hand for shovelling the ready-mixed concrete directly from the delivery lorry into the foundation trenches up to the level of the pegs. It is important to work quickly at this point before the concrete sets or the weather conditions change.
4 More ready-mixed concrete is shovelled into the patio area and levelled off with a tamping beam using the formwork as a guide.
5 The formwork is left in place until the compacted concrete sets hard. It can then be removed altogether.

2

4

5

Additives Chemicals added to mortar and concrete mixes to improve their performance. The commonest include plasticisers, waterproofers and frostproofers.

Aggregate Sand or gravel added to cement to make mortar or concrete respectively. In Britain the term is normally used for all-in aggregate (also known as hoggin), a mixture of sand and gravel mixed with cement to make concrete. In South Africa, all-in aggregate refers to inferior material which should not be used.

Auger Machine or hand tool used to bore holes in the ground.

Bargeboard Timber used to neaten the edge of a roof at the gable ends of a building.

Basketweave bond A pattern used when laying block pavers, consisting of pairs of blocks which are laid at right angles to adjacent pairs.

Batching Method of measuring materials for one batch of concrete, mortar or render.

Batten Lengths of timber commonly used as part of a roof structure.

Batter frame A home-made timber building guide used in the construction of dry-stone walls to ensure an even backward slope to the wall face.

Baulk A stout length of timber.

Beading Narrow moulding for neatening edges.

Beam Squared timber used horizontally at the base of a roof structure and supported at both ends.

Bearer Large supporting beam or girder used at the base of a floor structure.

Bedding plane The lines of natural stratification in sedimentary rocks.

Bitumen Tar-like substance used to protect and waterproof timber.

Blinding layer A layer of sand used to cover a base of hardcore or crushed stone.

Block paver A reconstituted stone or concrete paving block designed to be dry-laid on a bed of sand in a variety of different interlocking patterns such as basket-weave, herringbone or running bond.

Bolster A steel chisel with a wide blade, used for cutting stone blocks and slabs in conjunction with a club hammer.

Bond The arrangement of blocks in a wall, designed to increase the wall's strength as well as to enhance its appearance.

Bore Hollow part of piping; term used in relation to internal diameter.

Bricklaying sand Masonry sand.

Bricklaying trowel (mason's trowel) A broad-bladed tool used for spreading mortar when laying masonry or paving.

Builder's square A rough wooden triangle made up from sawn timber with sides in the ratio 3:4:5, and is used to check the squareness of masonry and concrete. Metal squares are used for fine work.

Buttering Technique used to apply mortar or adhesive to tiles or bricks.

Carriage (trucking) costs The charge made for delivery of stone from a quarry or other supplier.

Cement The adhesive from which mortar and concrete are made. Portland cement is the commonest type. It is usually sold in 50 kg (112 lb) bags, although smaller sizes are also available.

Chestnut paling Snow fence - split pole fence.

Chicken-wire Wire netting with a hexagonal mesh, traditionally used to fence-in chickens. Useful for DIY concrete ponds.

Chipboard A man-made constructional board formed by binding wood chips together with resin. Exterior-grade board is essential if to be used outside.

Chisel An all-steel tool with a wedge-shaped or pointed cutter, made in a range of sizes and used to cut and shape masonry in conjunction with a club hammer.

Chop saw Bench-top mitre saw - cut off saw.

Circular saw Skil saw.

Cladding Material used to cover and finish the timber framework of dry walling.

Clout nails A galvanised nail with a large flat head, mainly used to fix sheet roofing materials. Also known as roofing nails.

Club hammer (lump hammer) A hammer with a heavy squared-off head and a short wooden handle, used to drive masonry chisels and similar tools.

Coach bolts Carraige bolts.

Cobbles Small rounded pebbles set in mortar to form a path or other decorative surface detail.

Cold-roll macadam Macadam pre-packed in bags and specially formulated for laying when cold, unlike ordinary macadam which is laid hot.

Concrete A mixture of cement, sand and gravel (all-in aggregate) or crushed stone, used to cast foundations and slabs. It can be mixed by hand from dry ingredients, or ordered ready-mixed.

Coping stones Flat or ridged stones used to weatherproof the top of masonry walls. A coping can also be formed by a course of blocks laid on edge.

Course A continuous row of bricks. Several courses form a wall.

Coverband A stone spanning the width of a dry-stone wall, laid immediately before the coping stones.

Crazy paving (random paving) Paving consisting of irregularly-shaped pieces set on a mortar bed and pointed.

Crushed bark Shredded bark or wood chips used to discourage weed growth or to act as an informal path surface.

Curing Keeping concrete or mortar moist to ensure a chemical reaction which gives it strength as it hardens.

DPC or Damp-proof course (vapor barrier) A layer of impervious material incorporated in a masonry structure to prevent dampness rising into it from the ground.

Dressing The process of shaping the faces of a piece of quarried stone.

Dry wall A timber-framed wall which, unlike conventional brick and block walls, does not involve any 'wet' work (bricklaying, etc) during construction.

Facebrick Clay or concrete brick manufactured for use without plaster.

Fascia Timber used to neaten the back and front of buildings at the ends of rafters; this is the surface to which gutters are usually affixed.

Fibrecement Material composed of cement, organic fibres and sometimes a small percentage of asbestos, which can be moulded to form pond shells, fountain features and pot plant containers.

Flagstone (stone paver) A large square or rectangular slab of natural or man-made stone used for paving.

Flashing Waterproofing which seals the joins between the roof and protrusions.

Flat bit Space bit.

Formwork (shuttering) Timber used to support the edges of concrete slabs, paths etc while the concrete is placed. The boards making the formwork are nailed to stout pegs.

Foul water drain Underground pipework carrying water from household plumbing equipment.

Foundations Cast concrete strips or slabs laid to support walls and other stone garden structures.

Galvanise Method used to coat iron with zinc to stop it from rusting.

Granite The commonest of the igneous stones, very dense and hard and widely used in the form of setts for paving.

Hardcore Crushed stone, broken brick, concrete etc used as an infill and support beneath concrete foundations on clay or other unstable ground.

Hardwood Botanical classification identifying broad-leafed species of trees.

Header Brick laid with face at right angles to the wall. Also head or short side of a brick.

Hearting (pinning or chinking) Small stones used to pack the heart of a dry-stone wall.

Herringbone bond A pattern used when laying block pavers. Each block is laid at 90° to its neighbour, and overlaps it by half the length of the block.

Hiring (renting) An alternative to buying tools and equipment, often more economical for seldom-used items.

Hoggin See Aggregate.

Honeycomb wall A supporting wall built with gaps between the building blocks to save on materials where the wall structure is subsequently hidden, as within a flight of steps.

Interference or Interlap fencing Alternate board - board and board.

J-Bolt Anchor bolt.

Jointing Method used to neaten the joints in brickwork where facebricks are used.

Limestone A sedimentary stone consisting mainly of calcium carbonate, widely used for all sorts of garden stonework.

Masonry cement Ordinary Portland cement with added plasticiser.

MDF/Medium Density Fibreboard MDO/Medium Density Overlay. Constructional board made by bonding wood fibres with resins. Exterior grade board for use outside. Also known as chipboard.

Micro-porous paint Latex stain.

Mortar A mixture of sand and cement with added plasticiser, used for building walls and bedding paving slabs.

mpa (mega pascals) Units to measure the compressive strength of concrete.

Nail punch Nail set.

pH Degree of acidity or alkalinity of water, measured on a scale from 0-14.

Paver (patio paver) A man-made hydraulically-pressed paving slab or block.

Pier A thickened section of masonry built at the ends of a wall and at intervals along its length for extra support.

Piling Post driven into soft sand to support a structure. For pile foundations, holes are bord into the ground and filled with reinforced concrete.

Planed timber Dimensional lumber - PAR timber.

Planning permission Zoning approval.

Plant hire firm Equipment rental company.

Plaster Protective coating applied to bare brick or cement block walls. Some refer to plaster as a cement and sand mixture (see render), in parts of the world it refers only to gypsum plasters.

Pointing The use of mortar to fill and finish the joints in walls and areas of rigid paving.

Pole-building Term used for construction using a framework of posts set in the ground.

Plumb Flat, vertical plane.

Polyethylene Polymerized material, including polythene, often referred to as 'plastic'.

Post anchor Metal base set in a concrete foundation to anchor timber posts.

Preservative-treated timber (pressure-treated lumber) Wood that has been pre-treated with wood preservative.

Plywood Constructional board made by bonding thin plies of wood together. Exterior grade is essential if to be used outside.

Prime Procedure used to make some pumps start working. Certain surfaces must also be primed before being painted.

Punner Ramming tool used to compact earth or hardcore.

PVC Abbreviation for polyvinyl chloride, a thermoplastic made from a polymer of vinyl chloride.

Railway sleepers Railroad ties.

Re-decorate Re-paint externally.

Render coat (stucco coat) A coat of mortar applied to a masonry surface to weatherproof or decorate it.

Ridged roof Pitched roof.

Riven stone (splitface stone) Stone with a natural rough face, not dressed.

Running bond A pattern used when laying block pavers. The blocks are laid end to end throughout with joints in adjacent rows staggered, imitating stretcher-bond brickwork.

Sand Fine aggregate, graded as fine or soft sand used in mortar, or as coarse or sharp sand used in making concrete.

Sandstone A sedimentary stone consisting of fine or coarse particles of quartz bound together by a cement of other minerals, widely used for paving and walling projects.

Screed A smooth mortar layer spread over concrete to create a flat surface.

Scutch holder A chisel-type tool consisting of a metal holder into which a variety of cutting edges - the scutches – are fitted; used when cutting stone to shape.

Services Utilities.

Sett A small square block of stone, usually granite, used for paving.

Shingle (pea gravel) Clean washed gravel, used as a path surface or for other decorative purposes.

Shuttering Framework of wood or steel, erected as a temporary support for concrete to be cast on site.

Silver sand Sharp sand - river sand.

Slate A metamorphic stone formed by the action of heat and pressure on clay, used mainly for paving and walling.

Softwood Botanical specification identifying conifers.

Spanner Wrench.

Spirit level Level.

Stack bond A blocklaying bond used chiefly with square screen walling blocks.

Stretcher bond A building bond consisting of a single skin of walling blocks, overlapping each other by half their length in successive courses.

Stud Vertical post of timber-frame houses and panelling.

Stud frame Framework for dry walling or partitions made with studs and rails.

Tamp down Compact.

Tarmacadam (asphalt or black top) A mixture of crushed stone and tar used for paths and other surfaces.

Through stones Long stones running the whole width of a dry-stone wall.

Timber Lumber.

Timber cladding Clapboarding.

Timber mechant Lumber yard.

Try square Carpenter's square.

Turf Sod.

Waney-edged board Rough sawn plank.

Water head The height a pump can spurt from the surface of the water in a pond or pool.

Weep holes Unpointed gaps left between the blocks in retaining walls to allow drainage to occur through the wall.

Willow hurdle Woven sapling fencing.

SUPPLIERS

UK

Aquatek
33 Bruce Grove
North Watford
WD2 5AQ
Tel: 01923 246312

Asphalt & Coated Macadam Association
25 Lower Belgrave Street
London
SW1 0LS
Tel: 0207 730 0761
(Advice on specifications)

B & Q plc
Portswood House
Hampshire Corporate Park
Chandlers Ford
Eastleigh
Hants
SO5 3YX
Tel: 01703 256256
(Branches throughout the UK)

Blagdon Water Garden Products Ltd
Bristol Road
Bridgwater
Somerset
TA6 4AW
Tel: 01278 446464

Brick Development Council
Woodside House
Winkfield
Windsor
Berks
SL4 2DX
Tel: 01344 885651

British Aggregate Construction
Materials Industries
156 Buckingham Palace Road
London
SW1W 9TR
Tel: 0207 730 8194
(Lists of members supplying materials
and laying drives)

Building Centre Group
26 Store Street

London
WC1E 7BT
Tel: 0207 637 1022 (technical advice)
Tel: 01344 884999 (useful literature)
Also in Bristol, Glasgow and Manchester

Building Employers Confederation
82 New Cavendish Street
London
W1M 8AD
Tel: 0207 580 5588
(Supply lists of BEC-registered builders)

Cement & Concrete Association
Wexham Springs
Slough
Berks
SL3 6PL
Tel: 02816 2727
(Technical advice plus useful literature)

Do-It-All
Falcon House
The Minories
Dudley
West Midlands
DY2 8PG
Tel: 01384 456456
(Branches throughout the UK)

Federation of Master Builders
33 St John Street
London
WC1N 2BB
Tel: 0207 242 7583
(Supply lists of members)

Great Mills Retail
RNC House
Paulton
Bristol
BS18 5SX
Tel: 01761 416034
(Branches throughout the UK)

Harcross Timber and Building Suppliers
1 Great Tower Street
London
EC3R 5AH
Tel: 0207 711 1444

Homebase Ltd
Beddington House
Wallington
Surrey
Tel: 0208 784 7200
(Branches throughout the UK)

Jewson Ltd
Intwood Road
Cringleford
Norwich
NR4 UXB
Tel: 01603 56133
(Branches throughout the UK)

Onduline Building Products
Eadley Place
182-184 Campden Hill Road
Kensington
London
W8 7AS
Tel: 0207 277 0533

Surrey Water Gardens
Clandon Park
Clandon
Nr Guildford
Surrey
Tel: 01483 224822

Texas Homecare
Homecharm House
Parkfarm
Wellingborough
Northampton
NN5 7UG
Tel: 01933 679679
(Branches throughout the UK)

The Water Gardener Magazine
9 Tufton Street
Ashford
Kent
TN23 1QN
Tel: 01233 621877

Travis Perkins
Lodge Way House
Lodge Way
Harlestone Road
Northampton

NN5 7UG
Tel: 01604 752424
(Branches throughout the UK)

Waterworld
Kingswood Nurseries
Bullsmoor Lane
Enfield
EN1 4SF
Tel: 01992 761587

Wickes
120-138 Station Road
Harrow
Middlesex
HA1 2QB
Tel: 0208 863 5696
(Branches throughout the UK)

Tool manufacturers

De Walt Tools
210 Bath Road
Slough
SL1 3YD
Tel: 01753 567 055

Black & Decker
210 Bath Road
Slough
SL1 3YD
Tel: 01753 567 055

Stanley Tools
The Stanley Works
Woodside
Sheffield
S3 9PD
Tel: 0114 276 8888

Tool retailers

Tilgear
Bridge House
69 Station Road
Cufflry
Herts
EN6 4TG
Tel: 01707 873 434

S J Carter Tools Ltd
Gloucester House
10 Camberwell New Road
London
SE5 0TA
Tel: 0207 587 0306

Router tables & accessories

Trend Machinery & Cutting Tools Ltd
Penfold Works
Imperial Way
Watford
WD2 4AF
Tel: 01923 249 911
Email: Mailserver@trend.co.uk

Health & safety equipment

Tecmark Ltd
St John's Innovation Centre
Cowley Road
Cambridge
CB4 4WS

Hardwood retailers & timber yards

South London Hardwoods
12 Belgrave Road
London
SE25 5AN
Tel: 0208 771 6764

North Heigham Sawmills Ltd
Paddock Street
Norfolk
NR2 4TW
Tel: 01603 622 978

AUSTRALIA

DIY stores

Mitre 10
319 George Street
Sydney 2000
Tel: 1800 803 304
(outlets nationwide)

BBC Hardware
Head Office, Bldg A

Cambridge Street
NSW 2121
Tel: (02) 9876 0888

Timber suppliers

ABC Timbers and Building Supplies Pty Ltd
Auburn Road
Regents Park 2143
Tel: (02) 9645 2511

Australian Treated Timber Sales
Brisbane 4000
Tel: (01) 800 06 0685

Bowens Timber and Building Supplies
Macaulay Road
North Melbourne 3051
Tel: (03) 9328 1041

NEW ZEALAND

DIY stores

Mitre 10 Support Centre
182 Wairau Road
Glenfield
Auckland
Tel: 09 443 9900

Placemakers Support Office
150 Marua Road
Auckland
Tel: 09 525 5100

SOUTH AFRICA

Timber suppliers

Federated Timbers
14 Mckenzie Street Ind Sites
Bloemfontein
Tel: (051) 447 3171
Fax: (051) 447 5053

Federated Timbers
39A Commercial Road
Arcadia
East London
Tel: (0431) 43 3733
Fax: (0431) 43 5240

P G Bison
161 Industrial Road
Pretoria West
Tel: (012) 376 6554
Fax: (012) 386 6560

P G Bison
4-5 Kwaford Road
Port Elizabeth
Tel: (041) 43 1250
Fax: (041) 43 5046

P G Bison - for timber
45 Gypsum Street
Pietersburg
Tel: (015) 292 0523
Fax: (015) 292 1112

DIY & hardware

Hardware Centre
14 Bree Street
Cape Town
Tel: (021) 421 7358
Fax: (021) 419 6792

Feds DIY
16 Mill Street
Gardens
Cape Town
Tel: (021) 461 7202
Fax: (021) 461 0524

Hardware Centre
Union Main Centre
Old Main Road
Pinetown
Durban
Tel: (031) 722 629
Fax: (031) 722 581

Feds DIY
329 Sydney Road
Durban
Tel: (031) 25 1551
Fax: (031) 25 6098

Hardware Centre
c/o Hans Strijdom and CR
Swart Drive

Randburg
Johannesburg
Tel: (011) 791 0844
Fax: (011) 791 0850

Feds DIY
26 Paterson Road
Port Elizabeth
Tel: (041) 54 2535
Fax: (041) 57 1855

Tool retailers

J & J Sales
38 Argyle Street
East London
Tel: (0431) 43 3380
Fax: (0431) 43 5432

Tooltrick - for tools
55A Bok Street
Pietersburg
Tel: (015) 295 4957
Fax: (015) 295 6151

First published in the UK in 2000 by
New Holland Publishers (UK) Ltd
24 Nutford Place, London W1H 6DQ
London • Cape Town • Sydney • Auckland

10 9 8 7 6 5 4 3 2 1

ISBN 1 85974 407 9

Consultant Editors: David Holloway, Mike Lawrence
Editors: John Boteler, Dek Messecar, Elizabeth Rowe
Editorial Co-ordinators: Kate Latham, Emily Preece
Designers: Paul Cooper, Phil Gorton
Illustrators: Tom Cross, Rob Shone, Bruce Snaddon
Co-ordination and picture research: Elizabeth Whiting & Associates
US consultant: Derek Bradford AIA RIBA

Printed in Malaysia by Times Offset (M) Sdn. Bhd.

The author would especially like to thank the following for their invaluable
assistance: Armatool Distributors Ltd, Black & Decker, Clifton Nurseries,
Lloyd Christie Garden Architects and Stanley Tools for loan of tools for
special photography, Jennifer Tetlow, stonemason, for allowing us to photograph her at work, Marshalls, for loan of photographs and advice. Design of
aviary: Anne Kelly. Special project design: D.K.M. Design.

INDEX

CONVERSION CHART

To convert the metric measurements given in this book to imperial measurements, simply multiply the figure given in the text by the relevant number shown in the table along-side. Bear in mind that conversions will not necessarily work out exactly, and you will need to round the figure up or down slightly. (Do not use a combination of metric and imperial measurements — for accuracy, keep to one system.)

To convert	Multiply by
millimetres to inches	0.0394
metres to feet	3.28
metres to yards	1.093
sq millimetres to sq inches	0.00155
sq metres to sq feet	10.76
sq metres to sq yards	1.195
cu metres to cu feet	35.31
cu metres to cu yards	1.308
grams to pounds	0.0022
kilograms to pounds	2.2046